THE PRIMITIVE CHURCH

THE PRIMITIVE CHURCH

STUDIED WITH SPECIAL REFERENCE TO THE ORIGINS OF THE CHRISTIAN MINISTRY

THE HEWETT LECTURES, 1928

BY

BURNETT HILLMAN STREETER

READER IN CHRISTIAN ORIGINS IN THE UNIVERSITY OF OXFORD
FELLOW OF THE QUEEN'S COLLEGE, OXFORD ; CANON OF HEREFORD
FELLOW OF THE BRITISH ACADEMY
HON. D.D. EDIN.; HON. D.D. DURHAM

MACMILLAN AND CO., LIMITED
ST. MARTIN'S STREET, LONDON
1929

MACMILLAN AND CO., Limited
LONDON · BOMBAY · CALCUTTA · MADRAS
MELBOURNE

THE MACMILLAN COMPANY
NEW YORK · BOSTON · CHICAGO
DALLAS · SAN FRANCISCO

THE MACMILLAN COMPANY
OF CANADA, LIMITED
TORONTO

CONTENTS

EXTRACT FROM THE WILL
OF
WATERMAN THOMAS HEWETT

I desire to place on record at the close of my life, my profound *FAITH* in the Christian religion. I believe that the future of the human race and the highest individual character are dependent upon realising in life, consciously or unconsciously, the spirit of our Lord and Master, Jesus Christ. Every successive generation must apprehend anew these truths, and a fresh statement of them by the ablest and most reverent scholars is desirable to secure their intelligent acceptance and recognition.

It is provided that the Lectures be delivered in Union Theological Seminary, New York, and the Episcopal Theological School, Cambridge, Massachusetts. They were so delivered—the course at Cambridge, by the courtesy of President Lowell, being given in Emerson Hall, Harvard University, to which the Episcopal Theological School is affiliated.

INTRODUCTION

WHEN I first began to read Theology more than thirty years ago, I found Church History so dull—especially after reading Greek and Roman history for ' Greats '—that I dropped the subject, and offered for examination Textual Criticism instead. I discovered later what the matter was ; it was not that ' Church ' history was dull, but that what was then presented to me as such was not really history. Whether the present volume is dull, or even history, it will be for others to pronounce. I only know that I have enjoyed the writing of it—the hue and cry after new discovery, the following up of hitherto unnoticed clues, the delimitation of conflicting tendencies, envisaging the interaction between personality and circumstance in testing situations, noting the intermittent ironies emergent in all things human.

The special reference to the Origins of the Christian Ministry was due in the first place to the importance of that topic in relation to the present-day discussion of Christian Reunion. But as my investigations led me to detect the existence of a far greater diversity and variegation in Primitive Christianity than is commonly recognised, I came to see in the study of Primitive Church Order the most convenient skeleton, so to speak, round which to form the living body of early Church history. It led me also to a fresh survey of the surviving literature of the first hundred years of Christianity—

including the New Testament—as a result of which I seemed to see the several documents in a new way. Each had its special place in the development of the organism, as well as of the thought, of the Christian community ; and most of them, though in different ways, exercised a determinative influence on that development. Indeed, unless a writing produced a profound impression on contemporaries—or, like Philemon and 2 and 3 John, bore the name of an outstanding leader—in the circumstances of the early Church it would have little chance of being copied and, therefore, of survival.

It is my hope that many who take no special interest in the history of Church organisation may find this book of value as a general introduction to the literature of early Christianity, seen from this point of view. A past age lives in its architecture, its art, and its literature ; but where, as in this case, hardly anything remains of the art or architecture, it is the more necessary, if that literature is to be heard again speaking with a living voice, to see it in the right historical framework.

For four hundred years theologians of rival churches have armed themselves to battle on the question of the Primitive Church. However great their reverence for scientific truth and historic fact, they have at least *hoped* that the result of their investigations would be to vindicate Apostolic authority for the type of Church Order to which they were themselves attached. The Episcopalian has sought to find episcopacy, the Presbyterian presbyterianism, and the Independent a system of independency, to be the form of Church government in New Testament times. But while each party to the dispute has been able to make out a case for his own view, he has never succeeded in demolishing the case of his opponent. The explanation of this deadlock, I have come to believe, is quite simple. It is the uncriticised assumption, made by all parties to the controversy, that in the first century there existed a single type of Church Order.

Approach the evidence without making that assumption and two conclusions come into sight:

(1) In the New Testament itself there can be traced an evolution in Church Order, comparable to the development in theological reflection detected by the scholarship of the last century.

(2) The most natural interpretation of the other evidence is that, at the end of the first century A.D., there existed, in different provinces of the Roman Empire, different systems of Church government. Among these, the Episcopalian, the Presbyterian, and the Independent can each discover the prototype of the system to which he himself adheres.

The hypothesis of a primitive diversity in Christian institutions may, or may not, succeed in commending itself to the judgment of scholars ; but in the meantime it has, at any rate, one merit: it is not likely to add fuel to the flames of ecclesiastical controversy. Indeed, if my hypothesis is correct, then, in the classic words of *Alice in Wonderland*, ' Everyone has won, and all shall have prizes '. At any rate, I am entitled to presume that—among those who profess and call themselves Christians—there will be but few of those unfortunates, to whom it is no satisfaction to be right unless they can thereby put others in the wrong.

The clarification of my ideas on this matter has been gradual. Considerations of space prevented me from including a discussion of the subject in my book *The Four Gospels*—to which this volume is, in some respects, a sequel. They were advanced a stage further by an invitation from the Theological Faculty of the University of London to deliver in May 1925 a short course of lectures embodying original research. The lectures then given, under the title of Primitive Church Order, formed the first draft for three of those comprised in this book. I have learnt much from members of a Seminar for post-graduate research, modelled on those held by Dr. Sanday, which I started in 1927 on my appointment as Reader in Christian Origins at Oxford. Many valuable suggestions from Dr. J. Vernon Bartlet, Prof. F. C. Burkitt, Mr. H. J. Carpenter, and Dr. P. N. Harrison, made after reading the galley-proofs, I have been able to embody. Lastly, this book owes much to the vigilant reading of the page-proofs by Mr. J. S. Bezzant and Canon Lilley. For the Index I am indebted to Mrs. C. W. Sowby.

The Lectures here printed were, I should explain, the first to be given on a Lectureship founded by the late Prof. W. T. Hewett of Cornell—an extract from whose will is printed above (p. vi). It is fitting, therefore, that I should put on record my sense of the compliment implied in the invitation by the Hewett Trustees to deliver the inaugural course on a Lectureship of this importance. I should like also to express my appreciation of the more than gracious hospitality of my several hosts and hostesses on a visit to the United States to which I shall always look back as one of the most enjoyable experiences that have fallen to my lot.

B. H. STREETER.

THE QUEEN'S COLLEGE, OXFORD,
    6th May 1929.

SOME NOTABLE DATES

A.D.

81–96 *Domitian.*
Matthew, Luke, Acts, Apocalypse.
Josephus writes and Plutarch lectures in Rome.
Agricola conquers Britain south of Forth.
Emperor-worship pressed, especially in Asia.

96 Persecution of Christian aristocrats at Rome.

96–98 *Nerva.*
96 Epistle of Clement.
97 Trajan becomes co-emperor.
Tacitus' *Life of Agricola.*

98–117 *Trajan.*
Gospel of John.
Martyrdom of Symeon of Jerusalem.
107 Juvenal, Book I. of Satires.
112 Pliny persecutes Christians in Bithynia (Pontus).
115 Ignatius martyred in Colosseum.

117–138 *Hadrian.*
135 Jerusalem destroyed, rebuilt as *Aelia Capitolina.*

138–161 *Antoninus Pius.*
140 Marcion comes to Rome.
156 Polycarp martyred at Smyrna.

161–180 *Marcus Aurelius.*
This reign marks culturally ' the end of the ancient world '.
163 Justin martyred at Rome.
165 Hegesippus visits Rome.
177 Persecution at Lyons.

180–192 *Commodus.*
185 Irenaeus of Lyons (Lugdunum).
190 Victor of Rome excommunicates churches of Asia.

193–211 *Septimus Severus.*
192 Tertullian converted (Carthage).
202 Persecution drives Clement from Alexandria.
203 Origen (aet. 18) takes charge of Catechetical School.
204 Birth of Plotinus.

211–217 *Caracalla.*
212 Edict conferring Roman citizenship on all freeborn subjects of
Empire.

NOTE.—The purpose of the above selection of dates is to assist the
student to see the events of Church history against their background in
European history. When, therefore, the exact year is disputable, I have
usually given, ' without prejudice ', the approximation most generally
accepted.

I

HISTORY AND LEGEND

SYNOPSIS

The Apocryphal Acts

WHAT became of the Twelve Apostles ? History tells surprisingly little ; legends abound, but they go back to romances artificially concocted as party propaganda—Gnostic (or Gnosticising) and Ebionite. Thus the *Acts of John*—and to a varying extent those of Paul, Peter, Andrew, and Thomas—condemn marriage ; the *Clementine Homilies* (the *Recognitions* are only another recension of these) make it an obligatory duty.

The Manichaean Canon, and the ' Catholic ' recensions of the Apocryphal Acts. Their influence on Christian art and liturgies ; on statements made by the Fathers, and even by the historian Eusebius. Possibility that the *Acts of Paul* may contain scraps of authentic tradition. The Gnostic Hymn in the *Acts of John*.

The *Clementines* depict a contest between Peter and Simon Magus. They are based on an earlier Ebionite document, which aimed at delivering a veiled attack on the Apostle Paul under the name of Simon Magus. Much more of this Ebionite propaganda is preserved in the *Homilies* than in the *Recognitions*. The *Homilies* open with two fictitious letters : I. Of Peter to James, the brother of the Lord, saluting him as the supreme Bishop of the Church, and affirming his (Peter's) adherence to the Mosaic law. II. Of Clement to James, notable as the earliest statement that Peter was himself Bishop of Rome, and that he consecrated Clement as his successor in that See.

In the *Acts of Peter* the story of the Apostle's conflict with Simon Magus is carried to its conclusion in Rome. These *Acts* include the noble *Quo Vadis* legend, and an account of Peter's crucifixion head-downwards. Peter's journey to Rome to confront Simon Magus is dated twelve years after the Resurrection, or A.D. 42. If this date be set in conjunction with the date A.D. 67—mistakenly assigned by Eusebius to Nero's persecution, in the course of which, he says, Peter and Paul were put to death —a simple sum in subtraction gives the period of twenty-five years, which tradition assigns to the Episcopate of Peter in Rome.

1

TRADITION AND THE FATHERS

The 'tradition' which the Fathers take seriously is the tradition of sound doctrine. With the correctness of this they were gravely concerned. 'Traditions', in the sense of anecdotes about the doings of Apostles, they were prepared to accept on very slight evidence. It is evident that many of the stories they tell are derived, directly or indirectly, from Apocryphal Acts.

Church historians have been sometimes misled through overlooking the fact that the Fathers quote one another—usually with some amplification of the statements made by their predecessors. This *crescendo* illustrated by a series of statements made by Fathers in regard to the origins of the Gospels of Matthew and Mark. The evidence of Irenaeus as to the residence of the Apostle John in Asia must be scrutinised in the light of this tendency. But the Fathers must not be judged too harshly; historical accuracy was for them a thing difficult to attain owing to the lack, until the age of Constantine, of a standard text-book of Church history. The pioneer attempt to write a history of the Church made by Eusebius *c.* A.D. 311. The task presented great difficulties; but these were largely overcome by the fact that Eusebius was, for his age, a really great historian.

It is largely due to Eusebius—and the ancient materials which he preserves—that the history of the origins of Christianity is so much less obscure than that of the other great Religions. But in this regard, of still greater importance was the conflict with Gnosticism in the second century. In order to rule out Gnosticising Gospels and Acts, the Church was compelled to select, and to attribute canonical authority to, that portion of its *most ancient* literature which it believed to be authentically apostolic in origin. This primitive literature, once it was regarded as 'inspired'— *i.e.* as a New Testament alongside the Old—could no longer be seriously amplified or rewritten; and is therefore still available for the purposes of the historian in approximately its original form. In addition to the collection of early literature included in the New Testament, there fortunately survives another collection known as the 'Apostolic Fathers'. In point of date the two collections overlap; together they form a solid basis—and the only solid basis—on which to build a history of the primitive Church.

The nature of the task set before a writer of early Church history.

I

HISTORY AND LEGEND

THE APOCRYPHAL ACTS

WHAT became of the Twelve Apostles? That is a question to which legend will give a vivacious answer; but history is strangely silent. For stories about great men there is always a popular demand; in the Christian Church this demand was catered for in the first instance by persons who saw here an opportunity for commending a particular type of doctrine and ethical practice. The earliest to perceive and exploit to the full this opportunity was one 'Leucius', who produced (A.D. 150-170) a work of pure imagination, the *Acts of John*—a novel with a religious purpose, that of advocating a Gnostic or semi-gnostic interpretation of Christianity. His success encouraged others; there followed rapidly *Acts of Paul*, *Acts of Peter*, and an earlier recension of the *Clementines*,[1] then *Acts of Andrew*, and *Acts of Thomas*—all probably between A.D. 175 and 250.

From the standpoint of doctrine and ethics the *Acts of John* and the *Clementine Homilies* represent directly opposite tendencies — the Gnostic and the Ebionite.

---

[1] Extant in two later recensions, known respectively as the *Recognitions* and the *Homilies*. F. J. A. Hort, in his lectures on the *Clementine Recognitions* (Macmillan, 1901), argues that these are two independent abbreviations of a work referred to by Epiphanius as popular among Essene Ebionites—the περίοδοι, or *Circuits, of Peter*, 'written by the hand of Clement'. The *Recognitions* preserve more of the original story, the *Homilies* more of the Ebionite discourse. See also Dr. Vernon Bartlet's article, 'Clementine Literature', in *Encyclopædia Britannica*.

Probably the authors wrote with a definite intention of commending these heresies to the orthodox, though some scholars think that they represent the extreme limits of what was still tolerated within the Church at the time of writing. In the *Acts of John*, Christ is a Divine Being essentially incapable of suffering, and is depicted as calmly talking to the disciples on the Mount of Olives while the spectacle of the Crucifixion—a pure illusion— is being enacted on Calvary before the eyes of the multitude. In the *Homilies*, Christ is regularly styled ' the True Prophet ', and is not much more than a kind of super-human Moses. Again, the *Acts of John* is largely concerned with a polemic against marriage, whereas in the *Homilies* marriage is commanded as a matter of obligation.

The other works mentioned above, with the possible exception of the *Acts of Thomas*, seem to represent different strains in popular Christianity within the Church at the end of the second century. But at a later date the five volumes of *Acts* were adopted by the Manichees into their Canon of sacred books in place of the Lukan Acts— doubtless because, in a greater or less degree, their attitude towards marriage is that which the Manichees themselves adopted. This damaged the reputation of these *Acts*, and, with the exception for a time of the *Acts of Paul*, they came to be regarded definitely as heretical. But to the taste of that age they were too interesting to be completely discarded, and various editions of them —often spoken of as ' Catholic Acts '—were produced, in which the heretical speeches were altered or excised, while the adventures and miracles received further embellishment. At the same time similar *Acts* of the remaining apostles were produced, beginning with those of Philip *c.* A.D. 250. In these *Acts* are to be found numerous legends immortalised in Christian art; and by them the mediaeval liturgies have been profoundly influenced. Even in the revised Calendar of the Church of England the commemoration as martyrs of all the Apostles except John rests ultimately on the authority of these apocryphal Acts.

What is less commonly realised, is the extent to which statements by Fathers of the third and fourth centuries, and even by our primary historian Eusebius, are dependent upon the earlier examples of this type of romance. For this reason a great service has been done to the ordinary student of Church History by Dr. M. R. James, who has collected and translated into English, in one convenient volume, *The Apocryphal New Testament*,[1] all that survives of this kind of literature from the second and the third centuries—with the exception of the *Clementines*, which were already conveniently accessible to English readers in the Ante-Nicene Library.

The *Acts of Paul*, we are told by Tertullian, was produced shortly before his own time by a presbyter of Asia. For this exploit the presbyter was degraded from office, in spite of his plea that he did it from 'love of Paul'. It was doubtless the attribution to the Apostle of speeches roundly denouncing marriage that secured his condemnation, not the venial—indeed all but commendable—offence of providing him with fictitious adventures and bogus miracles. At any rate, in spite of the widely known fact of its author's condemnation, the *Acts of Paul* was treated as a serious historical authority by Hippolytus in Rome, c. A.D. 220, by Origen in Alexandria, and even by St. Augustine, who must have read what his African predecessor Tertullian had said on the subject. The historian naturally asks, How many statements

[1] Clarendon Press, 1924.

made by other Fathers from A.D. 200 onwards may not be derived from some of the other apocryphal Acts?

The *Acts of Paul*, however, may preserve scraps of authentic tradition. Prof. Ramsay [1] has argued that there is a historical basis to the story of Thecla. And there is a personal description of the Apostle's appearance, given near the beginning of this episode, which is so uncomplimentary that it may be surmised to rest on some local memory, especially as this romance comes from Asia Minor,[2] the main field of the Apostle's activity.

And he saw Paul coming, a man little of stature, thin-haired upon the head, crooked in the legs, of good state of body, with eyebrows joining, and nose somewhat hooked, full of grace ; for sometimes he appeared like a man, and sometimes he had the face of an angel.

The imaginative faculty of the author of the *Acts of John* operated untrammelled by any regard for history or authentic local tradition ; but, considered as a novelist, he shares with the author of the *Acts of Thomas* the distinction of being skilled in his craft. Fortunately he incorporates a hymn of great beauty, which gives us a glimpse of Gnosticism on its more attractive side. In general, what survives of Gnostic literature, the *Pistis Sophia* for example, is incredibly tedious ; and what we know of Gnostic theosophical speculation is so grotesque that we are apt to wonder what there was about the movement which made it so alluring to that age as to become a really formidable enemy to the Church. No doubt its chief appeal lay in the dualism which offered a solution, theoretical and practical, to the problem of evil. This hymn reveals another and a completely different aspect of it—mystical, devotional,

---

[1] *The Church in the Roman Empire*, ch. xvi.   (Hodder & Stoughton, 1893.)
[2] Possibly from Iconium.   Cf. M. R. James, *op. cit.* p. xx.

poetical. For that reason I print it, in an Appendix at
the end of this volume, from a version familiar, from its
musical setting by G. Holst, to those who resort to
choral festivals.

The *Clementine Homilies* and *Recognitions* purport
to be the work of Clement, represented as a personal
disciple of Peter, who appoints him his successor as
Bishop of Rome. Though not commonly classed among
the Apocryphal Acts, the *Clementines* are romances of
a similar character. They are equally novels with a
purpose, the centre of interest lying in the adventures and
teaching of the Apostle Peter. But there is some difference between the *Clementines* and the *Acts* in the literary
form adopted, and still more in the theological position of
the writers. In the Apocryphal Acts startling miracles
are the conspicuous feature of the narrative setting,
which is, so to speak, the jam supplied to make more
palatable the solid nutriment of the doctrinal harangues;
and the Apostle who is the hero of the romance is brought
into contact with a large variety of persons in divers
situations. In the *Clementines* the plot is tamer, and
the range of incident less varied. The under-plot is a
familiar Greek and Latin comedy *motif*—the discovery,
after a long lapse of years, of parents by children, brothers
and sisters by one another, having been separated and
sold into slavery in early youth. In this subordinate
plot Clement is the hero. The main plot is the contest
between Peter and the sorcerer and heresiarch Simon
Magus, whom Peter follows from place to place, confutes
in doctrinal argument, and finally vanquishes—out-
trumping the sorcerer at Antioch by opposing to his magic
a happy mixture of miracle and ruse.

Either the whole romance of which the extant *Clementines* are divergent recensions, or else a document em-

bodied in it containing the series of conflicts between
Peter and Simon Magus, as well as a great deal of the
substance of the speeches of the combatants, was a piece
of Ebionite propaganda — most probably emanating
from an Essene Jewish-Christian sect, the Elkesaites.
In it the character of Simon Magus is made use of
to mask an attack on the Apostle Paul, whom all
Ebionites hated for his attitude towards the law of
Moses. For that reason this Ebionite document was
supposed by the Tübingen school to be prior to the
Lukan Acts, and to afford a key to the true interpretation
of the history of the Apostolic Age. This was a grand
mistake. So far from being prior to the work of Luke, it
comes much nearer to being a reply to it. In the Acts,
Peter is represented as being the precursor of Paul in
throwing open Christianity to the Gentiles. The author
of the Ebionite work (or the earlier source he followed)
finds both the Acts and the corpus of Pauline Epistles
already accepted as religious classics by the majority of
Christians. He dislikes Paul—and still more the docetic,
ascetic, Gnostic section of his followers—but he is not
in a position to deliver a frontal attack on the Apostle
in person. He therefore takes from the Acts (viii. 9 ff.)
the character of Simon, the sorcerer whom Peter rebuked
in Samaria, and under cover of that name develops his
assault on the Paulinists of his own time—believing,
no doubt with good reason, that his work would have a
wider circulation if the attack on Paul himself was, to
this extent, veiled.

The *Homilies* conserves much more of this Ebionite
polemic than the *Recognitions*, and so is of far more
value to the historian. It also includes two letters
which, though palpable inventions, are of considerable
moment.

(I.) The letter of Peter to James. In this Peter salutes James as his superior, ' the lord and bishop of the holy church, under the Father of all ', and explains that he had taught adherence to the Law of Moses, but that his teaching had been misrepresented.

Some from among the Gentiles have rejected my legal preaching, attaching themselves to certain lawless and trifling preaching of the man [*i.e.* Simon Magus = Paul] who is my enemy.

Of the quasi-Papal supremacy here ascribed to James, the brother of the Lord, I shall have something to say later.

(II.) Rufinus, in his preface to the Latin translation of the *Recognitions*—the original Greek is lost—says :

The letter in which the same Clement, writing to James the Lord's brother, informs him of the death of Peter, and that he had left him (Clement) as his successor in his chair and teaching ; and in which the whole subject of church order is treated of, I have not prefixed to this work . . . because I have already translated and published it.

The Greek text is preserved in the *Homilies*. This letter of Clement to Peter contains the earliest statement that Peter was himself actually Bishop of Rome ; Irenaeus reckons Linus as the first bishop, appointed by Peter and Paul. Also it makes Clement the first bishop after the Apostles ; whereas in the old Roman tradition, found in the Canon of the Mass and in Irenaeus (cf. p. 184), he is preceded by Linus and Cletus (= Anencletus). Now Tertullian,[1] it should be noted, though he had read Irenaeus, places Clement first—most probably on the authority of this apocryphal letter. Still more influential was Rufinus' Latin translation of the letter. This became the nucleus of the *False Decretals*, which through-

---

[1] *De Praescr. Haeret.* 32, written c. A.D. 199.

out the Middle Ages constituted the chief documentary basis for the more grandiose of the Papal claims.

The author of the *Acts of Peter* had read the *Acts of John*, and sympathised with its views on marriage ; but the greater part of what is preserved of his work— apart from the account of the arrest and death of Peter— is a continuation of the story of the conflict between Peter and Simon Magus. Simon, defeated by Peter in Palestine, has gone to Rome. There he works desolation among the believers until Peter is summoned by a divine vision to go to Rome and undo the mischief caused. Since the author of these Acts never mentions the name of Clement, it is possible that he derived the idea of the conflict between Peter and Simon Magus, not from the Clementine Romance—the immediate source of the extant *Recognitions* and *Homilies*—but either from an older Ebionite work embodied therein, or from a legendary amplification of the incident mentioned in Acts (viii. 9 ff.) current in non-Ebionite circles. At any rate he clearly intended to write a sequel in which the conflict was carried to a finish in Rome.

The idea of a visit of Simon Magus to Rome originated in a mare's nest discovered by Justin Martyr, *c.* A.D. 152. Justin speaks of a sect founded by a Samaritan named Simon, who gave himself out to be an incarnation of the Supreme God, and was worshipped as such by a large following in Samaria, 'though very few of other nations'. He goes on to say that in the time of Claudius Caesar :

Simon . . . by his magic arts with the powers of darkness, did such wonderful feats in the imperial city of Rome, that he gained the reputation of a god, and accordingly is honoured by you [Romans], like your other gods, with a statue erected upon the Tiber between the two bridges, with this Latin inscription, *Simoni Deo Sancto,* ' To Simon the Holy God '. (*Apol.* i. xxxiv.)

This astonishing statement could never have been made by a native of Rome ; but Justin was born in Samaria and had then lived in Ephesus, and on the spot which he indicates, an island in the Tiber known as *inter duos pontes* (' between the two bridges ') there was discovered in A.D. 1574 an altar with a dedication *Semoni Sanco Deo* (*C.I.L.* vi. 567). Semo Sancus was an ancient Sabine deity, of whose existence Justin could hardly be expected to be aware. Justin's veracity, then, is completely vindicated, somewhat at the expense of his intelligence, if, familiar as he was with the cult of the Samaritan Simon, he confused him with the Sabine deity.[1] That the Samaritan Simon ever came to Rome is improbable. Justin expressly says that he had a very small following outside Samaria ; and Hegesippus ranks the Simonians as one of five Jewish sects. It is not certain that he is the same person as the magician Simon, whose rebuke by Peter is recorded in the Acts (viii. 20-24), and who has provided ecclesiastical law with the technical term ' simony '. Since, however, the Simon of the Acts was regarded by his followers as ' that Power (*i.e.* emanation) of God which is called Great ', I incline to think they are identical ; at any rate, they were identified.

Any Christian who had read the Ebionite story of the contest of Peter with Simon Magus, and then read Justin Martyr, would receive a shock. Simon Magus, vanquished by the Apostle in Syria, had succeeded in getting himself deified in Rome. Neither divine nor poetic justice could allow the villain of the piece such a signal triumph in the end. Clearly, something had to be done about it ; Peter must once more pursue the

[1] Prof. Merrill suggests that the statue may have been set up or repaired by Claudius (who had an antiquarian interest in reviving moribund cults) and bore an inscription to this effect. If so, this would be Justin's evidence that Simon came to Rome ' in the time of Claudius '.

sorcerer, and must finally vanquish him on the field of
his apparent victory. This is the principal *motif* of the
Acts of Peter. . . . And in Eusebius it reappears as
sober history (*H.E.* ii. 14-15).

The romantic necessity that Peter should crush
Simon carried with it chronological consequences. Simon
had come to Rome in the days of Claudius; Peter, therefore, must have done the same. St. Luke tells us that
Peter, after his escape from prison under Herod Agrippa
I., left Jerusalem and ' went to another place ' (Acts xii.
17). How obvious the conjecture that the ' other place '
was Rome! And the date of Peter's escape from prison,
and therefore of his journey to Rome, could very
naturally be fixed at *twelve years* after the Crucifixion.
Judaea and Samaria were added to the previous do-
minions of Herod Agrippa I. by Claudius on his accession
in A.D. 41 ; and Agrippa died in A.D. 44. Hence the
execution of James the son of Zebedee and the imprisonment of Peter must have taken place between
these years. If the Crucifixion be dated A.D. 30,
Peter's departure ' to another place ' *may* have been
exactly twelve years later. But the ancients took
sacred numbers seriously ; there are twelve tribes,
twelve signs of the Zodiac, ' twelve months of the sun ',[1]
etc. Twelve years would be the *right* period for the
College of Twelve Apostles to remain in Jerusalem,
working for the conversion of Israel before they separated
to go on the Gentile Mission. This *a priori* sense of the
appropriate—*plus* the actual fact that Peter left Jerusalem about twelve years after the Crucifixion—was
translated into an express command of the Lord
addressed to all the Apostles. This already appears in
the *Preaching of Peter*, an apocryphal writing not later

---

[1] The phrase occurs in *Clementine Homilies*, ii.

than A.D. 150, from which Clement of Alexandria quotes as follows :

> The Lord said to the Apostles : If then any of Israel will repent, to believe in God through my name, his sins shall be forgiven him ; . . . after twelve years go ye out into the world, lest any say: We did not hear (*Strom.* vi. 5).

The *Preaching of Peter* was presumably known to the author of the *Acts of Peter*. At any rate he refers to this command ; and had evidently recorded it in the early portion of his book, which is now lost.

> And as they [*i.e.* the Christians at Rome] prayed and fasted, God was already teaching Peter at Jerusalem of that which should come to pass. For *whereas the twelve years which the Lord Christ had enjoined upon him were fulfilled*, he showed a vision after this manner, saying unto him : ' Peter, that Simon the sorcerer whom thou didst cast out of Judaea, confuting him, hath again come before thee at Rome. . . . Delay thee not ; set forth on the morrow, and then thou shalt find a ship ready, setting sail for Italy. . . .'

In Jerome's translation of the *Chronicon* of Eusebius —the standard authority for all later ecclesiastical writers—the entry opposite the second year of Claudius (A.D. 42) is :

> Peter the Apostle, after first founding the Church of Antioch, is sent to Rome, where he preached the Gospel and continued for twenty-five years as Bishop of the same city.

The ultimate authority for Peter's arrival in Rome in A.D. 42 would seem to be the passage of the *Acts of Peter* quoted above. The earliest statement that Peter exercised the office of Bishop in Rome is the apocryphal letter of Clement to James, now extant, in the *Clementine Homilies*. Whence comes the period of twenty-five years ? The answer to this question lies near at hand.

A few pages later in the *Chronicon*, against the last year of Nero (A.D. 67–68), we read :

> Nero, to crown his enormities, was the first to carry out a persecution of the Christians, in which Peter and Paul died gloriously at Rome.

According to Tacitus, the persecution took place shortly after the great fire of A.D. 64, so that the date given by Eusebius, A.D. 67, is, in point of fact, three years out. But A.D. 67 *is* the Eusebian date ; and a simple sum in subtraction $(67 - 42 = 25)$ gives as the interval between Peter's first arrival in Rome and his martyrdom in the same city (and therefore, as the duration of his episcopate), the famous twenty-five years.

The *Acts of Peter* is probably the ultimate source, not only of the traditional chronology of Peter's life, but also of the story, repeated later by Origen, that Peter at his own request was crucified head-downwards. And like the *Acts of John*, it includes one item which is really great—the glorious legend commemorated by the Church *Domine Quo Vadis* on the Appian Way outside the walls of Rome. Peter is warned that Agrippa the prefect is about to arrest and put him to death. The brethren exhort him to save his life ' that he might yet be able to serve the Lord ', and he decides to leave Rome in disguise.

> And he obeyed the brethren's voice and went forth alone . . . and as he went forth out of the city, he saw the Lord entering into Rome. And when he saw Him, he said, ' Lord, whither goest thou ? ' And the Lord said unto him, ' I go unto Rome to be crucified '. And Peter said unto Him, ' Lord, art thou being crucified again ? ' He said unto him, ' Yea, Peter, I am being crucified again '. And Peter came to himself . . . and returned to Rome.[1]

[1] The version quoted is that of Dr. James's *Apocryphal New Testament*, p. 333.

Tradition and the Fathers

At times it is clear that the Fathers make historical statements directly on the authority of Apocryphal Acts. Hippolytus, for example, in defending the credibility of the story of Daniel in the lions' den, writes : [1]

> If we believe that, when Paul was condemned to the beasts, the lion that was set upon him laid down at his feet and licked him, how shall we not believe that which happened in the case of Daniel ? (*Commentary on Daniel*, iii. 9).

No one could appeal to an event supposed to have taken place a hundred and fifty years ago as evidence for the credibility of an incident recorded in Scripture merely on the authority of floating tradition ; it must have been recorded in a *book* known to and valued by Hippolytus and his readers. And the story of St. Paul and the lion does occur in the *Acts of Paul*.

In the majority of cases, however, when the Fathers quote a ' tradition ', it is probable that they are not referring directly to the text of Apocryphal Acts, but to stories current by word of mouth. But whenever a story occurs in one of the Apocryphal Acts, and is *first* quoted by a Father who wrote *later* than the earliest edition of those Acts, it is open to the suspicion of being part of the output of those factories of legend. Human nature changes but slowly ; and stories spread in those days as now, not because they are true, but because they are interesting. And once a good story becomes current, it is widely believed—unless immediately and repeatedly contradicted, either by glaring incompatibility with some notorious fact, or by powerful influences which have an interest in its suppression.

[1] *Cf.* M. R. James, *op. cit.* p. 291 f.

In the third century, as to most people in the twentieth, ' everybody says so ' is a quite sufficient reason for accepting any anecdote which is really interesting.

In the Fathers, ' tradition '—or rather the various words and phrases which we translate by that word— means two very different things. There is the tradition of sound doctrine, of which the Bishops of the great sees were regarded as in a special sense the custodians ; and there are stories current about historical personages or events. It is only where the tradition of sound doctrine is in question—more especially as regards the Unity of God and the reality of Christ's Manhood as against the Gnostic challenge—that the early Fathers are serious about the appeal to history. Anecdotes about apostles or other personages of that age, like common - room stories at the present day about persons regarded as 'characters', were told and re-told without anyone feeling the need of conformity to an exacting standard of historical accuracy.

There is another reason why writers of Church history often misconceive the nature and value of a catena of statements of Church writers, when these occur in a chronological series in regard to some one set of facts. They forget that the ancients read one another. Indeed, save in exceptional and more or less accidental circumstances, no ancient writer has survived at all unless his work was highly esteemed by those who followed after ; and where a statement appeared in a previous writer of esteemed reputation, a later writer naturally accepted it on his authority. Most commonly, however, instead of word for word quotation, the later writer reproduced what he took to be the general meaning of his authority— which means in practice that he reproduced the original statement with amplifications and modifications of his own. Students of the Old and New Testament are trained to study carefully the way in which, in ancient historical writings, the sense of fitness or the desire for greater explicitness has led to the amplification of the account of an earlier author. They are familiar, for example, with the twist which the Chronicler has given to many of the statements taken by him from older books like Samuel or Kings; or with the way, rather more conservative yet not in principle dissimilar, in which Matthew and Luke have rewritten certain sections which they have derived from Mark. Curiously enough, it is less generally recognised that the relation between earlier and later ecclesiastical writers is of a very similar character. Irenaeus derived materials from Papias, Hegesippus, and Justin Martyr; Clement of Alexandria, Tertullian, and Hippolytus used Irenaeus; Origen read most of his predecessors; and Eusebius, the real ' father of Church history ', used all these earlier writers. Jerome, the greatest scholar of the Western Church, copied and improved upon Eusebius. But even Eusebius rarely, if ever, perceived that a later writer was merely repeating, with his own comments or conjectural amplification, the statement of an earlier writer; and he thus sets their evidence side by side, as if they were independent witnesses who corroborated one another's testimony. And not a few modern writers have followed his example.

An instructive illustration of the *crescendo* in a series of statements which can originate in this manner is to be seen by studying what these authorities respectively have to say in regard to the relation of the Gospel of Mark to the Apostle Peter. Papias states that, ' Mark, having become the interpreter of Peter, wrote down accurately everything he remembered ', with the disparaging qualification 'without, however, recording in order what was either said or done by Christ'.

Irenaeus adds the detail that Mark wrote ' after the death of Peter and Paul '. Clement of Alexandria (*ap.* Eus. *H.E.* vi. 14. 5 ff.) says that this Gospel was written during the lifetime of Peter, but in his absence, at the request of those who had heard Peter preach; and that, 'when Peter heard of it, he neither strongly hindered nor encouraged it'. Origen improves on this, saying that Mark ' wrote it in accordance with Peter's instructions ' (Eus. *H.E.* vi. 25. 5). Eusebius (*H.E.* ii. 15. 2) reports substantially the story as told by Clement, and adds:

It is said that the Apostle, learning by the revelation of the Spirit what was done, was delighted with the zealous ardour of these men, and authorised the book to be read in the Churches.

Jerome brings the series to a climax by making the relation of Peter and Mark a matter of simple dictation, saying that the Gospel was composed *Petro narrante, illo scribente* (*Ad Hedibiam,* xi.). The last two cases are particularly enlightening as to the standard of accuracy in reproduction of earlier authorities, for Eusebius expressly gives us to understand that he is merely repeating the statements previously quoted from *Clement of Alexandria*[1] and Papias :

This account is given by Clement, whose testimony is corroborated also by that of Papias.

Jerome, again, in another work (*De vir. illustr.* viii.), repeats from Eusebius the statement in the form given by Clement ; so that in his letter to Hedibia we catch him out in a conscious exaggeration.

---

[1] I cannot accept Zahn's contention that the added details are derived from a sentence which Eusebius *omitted* in his previous quotation from Papias. Eusebius was not the man to omit the most telling words from the earliest ' testimony ' available.

A similar evolution in tradition, as represented in patristic writers, can be traced from its origin in the single bald sentence of Papias :

So then Matthew composed the oracles in the Hebrew language, and each one interpreted them as he could.

This by the time of Eusebius has become :

Matthew and John alone have left us memoirs of the Lord's discourses ; and they, it is recorded, only came to write under compulsion.[1] For Matthew first of all preached to Hebrews ; and when he was about to go also to others he committed his Gospel to writing in his native tongue ; thus he made his writing compensate those from whom he was departing for the lack of his bodily presence (*H.E.* iii. 24. 5 f.).

This example is in some ways even more instructive than the former ; for there is no doubt that the Greek Gospel of Matthew is *not* a translation of a Hebrew original ; and therefore *the whole* of the patristic tradition has arisen from a misapprehension of the fact (whatever it may be) which lies behind the original, and unfortunately enigmatical, sentence of Papias. The historian, then, has not done his duty unless he has tested every item of patristic evidence in the light of the tendency of the Fathers to copy and improve upon the statements of their predecessors, of which the passages quoted above are not exceptional, but fairly representative, examples.

The case of Irenaeus (A.D. 185) is, perhaps, the most important. He stands to the theologians who succeeded him in a relation not unlike that in which Hooker stands to the series of Anglican Divines. He is the first of the 'Fathers'—in the strict sense of that term, which excludes the still earlier 'Apologists' and 'Apostolic Fathers'.

---

[1] The story that John wrote under pressure from his disciples is found in the *Muratorianum*, and is probably derived from a lost section of the *Acts of John*.

And every influential Church writer in the next two
hundred years had studied his work. His theology,
however, was better than his history. The way in which
he reproduces the statement of Papias about Matthew
(quoted p. 187) shows that same tendency to improve
upon earlier authorities which later writers exhibit in
their improvements upon him. This tendency on his
part will assume a vital import when we come to consider the exact value of his evidence as to the residence
in Asia of the Apostle John.

In fairness, however, to Irenaeus and other early
Fathers, it should be insisted that it was far more difficult
than we are apt to suppose for them to draw a clear
distinction between history and legend. That distinction is one which can never be effectively drawn for any
period until and unless there are standard written
histories dealing with that period. It is a fact, in itself
remarkable and of immense consequence to the modern
student, that between St. Luke—whose second volume,
the Acts, brings the history of the Church down to
about the year A.D. 62—and Eusebius, who seems to have
published the first edition (Bks. i.-viii.) of his work about
A.D. 311,[1] no one thought it worth while to write a history
of the Church. Hegesippus has been miscalled 'the
father of Church history'; it is now realised that he did
not write a history at all, but an apologetic and controversial treatise in the course of which—mainly, it would
seem, in the fifth book—he gave some interesting information about the early Church of Jerusalem and a list
of the bishops of Rome.[2] Julius Africanus in A.D. 221
produced his *Chronographies*, a table of dates of important

---

[1] Eusebius seems to have published a final edition, A.D. 325, just before
the Council of Nicaea. See the discussion in the indispensable edition of the
Ecclesiastical History by Lawlor and Oulton, ii. p. 2 ff. (S.P.C.K., 1928.)

[2] H. J. Lawlor, *Eusebiana*, p. 1 ff. (Clarendon Press, 1912.)

events. But this work dealt mainly with pre-Christian
history, though giving dates to a few important events of
Church history and to the accessions of the bishops of
certain sees down to the time at which he wrote.

Eusebius was thus a pioneer ; he was actually the
first to write the history of the Church during the pre-
ceding 250 years. Fortunately he had at Caesarea
access to a unique library of early Christian literature ;
and this, though mainly consisting of hortatory and
controversial works, included collections of letters and
descriptions of martyrdoms. He had also an insight, for
that age quite exceptional, into the possibility of con-
structing history out of the incidental allusions in such
literature to persons and events contemporary with the
writers. Inevitably he sometimes gets his facts wrong ;
sometimes, though less often than might have been
expected, he mistakes legend for history. He accepts
as genuine, for example, the apocryphal correspondence
between our Lord and Abgar, King of Edessa (*H.E.* i. 13).[1]
Again, though he mentions the *Acts of Peter* as a book
having no claim at all to inclusion among the canonical
books of the New Testament (*H.E.* iii. 3. 2), he repeats
as history Peter's pursuit of Simon Magus to Rome in the
reign of Claudius (*H.E.* ii. 14. 6)—and that with details
nearer to the account in the *Acts of Peter* than to the bare
allusion in Hippolytus (*Ref.* vi. 15), who is the earliest
reputable Church writer to allude to the incident.

Nevertheless the debt which the historian owes to
Eusebius cannot be. overestimated. His matter is ill-
arranged, his style is both sententious and pretentious ;

---

[1] Abgar is converted by Thaddaeus, who is not one of the Twelve (as in
the B ℵ text of Matthew and Mark), but one of the Seventy. But Thaddaeus
is Eusebius' own rendering of the Syriac name Addai, whom Burkitt attract-
ively identifies with Tatian, the historical founder of the Church in Edessa
about A.D. 170. The name Abgar was borne by many kings of Edessa.

yet he is one of the very few great historians of antiquity.
He was, unless I am mistaken, actually the first writer
of history to quote original authorities consistently and
on a large scale ; and his method of using, and his com-
ments upon, the sources available show an insight into
the nature of historical evidence far in advance of his
time. Moreover, he set an example which others followed.
His *Ecclesiastical History* at once became a standard
authority ; and from time to time thereafter it was
brought up to date by a succession of historians whose
works aimed at being in some sense continuations of his.
But until the reign of Constantine the Fathers had no
textbook of Church history.   And if we reflect on what
the general knowledge of modern Church history would
be like, if in the Universities or Theological Colleges of
Europe no textbook was available which brought that
history down later than the death of Charles II., we shall
marvel, not that the Fathers sometimes mistake legend
for history, but that they do not commit historical
blunders more frequent and more outrageous than is
actually the case.

The early history of Christianity is far less obscure
than that of any of the other great religions ; we are apt
to forget how largely this is due to the initiative, learning,
and historical gifts of Eusebius.   But in this regard, even
more important than the emergence shortly after the
year A.D. 300 of a historian of real capacity was the
collection (probably made before A.D. 180) into a sacred
Canon—to form a New Testament, alongside of the Old—
of certain books which had already won their way into
general estimation in the Church as religious classics.
The list of books comprised in this New Testament varied
in different churches ; but all recognised the Four
Gospels, Acts, and a collection of epistles of Paul, while

most had the Apocalypse and some (these varied from church to church) of the Catholic Epistles. The formation of the Canon was due, not to any historical interest, but to the necessity of ruling out apocryphal Gospels and Acts produced by the Gnostics for the dissemination of their views. But though the motive was not historical, the result has saved the situation for the modern historical investigator. As against the Gnostics, the appeal of the Church *had* to be to books which were universally known to be *ancient*, as well as orthodox. Hence legendary works arising in orthodox circles (like the *Protevangelium of James*) were ruled out along with works of Gnostic origin ; and the orthodox revisions made at a later date of Acts originally Gnostic were unable to force an entrance into the Canon. Had the Church waited till the year A.D. 500 before drawing a sharp distinction between inspired scripture and all other religious writings, the greater part of the literature contained in Dr. James' *Apocryphal New Testament* would almost certainly have been included among the sacred books of Christianity. Again, the books of the New Testament themselves, but for the fact that (from A.D. 180 on, if not earlier) they were regarded as verbally inspired, would, like this Apocryphal literature, have been subjected to constant amplification and adaptation. We owe more to the Gnostics, or rather to what they forced the Church to do, than is usually supposed. But for the conflict with these early heretics, and the resultant canonisation of the New Testament, the early history of Christianity would have been as hard to trace, and the earliest forms of its sacred books might have been as difficult to determine, as is now the case with the history and literature of Buddhism.

By a fortunate series of accidents there has also survived the handful of early documents known collectively as the *Apostolic Fathers*—the epistles of 'Barnabas', Clement, Ignatius, and Polycarp; the *Didache* (a manual of ethics and Church Order), and a book of Visions, *The Shepherd of Hermas*.[1] The original Greek of two of these has come down in a single MS.; of two more in a couple of MSS. of which one is incomplete; and of two, part of the Greek text is lost, and the gaps must be supplied from an old Latin translation. The determination of their several dates and place of writing is of so great importance to the historian that each case merits careful discussion in the appropriate place in this volume. In point of date this collection of writings, and that other which we call the New Testament, overlap—the earlier 'Apostolic Fathers' being contemporary with some of the later writers of the New Testament. For that reason, though in spiritual value the Apostolic Fathers are in general much inferior, as historical evidence for the first hundred years of Christianity they must be studied side by side with the later writings of the New Testament.

Only upon the foundation of a critical study of these two collections of primitive writings can an authentic history of the early Church be built. The total extent of the material provided by both of them together is not large; but for the historian it has a very special quality. These documents are not like the casual hoards of old letters and diaries, which a dip into the lucky bag of history brings to light in some country house. Nor are

[1] The *Apostolic Fathers* are collected into a single volume (with original text, translation, and brief Introductions) by Lightfoot and Harmer, which includes also the (somewhat later) *Martyrdom of Polycarp, Epistle to Diognetus,* and fragments of Papias, etc. (Macmillan, 1893). All these, except the *Didache,* with comprehensive Introductions and notes in Latin, are contained in the three volume edition by Gebhardt and Harnack. A still more elaborate edition of the letters ascribed to Clement and Ignatius, in five volumes, is that of Lightfoot. By anyone who aspires to a real grasp of the history of the early Church, both these great editions should be studied and re-studied.

they that flotsam and jetsam of a bygone age which
chances to be left stranded in the inscriptions of a
cemetery or a buried city. They are the writings of men
who made history; often the very writings which were
the implements with which they made it. Such documents—once we can correctly date, place, and correlate
them—take us back to the storm centres of the Church
in an age which, like every other creative epoch in the
history of man, was essentially an age of conflict.

The historian of primitive Christianity is like an
architect called in to restore to its original form the
chapel of some ruined abbey which, partially rebuilt as
a village church in the eighteenth century, was further
renovated and enlarged during the Gothic revival.
First, he must clear away all later work; yet in so doing
he will look out for fragments of the ancient stone-work
built into new structure by the first restorer, or stiffly
copied by the second. It will then appear that there are
places where the original walls and arches stand out
practically intact; in others the old work is still there
to perhaps half of its original height. Elsewhere a wall
or a column has completely disappeared; yet its position can still be traced with absolute certainty from
the old foundations. But these must be dug for to be
discovered. And sometimes their position can only be
inferred. The diggers will come across broken pinnacles
and fragments of tracery. Of these, some will be lying
so near the spot where they first fell that there can be
little doubt of their original position; others will have
been removed some distance away. Yet others may
turn up, built into the walls of a neighbouring farmhouse,
or ornamenting a cottage garden. Much, therefore, of
the restoration will be a matter for conjecture. But

it will not be mere guess-work; for conjecture will always be controlled by careful study of the architecture of the period. The trained eye can detect that this shaft once stood in the clerestory, whereas that moulding belonged to the upper part of a window, on the left-hand side. From two stones it may be obvious what was the original shape of a complete arch. But there will also be cases where all that can be said is, that a gap from which no original fragment survives would probably, in a building of this character, have been filled by a wall of approximately such a height, pierced by windows of a number that can no longer be determined.

On principles not very dissimilar the historian must seek to piece together into a consistent whole what evidence survives. Some of this is plain and incontestable, some consists of scraps and casual hints, often derived from out-of-the-way sources, supplemented by inference which at times amounts only to 'scientific guessing'. But in one respect he differs from the architect. Human personality and human motive are among the causes of the sequence of events which he aspires to reconstruct. Deeds are *done*; they do not happen; to the study, then, of this part of his material he must bring some understanding of psychology, and some sympathy with human nature—alike in its heroism and in its pettiness. While, therefore, the historian will always aim at the objectivity of science, success in this very aim will depend upon his capacity to bring to bear upon his subject an imaginative insight into character and its reaction to circumstance akin to the novelists' art. In a task so difficult he may fairly crave an indulgent judgment on the achievement, even if its imperfections be grave.

II

THE APOSTLES AND THE CHURCHES

SYNOPSIS

THE TWELVE APOSTLES

WE ask again, What became of the Twelve Apostles ? According to the Gnostic Acts of Thomas (*c.* A.D. 250) they cast lots, and divided the regions of the world between them as their field of preaching—India falling to the lot of Thomas. It has been recently argued that the visit of Thomas to India is historical. With regard to the others, sources which are indubitably authentic give solid information only about Peter, James, and John. Brief discussion of the traditions connected with Matthew, Bartholomew, and Philip. Uncertainty as to the actual name of the twelfth Apostle.

Possibility that the rest of the Twelve confined their preaching to Palestine. At any rate, there is no basis in history for the traditional picture of the Apostles sitting at Jerusalem, like a College of Cardinals, systematising the doctrine and superintending the organisation of the Church.

JAMES OF JERUSALEM

The remarkable position held at Jerusalem by James, the brother of the Lord. This due to the fact that he was the eldest male of the Messianic House. But for the catastrophes which overwhelmed Jerusalem and the Jewish Christian Church, a Caliphate, hereditary in the family of our Lord, might have been developed.

Between the original Jewish Christian Church of Jerusalem and the purely Gentile Church of the city re-founded there (with the name Aelia) after A.D. 135, there was a complete breach of continuity. Nevertheless, the Bishops of Aelia gradually established their claim to sit in the Chair of James, and Jerusalem was recognised as the fifth Patriarchal See by the Council of Chalcedon. The survival of the *Clementine Homilies*, which exalt James above Peter, may not be unconnected with these ambitions.

Historically, James was the leader of the Judaising section of the Church. Peter's position was intermediate between James and Paul. Since, however, James was one of the brethren who did not believe in our Lord during His earthly life, while Peter was His most faithful follower, it is reasonable to suppose the Petrine attitude towards the Law of Moses

27

represents much nearer the actual teaching of Jesus. The attitude of James would represent rather that of the home in which Jesus was brought up.

Gentile Christianity

A mistake to regard this as mainly the creation of Paul. He did more than any other one individual, but he was not the founder of the Church in the three largest cities of the Empire, Antioch, Alexandria, and Rome.

Probability that many Gentile churches began with individual Jews of the Dispersion, who, having come up to Jerusalem on a pilgrimage and being there converted, returned to spread the good news in their place of residence. At any rate, the founders of the Gentile churches were not, like modern missionaries, persons trained in communities which inherited a long tradition of doctrine defined through controversy, a collection of specifically Christian sacred books, and a carefully thought-out system of Church Order.

Inevitably, local churches which had arisen in these various ways would exhibit great diversity. *The history of Catholic Christianity during the first five centuries is the history of the standardisation of a diversity having its origin in the Apostolic Age.*

Summary of reasons why the conception of an ideal unity of the Church was powerful enough to make such a standardisation practicable.

Evidence of Local Diversities

Our *a priori* expectation, that churches so founded would exhibit diversity in the matter of organisation, is enhanced when we notice in how many other matters of high importance there was in early times considerable diversity—a diversity which later gave way to a more or less standardised uniformity. Six illustrations of this.

The Great Churches

Till its destruction, A.D. 70, Jerusalem was the natural capital of Christianity—with Caesarea and Antioch as subordinate centres. After the fall of Jerusalem, Antioch, Ephesus, and Rome are for a hundred years centres of more or less equal importance. After that the influence of Rome steadily increases, while Alexandria steps into the place once held by Ephesus.

Brief survey of the characteristic spirit of the churches in these five capitals, with special reference to the relation of each to the literature and development of the early Church.

The cosmopolitan character of the population of Rome ; and the importance, more especially in the struggle with Marcion, of the claim to be the heir to the teaching of both Peter and Paul.

II

THE APOSTLES AND THE CHURCHES

THE TWELVE APOSTLES

WE ask again, What became of the Twelve Apostles ? The Gnostic, or all but Gnostic, *Acts of Thomas*—which many scholars believe was originally written, not in Greek but in Syriac, *c.* A.D. 250, in the church of Northern Mesopotamia—answers our question as follows :

> At that season all we the apostles were at Jerusalem, Simon which is called Peter, etc., . . . and we divided the regions of the world, that every one of us should go unto the region that fell to him by lot, and unto the nation whereunto the Lord sent him. According to the lot, therefore, India fell unto Judas Thomas, which is also the twin. . . .

It has been recently argued by Dr. J. N. Farquhar [1] that in these *Acts*—all but hidden under the luxuriant overgrowth of legend and invention—is preserved an authentic fragment of historic fact. There was a trade route between Alexandria and India—by boat up the Nile to Andropolis, then by land to a port on the Red Sea, and thence by ship across the Indian Ocean to the mouth of the Indus. The *Acts* mention a stay *en route* at a royal city, Andrapolis (*sic*), and the name of a king Gudnaphar (Gundaphorus), with a brother Gad, at whose court the Apostle is received. The name is the actual name of a king who reigned at Taxila in the

[1] *The Bulletin of the John Rylands Library*, x. 1 and xi. 1. (Manchester Univ. Press, 1926, 1927.)

Punjaub until a date *c.* A.D. 50, when his dynasty was completely destroyed by invaders known as Kushans; and the name Gudi occurs as that of a neighbouring prince. The dynasty was of Parthian origin—which accounts, suggests Dr. Farquhar, for the tradition which had reached Origen, that Thomas went to Parthia. Moreover, the ancient native church of Southern India, which claims to have been founded by St. Thomas, dates his arrival A.D. 52—which would be explained if Thomas left the kingdom of Gudnaphar in view of, or just after, the invasion which led to its destruction.

Be this as it may, the opening scene in the *Acts of Thomas*, the Twelve casting lots for the regions of the world, is just a picturesque development of the story already discussed (p. 12 ff.) that they left Jerusalem twelve years after the Resurrection. It is possible that their twelve years' residence in Jerusalem may rest on genuine tradition, rather than merely on inference from Acts xiii. 7, as I have suggested above. But even so, it is still, I think, remarkable how soon, when we search the early authorities on which alone sober Church history can be built, we discover that there are only three of the Twelve about whose careers any detailed information exists—Peter, James, and John. About these alone have the Synoptic gospels, the Acts or the Epistles, anything in particular to record.[1]

The career of one, James the son of Zebedee, was very brief, as he was put to death in Jerusalem by Herod Agrippa I., who himself died in A.D. 44; and it is significant that in the second century even legend busies itself only with the names of Peter and John, and the two leaders who were not of the Twelve, James the Lord's brother and Paul; while the apocryphal Acts of

[1] On Matthew in Mt. ix. 9, see p. 32. Mark twice names Andrew—but only in connection with Peter (Mk. i. 16; xiii. 3).

the third century begin with Andrew, Thomas, and
Philip—apostles about whom only the Fourth Gospel
has anything to tell. The Twelve are said to have been
present on the Day of Pentecost, and at the choosing of
the Seven; and in the Acts (for the last time Acts xv.
22) 'the apostles', in the plural, are frequently spoken
of as being in Jerusalem. But none is mentioned by
name except Peter, John, and James; and in the
epistle to the Galatians (i. 19) Paul says expressly that
on his first visit to Jerusalem, three years after his
conversion, he met there of the Twelve only Peter; and
on his second visit (Gal. ii. 9) he speaks as if he saw
only Peter and John—the James there mentioned is
not the son of Zebedee (who was already dead) but the
brother of the Lord. It is stated in the Acts (ix. 27)
that on the former of these occasions Barnabas introduced
Paul to ' the apostles '; the author of Acts was therefore
either misinformed as to the facts, or else uses the plural
' apostles ' to cover only two names—one of them, James
the brother of the Lord, not being a member of the
Twelve. On either hypothesis the evidence for a continued residence of the Twelve in Jerusalem disappears.

Paul had lived in Jerusalem, so had Mark; his
mother's house was a place of resort for many members
of the Church there (Acts xii. 12). Luke knew some
Jerusalem traditions. The conjecture lies handy that
one reason—apart from their outstanding personalities
—why Peter, James, and John are the only three of
the Twelve of whom any definite action is recorded in
the Synoptics, the Acts, or Epistles, may be that they
alone did make Jerusalem a kind of headquarters, and
were thus familiar to that church. In any society the
anecdotes most frequently told concern persons well
known to it. But even legend gives the rest of the

Apostles only twelve years in the Holy City. The permanent resident head of the Church of Jerusalem is not one of the Twelve, but James the brother of the Lord.

To John are ascribed the Gospel, Epistles, and Apocalypse, which together make up nearly one-fifth of the New Testament. If that ascription is correct, we must accept the tradition that he migrated to Ephesus, and died there in extreme old age about A.D. 100. Personally, I am unable to accept the ascription of these works to an Apostle, and believe that the tradition that St. John lived in Ephesus is due to a confusion between him and the Elder John, about whom I shall have much to say in the next lecture. Accordingly, I am inclined to think that an authentic tradition lies behind the fragment of Papias which says that the Apostle John was 'killed by Jews', presumably in Palestine before the destruction of Jerusalem in A.D. 70.

The attachment of the name Matthew to the first Gospel creates a presumption that one of the sources which it incorporates—possibly Q—was the work of that Apostle ; but the substitution (Matt. ix. 9) of his name for that of Levi, the publican mentioned in the parallel passages in Mark and Luke, is open to suspicion of being merely a conjecture arising from the desire to give biographical distinctness to the author either of the Gospel or of its most important source.

If any of the Twelve left Palestine, we should expect them to go first of all to the Jews in the provinces bordering on Palestine, or to those in Babylonia. There is an obscure statement in Eusebius (*H.E.* v. 10. 3) that Pantaenus—subsequently, *c.* A.D. 180, founder of the Catechetical School of Alexandria—discovered among the Indians a copy of the Gospel of Matthew in Hebrew, handed down by persons converted by Bartholomew. It is not clear that their actual conversion took place in India ; also it has been suggested that the name India might apply to a district of South Arabia. But we may have here a scrap of evidence for the existence of a church founded by Bartholomew at some place (possibly in Arabia) which had trading connections with India.

Philip, one of the Twelve, is stated in a letter of Polycrates, Bishop of Ephesus (c. A.D. 190), preserved by Eusebius (*H.E.* iii. 31. 3), to have been buried at Hierapolis in Asia Minor. But a comparison of his statement with those of the Acts (xxi. 8-9) and of a Roman writer Gaius, c. A.D. 200 (both of which are quoted by Eusebius in the same chapter), makes it practically certain that the Philip in question was really Philip ' the Evangelist ', one of the Seven, whose earlier exploits are narrated in Acts viii., and who seems to have settled subsequently, with the prophetesses his daughters, in Caesarea.

Thus most of the Twelve are mere names ; and even the list of names varied with the tradition current in different localities. The twelfth name is given respectively as Thaddaeus, Lebbaeus, or as Judas son of James, in the first three Gospels. The MSS. have suffered, though in quite different ways, from assimilation of the parallel lists and from conflation. Origen, however, seems to me clearly to indicate the true text when he says, ' The disciple whom Matthew names Thaddaeus, Mark calls Lebbaeus; and Luke, Judas of James '.[1]

---

[1] The *Epistula Apostolorum*, a second-century document (included in M. R. James's *Apocryphal New Testament*) recently discovered, of either Asian or Egyptian origin, gives the following list : John, Thomas, Peter, Andrew, James, Philip, Bartholomew, Matthew, Nathaniel, Judas Zelotes, and Cephas— Paul, who is mentioned later, being probably regarded as the twelfth. This, however, is not an independent tradition but a selection and conflation from the various lists in the New Testament. The conflation Judas Zelotes occurs also in Matt. x. 3, in the Old Latin MSS. a b g h *gat*, and in the mosaics in the (fifth century) Baptistery of the Orthodox at Ravenna. In the *Acts of Thomas*

Again, it is by no means certain that the identification of Nathaniel, mentioned by John, with the Apostle elsewhere called Bartholomew, was intended by the author of the Fourth Gospel.

Of Peter, James, and John we learn something from the Epistles and Acts. Of what happened to the rest of the Twelve we can, I think, get a hint from the opening words of the ' Mission Charge ' in Matt. x. Schweitzer assumes that Matt. x. represents practically a word for word report of a discourse actually delivered on the occasion of the sending out of the Twelve ; and on that assumption bases the strange theory that Christ expected to be manifested in glory to judge the world before the disciples had returned from that preaching tour in Galilee. It is remarkable that so acute a mind should not have perceived that this assumption implies a degree of confidence in the accuracy of the report, legitimate only to a believer either in verbal inspiration or in the presence with the company in Galilee of a shorthand writer. Actually, of course, the sayings of Christ were collected long after they were spoken, and they were written down for a definite purpose—the guidance of the early Church on practical issues. Here, then, we have a collection of sayings giving advice to Christian missionaries which begins:

Go not into any way of the Gentiles, and enter not into any city of the Samaritans, but go rather to the lost sheep of the house of Israel (Mt. x. 5 f.).

That the reason for this prohibition is primarily the shortness of the time, appears later :

---

and other literature of the Church of Edessa—presumably because Thomas was regarded not as a name, but as a description, i.e. " twin "—we find the combination " Judas Thomas ". In the old Syriac the text of John xiv. 22 is emended accordingly ; for the usual " Judas (not Iscariot) ", *Syr. Cur.* reads " Judas Thomas ", and *Syr. Sin.* simply " Thomas ".

For verily I say unto you, Ye shall not have gone through the cities of Israel, till the Son of man be come (Mt. x. 23).

The natural inference is that this particular collection of sayings took shape in the period when the controversy as to the admission of Gentiles to the Church was at its height. We should naturally date it about the time of Paul's visit to Jerusalem (Gal. ii. 1 ff.), when James, Peter, and John made clear to him their conviction that, though God seemed to have called *him* to preach to Gentiles, *their* duty was to the circumcised.

We may, however, fairly question whether this collocation of sayings would have survived intact long enough to become incorporated in our first Gospel, unless it reflected the actual procedure of the Twelve. So interpreted, this passage supplies the one piece of evidence we have as to what really became of them. What they did was to continue going about two by two, avoiding cities of the Gentile and the Samaritan, confining their preaching to the lost sheep of the house of Israel—fearing that, even so, they would not have visited the cities of Israel till the Son of man should return to judge the world.

At any rate, that the Twelve did confine themselves to 'the lost sheep of the house of Israel', there are other indications. The promise to 'sit on thrones, judging the twelve tribes of Israel' (Mt. xix. 28 ; Lk. xxiii. 30), is enigmatic ; the function of 'judging' clearly belongs to them, not only in the present world-order, but in the life of the world-to-come. Nevertheless it implies a special association, both of their number and of their work on earth, with Israel as such. This same association best explains the importance attached to the filling up of the mystic number Twelve by the election of Matthias (Acts i. 15 ff.). Finally, the

passage in Galatians already referred to proves con-
clusively the baselessness of the later tradition that, after
twelve years in Jerusalem spent preaching to Jews, the
Apostles separated in order to carry the Gospel to the
Gentiles.   Here it is emphatically stated that—at a date
at least sixteen, possibly as much as twenty, years after
the Crucifixion—even Peter still regarded his mission as
limited to ' the circumcision '.   Nor is there any evidence
that Peter—even though (at one time) ready to eat and
drink with Gentiles—ever changed his conception of his
own call.   If, later on, he went to Rome, it might well
be to preach to the very large Jewish settlement there ;
or he may have gone unwillingly, like Paul and Ignatius
—a leading Christian arrested while working in an
Eastern city.

Whether any of the Apostles besides the three ' pillars '
were present at the so-called Council of Jerusalem (Acts
xv. 50 ff.) is a matter of dispute; the decision rests largely
on the answer given to the further question whether
the occasion is or is not the same as the second of the
visits of Paul to Jerusalem mentioned in Galatians.[1]
But even on the assumption that all were present, they
are not represented as recognising for themselves a
mission to the Gentiles, but merely as authorising certain
liberties in regard to the observance of the Law by
Gentile converts demanded by Paul and Barnabas, who,
in claiming such a mission, were held to have proved their
case.   What the Apostles present on that occasion did
was to exercise that power ' to bind and to loose ', which
in one place in the first Gospel (Mt. xvi. 19) is ascribed
specially to Peter; in another passage (xviii. 18)—probably from a different source—to the Apostles as a body.

Judaism is a religion with a single dogma—that God

[1] Cf. *The Four Gospels*, p. 556, footnote.

is One (cf. Jas. ii. 19) ; but this no Jew disputed. To
the Jew, then, the only ' orthodoxy ' about which controversy was possible concerned the stricter or laxer
interpretations of the Law ; here the Rabbi came in.
In technical Rabbinic phrase, ' binding ' or ' loosing '
means the allowing or disallowing of particular types
of action by a recognised exponent of the traditional
interpretation of the Law. So far, then, as the right
to exercise this power is conceived as vested in the
Apostles they would constitute, not so much a Christian
Sanhedrin, as a Christian School of Rabbis. As touching
the extent to which the obligations of the Law are
applicable to Christians, they speak with authority—by
the commission of Christ. But in the Palestinian Church
questions concerning definition of doctrinal belief or
ecclesiastical jurisdiction were simply not under consideration. If such questions had arisen, the Apostles
would have been the natural persons to consult ; but
that was *not* the purpose for which it was supposed they
had been called.

From the standpoint of such a situation both the
scope and the title of a document like the *Didache*
becomes clear. The title, *The Teaching of the Lord
through the Twelve Apostles to the Gentiles,* does not mean
that at about the year A.D. 90 Syrian tradition had it
that the Twelve actually, themselves, preached to the
Gentiles. It is meant, I shall argue later (p. 146, *n.*), to
suggest that the injunctions contained in the book are
ethical and ceremonial rules approved (at least in
principle) by the Apostles at the Council of Jerusalem
—the historic occasion on which, in regard to Gentile
Christians, they exercised the authority to bind and to
loose conferred on them by the Lord. The precepts
laid down in the *Didache* are conceived as being an

amplification of, if not almost a commentary upon, the epistle (usually called the *Apostolic Decree*) sent out by that Council to the churches of Syria. In no way is it implied that the Twelve themselves conducted a mission to the Gentiles ; still less that the authority inherent in their office was primarily of an administrative character.

There follows an important conclusion. To understand the history of early Christianity we must begin by eliminating from our minds the traditional picture of the Twelve Apostles sitting at Jerusalem, like a College of Cardinals, systematising the doctrine, and superintending the organisation, of the Primitive Church. They had a more urgent work to do. The Day of Judgment was at hand ; their duty was to call men to repent before it was too late. When the Lord might any day return in glory, it was unprofitable to build up an organisation about which the one thing certain was that it was never meant to last.

JAMES OF JERUSALEM

Dismissing, then, as a fancy picture drawn in a later age, the idea of a Board of apostolic legislators, we turn to the study of the evidence. Here we are at once struck by the remarkable position held at Jerusalem by James the brother of the Lord. About him we are in the fortunate position of being able to draw information from Josephus (*Ant.* xx. 9. 1) as well as from the New Testament.[1] From these sources, and from the position he occupies in Ebionite romance, it becomes clear that James of

---

[1] The account of his death given by Hegesippus (*ap.* Eus. *H.E.* ii. 23) is regarded as suspicious by Lightfoot as being derived from a lost Ebionite romance, the ἀναβαθμοί of James, mentioned by Eusebius and probably drawn upon in the *Clementines* (cf. *Galatians*, p. 330-66). But even if this be so, it probably rests on early Palestinian tradition.

Jerusalem ranks with Peter and Paul as one of the three outstanding individuals by whose personal gifts and influence was determined, humanly speaking, the future development of the Primitive Church. It is one of the ironies of history that his name does not appear in the Calendar of Saints in the Western Church—he having been wrongly identified with James the Less, the son of Alphaeus, one of the inconspicuous members of the Twelve.[1]

In the epistle to the Galatians, our earliest authority, three persons are named by Paul as the universally recognised 'pillars' of the Church, *i.e.* James—James the son of Zebedee was by this time dead—Peter, and John. Of the three, James has the first place, though not a member of the Twelve. It is also strange to find that there were persons in the Church who, alleging the authority of James, presumed to set Peter right for his behaviour at Antioch (Gal. ii. 12); it is hardly less strange that Peter gives way to them, at any rate for a time—thereby bringing down upon himself a fierce rebuke from Paul.

With the order of precedence in Galatians we may compare the actual superiority to most of the Twelve asserted in a passage of Clement of Alexandria—possibly derived by him from Hegesippus:

After the Resurrection the Lord imparted the (true) knowledge to James the Just, and John, and Peter. These handed it on to the rest of the Apostles; and the rest of the Apostles to the Seventy, one of whom was Barnabas (Eus. *H.E.* ii. 1. 4).

This pre-eminent position accorded to James seems remarkable to us, only because we moderns take for granted both an international spiritual conception of

[1] Cf. Dissertation II. in Lightfoot's *Galatians*.

Christianity and a more or less democratic view of the rights and qualifications of ruling persons. But to the Jewish Christian, Jesus was the national Messiah—destined to revive, on an infinitely grander scale, the glories of the golden age of David. And to the Jew both monarchy and priesthood were offices essentially hereditary in a sacred house. The Jewish Christian, then, would take it for granted that the most prominent male relation of Jesus was marked out to be His Vicegerent by Divine right, until He came again. Anything else would have seemed in the last degree unnatural. The prestige of birth was consolidated by personal character. James, styled the Just for his austere observance of the Law, lived on for many years, so Hegesippus states (*cf.* Eus. *H.E.* ii. 23), highly respected by orthodox Jews. In A.D. 62, accepting the date implied by Josephus—that is, at the beginning of the outburst of nationalistic and religious fanaticism which brought on the Jewish war—James was murdered by the mob ; and shortly afterwards the Christian community fled the city and took refuge in Pella, a Gentile centre beyond the Jordan. After A.D. 70 Jerusalem was slowly repopulated and some Jewish Christians came back ; Symeon, the nephew of James—that is, another member of the royal house—is at once recognised as their head. It was Harnack, I think, who first pointed out that Christianity, like Mohammedanism, might have developed a Caliphate, hereditary in the family of James. But three things made this impossible : first, the breach of continuity caused by the double destruction of Jerusalem, in A.D. 70, and again in A.D. 135 (after which no Jew was allowed to live in the city) ; secondly, the peculiar impetus given to Gentile Christianity by the genius of St. Paul ; thirdly, the enormous disparity in numbers, intelligence, and wealth between the rapidly growing Gentile churches and the decimated fragment of Jewish Christianity which still struggled on in Palestine.

Later writers uniformly speak of James as the first Bishop of Jerusalem. Epiphanius, probably on the authority of Hegesippus (who represents mid-second-century Palestinian tradition), says distinctly that James was appointed Bishop of Jerusalem by the Lord Himself.[1] I would venture the surmise that this statement (of Hegesippus) was an inference from the *Gospel according to the Hebrews*. We know that he used this Gospel as an authority ; and Jerome quotes a fragment of its account of the Appearance of Christ to James after the Resurrection. This account may well have included a special commission of the Lord to James, similar to the ' feed my sheep', spoken to Peter (John xxi. 15 ff.).

There was great rivalry between the Sees of Jerusalem and Caesarea for the primacy of Palestine ; Jerusalem based its case on the status of James. That is why Eusebius, as Bishop of Caesarea, prefers another statement of Clement of Alexandria (*H.E.* ii. 1. 3)—although he is later in date and obviously a much poorer authority for affairs in Palestine—that James was appointed Bishop of Jerusalem by the Apostles Peter, James, and John. But Eusebius, having something of the historian's conscience, does not quite suppress the statement of the earlier authority ; for he says elsewhere that James

received the episcopate of the Church of Jerusalem at the hands of the Saviour Himself *and* His apostles (*H.E.* vii. 19).

In the *Clementine Homilies*, we have seen, James

---

[1] Cf. H. J. Lawlor, *Eusebiana*, p. 16 f. (Clarendon Press, 1912). Also the Menology quoted *op. cit.* p. 44, *n.* 3.

is depicted as occupying a position of almost Papal authority. Peter is made to write a letter, which begins :

Peter to James, the lord and bishop of the holy Church, under the Father of all, through Jesus Christ.

Similarly Clement, writing explicitly as Peter's successor in the See of Rome, opens his letter :

Clement to James, the lord, and the bishop of bishops, who rules Jerusalem, the holy Church of the Hebrews, and the churches everywhere excellently founded by the providence of God.

The *Homilies* are party propaganda in the form of a historical novel ; and the passages quoted are not history but caricature. But caricature has no propaganda value unless it has a basis in something which is popularly believed.

Between the original Jewish Christian Church at Jerusalem and the church which grew up in the purely Gentile city of Aelia (built by Hadrian after the second destruction of Jerusalem, A.D. 135) there was a complete breach of continuity. But already in the second century there had begun the stream of pilgrims to see " the Place where the Gospel was proclaimed and the Gospel history was acted out ".[1] Soon the Gentile Church in the new pagan Jerusalem became, as Prof. Burkitt happily puts it, " like a new purchaser that has bought the Old Manor House, who after a while begins to collect old family portraits and souvenirs—coming at last to believe himself the genuine heir of the old line ".[2] For some years, evidently, before the time of Eusebius (cf. *H.E.* vii. 19. 1), pilgrims were shown the episcopal Chair actually used by James the brother of the Lord.

---

[1] So Melito of Sardis—who died some time before A.D. 190 (Eus. *H.E.* iv. 26) ; the term τόποι, " the Places ", became a technical term for the Sacred Sites of Palestine ; cf. C. H. Turner, *J.T.S.* i. p. 551.

[2] F. C. Burkitt, *Christian Beginnings*, p. 68. (Univ. of London Press, 1924.)

What explanation was given of its marvellous survival through two destructions of the city we are not told ; possibly no one asked so tactless a question. But at Rome what could they do—the point of honour would demand it — but retaliate by exhibiting a Chair of Peter ? And this, more fortunate than Jerusalem, Rome can still show.

The unimportant Gentile Church of Aelia-Jerusalem was naturally at first under the jurisdiction of the Metropolitan of Caesarea, the civil capital of Palestine ; but the possession of the Sacred Sites, and the claim to sit in the seat of James, enabled its bishops gradually to assert their independence of Caesarea. Later on, after a preposterous attempt by Bishop Juvenal to assert supremacy over Antioch itself, the Council of Chalcedon recognised the claim of Jerusalem to patriarchal pre-eminence—alongside of Rome, Alexandria, Antioch, and Constantinople. In the long struggle of which this was the triumphant climax, a letter written to James by Peter—whose successor the Patriarch of Antioch claimed to be—in terms of deference as marked as in the above quotation, would be an asset of great value to the successors of James. I have little doubt that, if we knew the details of the textual tradition, we should find that the *Homilies* (which embodies this letter) was the version of the Clementine romance most popular within the sphere of influence of the Patriarch of Jerusalem ; whereas the *Recognitions* (in which it does not appear) would be the recension circulating in that of Antioch— where, as in the West, the primacy of Peter had become a postulate of Faith and Order.

James was one of 'the brethren' who in the lifetime of Jesus did not believe in Him ; and even on one occasion

(Mark iii. 21, 31) made an attempt to restrain Him on the suspicion that He was beside Himself. This surely explains the conservative attitude of James in the controversy as to the position of Gentiles and the binding power of the Law. The attitude of James, as distinct from that of Peter, is only what we should expect if James reflects in the main the religion of the home in which Jesus was brought up—modified little save by the conviction that He was Messiah, which followed on a post-resurrection Appearance. Peter, who had actually followed Jesus and opened his whole soul to His preaching, does not hesitate to baptize Cornelius without any stipulation as to observance of the Law ; and later on at Antioch, when left to himself, he will go so far as actually to break the Law in order, in the spirit of full Christian brotherhood, to eat and drink with Gentile converts (Gal. ii. 12). Ought not the historian to look to Peter, rather than to James, as representing the real attitude of Jesus Himself towards the Gentile and towards the Law ? What Paul did was to work out with clear-sighted logic the full implications of an attitude of which Peter had merely an instinctive apprehension.

Gentile Christianity

Judaistic Christianity, then, should be regarded as the Christianity, not so much of the Twelve, as of James. What of Gentile Christianity ? The fundamental fallacy of histories of the Apostolic age inspired by the Tübingen school was the tacit assumption that Gentile Christianity was of one single type, and that that type was the creation of Paul.

Paul laboured more abundantly than they all ; more churches were founded by him than by any other one man. But he was *not* the first to preach to Gentiles; that was the glory (Acts xi. 20) of unnamed men of Cyprus and Cyrene. He was the first effectively to plant Christianity in the chief cities of Asia Minor, Macedonia, and Greece. But he was *not* the founder of the Church in the three cities which in size and influence stood out unique in the Mediterranean world—Antioch, Alexandria, and Rome. And these were the three churches whose traditions were destined ultimately to dominate the Catholic Church. In later years both Antioch and Rome were proud to recall their connection with him. But during his lifetime there was, even in Rome, as the epistle to the Philippians shows, a party vigorously hostile to him to the end. And in the Church of Antioch, with its far greater proportion of Jewish members and its propinquity to Jerusalem— the focus of the anti - Pauline counter - missions which visited the Churches of Galatia and Corinth—it is a fair presumption that his influence was considerably less. If we are to associate the outlook of Antioch—the first capital of Gentile Christianity—with the name of any Apostle it will be (cf. p. 58) with that of Peter.

There is little reason to suppose that the majority of Gentile churches were founded by persons who, like Barnabas and Paul, adopted the life of a wandering preacher as a life career. Doubtless there were some such ; but they differed in one essential point from the modern missionary. The modern missionary is a man with a professional training ; he goes out to heathen lands with a complete New Testament in his hands, which he interprets in accordance with a theology, and a tradition of discipline and devotion, which it has taken centuries to evolve. The Primitive Church had no New Testament, no thought-out theology, no stereotyped traditions. The men who took Christianity to the Gentile

world had had no special training, only a great experience—in which ' all maxims and philosophies were
reduced to the simple task of walking in the light since
the light had come '.

Jerusalem was a pilgrimage centre, like Mecca or
Rome to-day. To the great feasts from all parts of the
world came Jews of the Dispersion. At great cost, after
years of aspiration, perhaps once in his lifetime the exile
would approach the Mountain of immemorial sanctity.
Among these, as the story of the day of Pentecost
suggests, many would be found to listen eagerly to the
news that ' the hope of Israel ' had been fulfilled. When
such returned to Carthage or Cyrene, to Ctesiphon or
Rome, they would not keep quiet. Who first preached
Christ at Damascus ? We only know that it was done
some time before the conversion of Paul. Who brought
the new religion to Antioch ? Not Apostles or trained
missionaries, but unnamed Jews of the Dispersion
who had caught the fire in Jerusalem, and had therefore to flee the persecution in which Stephen fell (Acts
xi. 19-20).

The facts to which I have called attention are patent
and undisputed. It is, then, remarkable that so few
historians have pointed out that churches so founded
must have differed from one another indefinitely—
differed according to the degree of knowledge and insight
of the first enthusiast who preached there, according also
to the temper and type of their earliest converts. There
was ' one Lord, one faith, one baptism '—but the content
of that faith and its outward expression in the life of the
local community cannot but have varied enormously
from place to place. There follows the principle I have
had occasion to emphasise in another connection[1] : *The*

---

[1] Cf. *The Four Gospels*, p. 15.

history of Catholic Christianity during the first five centuries
is the history of a progressive standardisation of a diversity
which had its origin in the Apostolic age.

This standardisation would not have been possible, it
would not even have been desired, but for the fact that *in*
theory the Church was from the beginning and always
envisaged as one and indivisible. In modern times
all who would establish a community on international
lines—a League of Nations, a Federation of Labour, or
what not—are confronted at once with the tremendous
difficulty of getting men, originally grouped in national,
local, or sectional societies, to recognise a common bond of
union and to feel an *effective loyalty* to the larger brotherhood. Even when a central organisation has been
created to embody the wider idea, it is a long while before
this can elicit from the generality an allegiance strong
enough to outbalance the centrifugal tendencies of the
interests and traditions of the smaller constituent groups.
In the primitive Church this difficulty simply did not
exist, for the simple reason that the first Christians did
not regard themselves as a new society, but as the ancient
' People of God ', that is, as that portion of the Church of
the Patriarchs and Prophets which had not, by rejecting
the Messiah, forfeited its birthright and cut itself off from
the ' promises of Israel '. Many of the prophets had
proclaimed that only a ' remnant ' of Israel after the
flesh would repent and be saved ; others had foretold
that in the Messianic age Gentiles also would be brought
to share the religious privileges of Israel. The Christian
position was that, by recognising Jesus as Messiah, they
and they alone understood the prophets aright. The
number of Jews who had rejected the Messiah was larger
than might have been expected, so also was the number
of Gentiles who had accepted Him ; but that did not in

any way alter the fundamental position that only the community of those who did accept Him could claim to be the ' Israel of God '.

During the first fifty years of Christianity—but less so with every decade after that—the adoption of this conception of the Church as the ' remnant ' of Israel entailed four important consequences.

(1) Lack of definition, and even considerable diversity in regard to doctrine, caused small offence. The genius of the Jew was ethical; to him religious orthodoxy expressed itself in conduct, that is, in a strict observance of the Law. Indeed, precisely because to the Jew orthodoxy and patriotism alike centred in the Law of Moses, the controversy as to the observance of the Law did all but break up the Apostolic Church. In regard to this matter the situation was saved by the fact—of which the epistle to the Galatians is our chief first-hand evidence— that, while Paul and James were hailed as leaders of the factions most opposed, Peter (perhaps with some vacillation) held an intermediate position.

(2) Theoretically Christians were the ' new Israel '; and members of a ' nation ' scattered amid other peoples have a natural tendency to cohere with one another without the assistance of any external organisation. Hence the precise method of organisation would seem relatively unimportant. Membership of the Ecclesia, the ' congregation of Israel ', was the important thing ; and all who were baptized in the name of the Lord were *ipso facto* members of the ' remnant ', however it might locally be organised.

(3) By many this Divine society was conceived as being also the mystical body of Christ; and this could not but enhance their sense of a fundamental oneness of all believers. It was further intensified by the fact that the

weekly assemblage for solemn worship found expression in the Eucharist—ever renewing the union of the faithful with one another and with the One Lord.

(4) To the new Israel, as to the old, the Old Testament was the Holy Book, Jerusalem was the Holy City. These two provided a bond of unity, not only as between Jew and Gentile, but also as between the Gentile churches of different localities. It is evident that the carefully organised collection for the impoverished church in Jerusalem, mentioned so often in Paul's epistles, had a political, so to speak, as well as a purely philanthropic, object (Rom. xv. 26 f., 31). The Gentile churches were to be made to feel the essential unity of the Church by realising their debt to, and their unity with, the Mother Church; the Mother Church was to recognise the Gentile communities as true daughters of Israel.

But between A.D. 62–67 death removed the leaders, James, Peter, and Paul, on whose prestige and moderation so much had depended; in A.D. 70 Jerusalem and its Temple were destroyed, and the church there was decimated and forced to flee the city. For the next few decades the centrifugal tendency—inherent in the Gentile churches, from diversity of race, temper, and the circumstances of their foundation—was checked by little but a vivid consciousness of an ideal union and by the growing prestige of the writings which later came to form the New Testament—in the first generation only the Gospel of Mark, collections of sayings of the Lord like Q, and some of the epistles of Paul.

It follows that the historian should approach the study of the scanty evidence for the organisation of the early Church and the origin of the ministry with an antecedent expectation of discovering, not a uniform system, but a wide range of local diversity.

E

Evidence of Local Diversities

That expectation is intensified by the observation that in other matters of the first importance diversity rather than uniformity is the note of the Church even in the second and third centuries. For in every case this diversity appears to be, not a recent development, but the survival of a more primitive state of things. To marshal the evidence for this diversity and to discuss it in detail would be to digress too far from the main subject of this book. I can only call attention to the implications of the following facts.

(1) A divergency between the churches of Rome and Asia in regard to the day on which Easter should be observed was a matter of acute controversy throughout the second century, leading to the excommunication of Asia by Rome about A.D. 195. But when Polycarp of Smyrna visited Rome in A.D. 155, both he and the Bishop of Rome could urge as immemorial the practice of their respective churches. This divergence, then, must have gone back at least to the sub-apostolic period.

(2) The Gospels of Matthew and Luke coincide with one another over a large part of their contents. Their *coincidence* is adequately accounted for by their dependence on two earlier writtings, Mark and Q—written documents acquire authority in places very far apart. Less easy of explanation is the *startling divergence* in the traditions they follow in regard to the Birth and Infancy of Christ, and the Appearances after the Resurrection— let alone the glaring discrepancy between the genealogies in these Gospels, or between the accounts given by the same two writers of the end of Judas (Matt. xxvii. 3 ff. ;

Acts i. 18 ff.). This is only explicable if there existed
a high degree of local independence in the sub-Apostolic
age—even in regard to matters which must have been
considered as of supreme importance.

(3) It is a commonplace of the history of dogma
that the great doctrinal disputes tended to follow lines
of local cleavage corresponding roughly to the spheres of
influence of Alexandria and Antioch. Egypt tended to
favour a theology which was incarnationist to the verge
of docetism; Syria inclined to one which leaned towards
the adoptionist side. The Latin attitude, though verbally
often a synthesis of the two chief Eastern views, had an
individuality of its own.[1] But if we put side by side
the high Christology and mystical allegorising tendency
of the Alexandrian epistle of Barnabas (cf. p. 237, 246),
and the practical, ethical, non-theological interest of the
Syrian *Didache*, we see that the difference of emphasis—
not to say of actual doctrine—which we find between
Egypt and Syria in the fourth century is already present
in the sub-Apostolic age; though the fact that Ignatius
could represent Antioch shows that this point must not
be pressed too far.

(4) A study of the older MSS. versions and patristic
quotations enables us to recover the greatly variant
texts of the Gospels (and Acts) which were used in different churches about A.D. 230—and the main variations
clearly go back to a much earlier date. These local
texts were gradually replaced by a single standardised
text.[2] The actual evidence for this variety belongs to
a period somewhat later than that we are here discussing. Nevertheless, seeing that it is evidence of a
local diversity which lasted on *long after* the process

---

[1] Cf. *Essays on the Trinity and Incarnation*, p. 242 ff., ed. A. E. J. Rawlinson. (Longmans, 1928.)

[2] Cf. *The Four Gospels*, Part I.

of general standardisation had begun, it affords an interesting analogy.

(5) No student of Liturgiology will need to be reminded that each of the great centres of Christianity evolved its own type of Liturgy. But attempts to trace these back to their earliest form suggest that, apart from a very few constant features, there existed a maximum of freedom and diversity in the earliest period.

(6) The Canon of the New Testament seems to have been finally settled by the list promulgated in the *Festal Letter* of Athanasius, A.D. 367, which doubtless represents an agreement between Alexandria and Rome; at least this is the earliest list of the books of the New Testament which exactly corresponds to that which ultimately prevailed. Till then—and indeed for some time afterwards in the East—there was considerable local diversity among the churches as to the inclusion or exclusion of the Apocalypse and of certain of the Epistles. From about A.D. 180 all churches had included in their list at least the Four Gospels, the Acts, and a collection of epistles of Paul; but there were local differences as to the number of epistles in the *Corpus Paulinum*. In Alexandria there were fourteen, including Hebrews (cf. p. 129); Asia (cf. Polycarp's letter) had long recognised thirteen; but the exclusion by Marcion (and in part by Tatian) of the Pastorals, makes it probable that (perhaps till A.D. 170) the Roman collection included only ten. Again, in Asia the Four Gospel Canon is, I think, implied by Papias (A.D. 140 or earlier); [1] but in Rome—to judge by the use made of

---

[1] To Papias, Mark and Matthew are Church classics, yet his language is curiously disparaging in regard to the order (of events) in Mark, and to the correctness of the translation of the discourses (λόγια) in Matthew. This is most easily explained if he (or his informant, John the Elder) preferred the order of events, and the contents of the discourses, of the Fourth Gospel (cf. my *The Four Gospels*, p. 19 ff.). Since John seems to be dependent on Luke,

them by Justin Martyr—not more than three of the
Gospels were acknowledged as authoritative by A.D. 150.
And there is reason to suppose that even this measure
of standardisation had only been arrived at by a gradual
process.[1]

Standardisation is likely to be first attempted where
the need for it seems most urgent. In a community
beset with foes within and without, the development
of an organisation of proved efficiency may even be a
condition of survival. It is not disputed that by A.D. 200
a system of Church organisation, in its main structure
uniform, had come into existence throughout the
Christian world. But in view of the facts summarised
in this lecture, the hypothesis that this uniformity of
system displaced an earlier diversity is, I submit, one
that has a valid claim to serious consideration.

THE GREAT CHURCHES

Till A.D. 70 the Church looked to Jerusalem as its
capital. But the student of the history of the next
hundred years of Christianity must keep his eyes fixed
mainly on the Churches of Antioch, Ephesus, and Rome—
not, however, as yet on that of Alexandria.

Alexandria and Antioch—after Rome, the largest
cities in the civilised world—still retained, at any rate
in the East, much of the prestige which before their
absorption into the Roman Empire they had enjoyed
as capitals of the two largest kingdoms founded by the
successors of Alexander the Great. Cities of approxi-

---

the Third Gospel must have been recognised in Asia in the time of Papias ; but
if Papias, like the writer of the *Muratorianum*, merely emphasised the fact that
Luke did *not* see the Lord in the flesh, later writers would have found nothing
in Luke which it was worth while to quote, and 'the silence of Eusebius' in
regard to any mention of Luke by Papias needs no explanation.

[1] Cf. *The Four Gospels*, p. 526 f.

mately equal size, but reflecting very different racial temperaments and intellectual and religious traditions, they were destined, from the third century onwards, to reproduce in ecclesiastical controversy the immemorial rivalry between Syria and Egypt.

After the year A.D. 200 Alexandria rapidly became the intellectual centre of the Christian world, as it had long been of the Greek. A turning-point in the history of the Church there had been the inception (by Pantaenus about A.D. 180) of the Catechetical School. The famous Museum and Library of Alexandria really formed what nowadays would be called a post-graduate University ; and the relation of the Catechetical School to this has been happily likened to that of a denominational Theological College to the University in Oxford or Cambridge. But till the time of Clement of Alexandria— namesake and admirer of the much earlier Clement of Rome—who seems to have begun writing not much, if at all, before A.D. 200, this church, though it had produced Valentinus, the greatest of the Gnostics, seems to have had no influence on the development of orthodox Christianity outside Egypt. To *pre-Christian* Alexandria, or rather to its Jewish colony, the Church was early a debtor. Its apologetic rested mainly on the appeal to ancient prophecy ; the inheritance, then, in the Septuagint of a version of the Old Testament already invested with the glamour of antiquity was an invaluable asset. Again, before A.D. 40 Philo had utilised the conception of the Logos to lay the foundations of that synthesis between Hebrew and Greek thought which Alexandrian theologians were ultimately to work out. Yet it was not in Alexandria that the Logos doctrine was first applied to interpret Christianity to the Greek mind ; in the hundred years which followed the fall of Jerusalem, the part which in later centuries fell to Alexandria was played by Ephesus (p. 61).

In history formulae are misleading unless recognised as mere approximations. Subject to this proviso, we may say that the history of the early Church was always the history of three of its capitals—but at different periods the three were not the same. Up to A.D. 70 they are Jerusalem, Caesarea, and Antioch. From A.D. 70 till A.D. 200 the primacy is with Antioch, Ephesus, and Rome. After A.D. 200 Alexandria takes the place of Ephesus. The one factor always present is Antioch. Each of the five churches named has a clearly marked character and atmosphere of its own ; and, in each case, this may be associated with the name of an outstanding leader in the early Church.

Jerusalem is the church of James, the brother of the Lord. Its spirit is that which in the New Testament is associated with his name. It is conservatively Jewish, carefully observant of the Law, ready to accept, with reservations, the admission of Gentiles to the Church, but with hesitation and not really upon equal terms. James himself may possibly have come round completely on this last point ; but if so, as so often happens in political or ecclesiastical controversy, it was because the leader had a larger spirit than his followers. Thus persons claiming to represent James were able to put effective pressure upon Peter, when at Antioch he was associating with Gentile Christians on a basis of complete equality and freedom from the Law (Gal. ii. 11 f.). It was James who felt it vital, from the point of view of the rank and file of the Church of Jerusalem, that Paul should make clear his own personal respect for the Jewish Law by publicly associating himself with a piece of characteristically Levitical ritual (Acts xxi. 20 ff.). Moreover, as already mentioned, by his own rigid adherence to the Law, James gained the title of 'the Just' and retained the respect, and apparently even the goodwill, of a large section of the Pharisaic party until his murder, c. A.D. 62, in the outburst of fanaticism which preceded the Jewish war. But this respect would never have been accorded had not James adhered closely to the traditional scribal interpretation of the Law as well as to its actual letter. In our First Gospel we find attributed to Christ a few sayings of a markedly Judaistic type, which, whatever was their original meaning, must have suffered distortion in oral tradition.

The scribes and Pharisees sit in Moses' seat; all things whatsoever therefore they command you, that observe and keep (xxiii. 2 f.).

This actually sets the scribal interpretation on the level of the Law, and demands obedience to it. In another saying the words underlined seem definitely a hit at Paul, who *taught* that the Law was superseded.

Till heaven and earth pass away, one jot or one tittle shall in no wise pass away from the law, till all things be accomplished. Whosoever therefore shall break one of these least commandments, and *shall teach men so*, shall be called least in the kingdom of heaven: but whoever shall do and teach them, he shall be called great in the kingdom of heaven (Matt. v. 18-19).

Again, there is the prohibition on which I have commented already :

Go not into any way of the Gentiles, and enter not into any city of the Samaritans (Matt. x. 5).

We may reasonably infer that one at least of the sources of that Gospel is a tradition ultimately emanating from the church over which James presided.

Caesarea, on the coast of Samaria, was refounded and renamed by Herod the Great as the Hellenised capital of his still independent kingdom. Later on it was the usual

headquarters of the Roman governor of Palestine. The
incident of the conversion of Cornelius by Peter would
have given the Church of Caesarea as good a right to
claim Apostolic foundation as Antioch or Rome. But
Philip was its actual founder (Acts viii. 40), and for many
years he and his four daughters, noted for that gift of
prophecy so highly esteemed in the primitive community,
permanently resided in the city (Acts xxi. 8). Philip was
a Greek-speaking Jew of the Dispersion; and he had been
the first to preach the Gospel to the Samaritans. Later
on he seems to have migrated to Hierapolis in Asia Minor
(cf. p. 33). Caesarea, then, was the earliest centre of
a liberal Gentile Christianity. Thus, in the first half-
century of Christianity, Caesarea would to Jerusalem
and Antioch be very much what a little later Ephesus,
and what later still Alexandria, became to Antioch and
Rome. Caesarea, the city of the Herods and the gate
of Samaria, is the place where we should expect to find
preserved the memory of our Lord's dealings with
Samaritans and His relations with Herod or his *entourage*.
Both for that reason, and because we have definite
evidence that Luke knew Philip and his daughters
(Acts xxi. 8-9), and lived for two years in Caesarea while
Paul was in prison there, we can connect with that church
the bulk of the traditions concerning Christ found only in
the Third Gospel. In later years, as the second home
(after A.D. 231) of Origen, the master mind of Greek
theology, it renewed its glory in a quite different way ;
while the library of early Christian writers, collected
by the martyr Pamphilus, gave Eusebius the chance to
become 'the Father of Church History', as well as,
despite his shocking literary style, one of the greatest
historians of the Ancient World.

Antioch, before A.D. 70, was what Rome became

later, the capital of Gentile Christianity. Here the disciples were first called Christians (Acts xi. 26). Here, so far as we know, the first organised attempt at missionary enterprise was conceived (Acts xiii. 1-3). The accidental glimpse of Peter's movements afforded by Paul's epistle to the Galatians shows that at some quite early date he visited Antioch; and it is extremely unlikely that this was his only visit. With pardonable exaggeration, the Church of Antioch claimed Peter as its first Bishop; and does so to this day. Antioch was largely Jewish, but probably a majority of its Jews would incline towards the cosmopolitan Judaism of the Dispersion rather than the narrow Pharisaism of Judaea. The rest of the inhabitants—at any rate of the lower and middle classes to whom the Church mainly appealed— were less Greek than Hellenised Syrian. The Church of Antioch, therefore, was one whose traditions, hopes, and sympathies were strongly Jewish; but it was a Jewish Christianity of a philo-Gentile, universalistic type. Whatever, then, its exact relation to Peter, or the amount of time that he spent there, it is the church whose traditional outlook well expressed the spirit of Peter— that one of the original Twelve who ate and drank with Gentiles at Caesarea and at Antioch. If one of the sources of our First Gospel seems to represent a church owing allegiance to the views of James, the complete Gospel, as we have it, would seem rather to have been published in a church which, like that of Antioch, regarded Peter as the Great Leader. There is more about Peter in Matthew than even in Mark, though that Gospel is largely based on Peter's own recollections; and Matthew alone contains the notable saying:

Thou art Peter, and upon this rock I will build my church. . . . I will give unto thee the keys of the kingdom of heaven:

and whatsoever thou shalt bind on earth shall be bound in heaven ; and whatsoever thou shalt loose on earth shall be loosed in heaven (Matt. xvi. 18 f.).

In searching for the original meaning of the phrase ' the keys of the kingdom of heaven ', it is hard to feel sure that one is doing so with eyes undazzled by the glare of an ecclesiastical controversy that after 400 years is still ablaze. But the safest guide to an unbiassed exegesis would seem to be the simple maxim that the probable interpretation of any saying in the Synoptic Gospels will be one which starts by studying first the linguistic usage in other passages of those same Gospels. At any rate, if we merely set side by side Matt. xxiii. 13 and its parallel, Luke xi. 52, there emerges a simple and obvious meaning of the phrase. The scribes (or lawyers) and Pharisees are denounced, in Matthew's version—

because ye shut the kingdom of heaven against men : for ye enter not in yourselves, neither suffer ye them that are entering to enter ;

in Luke's version—

for ye took away the key of knowledge : ye entered not in your-selves, and them that were entering in ye hindered.

Here the *key* of the kingdom of heaven is evidently the *knowledge* which makes entrance to the kingdom possible. To Peter, then, is given that *true insight into the nature of the righteousness* taught by Christ—a righteousness that will ' exceed that of the scribes and Pharisees '— which is the indispensable qualification of one who is ' to bind and to loose ' (*i.e.* to expound the moral law) with such discrimination that what he shall ' bind on earth, shall be bound in heaven '. It was, I suggest, just the possession of that sound sense of moral values which enabled Peter instinctively to grasp the *via media* between legalism and licence, that made him—and has made men like-minded then and through the ages since—the solid rock on which the Church is built.

It is not surprising that it was to Peter, with his sympathy for freedom and experiment, not to James the hero of the conservative reactionaries, that Christ—so the more liberal Jews insisted—had given authority to ' bind and to loose '—to decide, that is, how much or how little of the Law the members of the new dispensation shall be required to observe.[1] Thus Matthew, while in some ways the most Jewish of the Gospels, yet is also the Gospel which ends with the command ' Go ye, therefore, and make disciples from all the Gentiles '. It reflects alike the missionary spirit, and the liberal Jewish atmosphere, of Antioch. At any rate, even if compiled elsewhere than in Antioch, we know that it soon became the most favoured Gospel in Syria ; for it is the Gospel most often quoted, indeed the only one undoubtedly quoted, both in that early Syrian work the *Didache* and by Ignatius of Antioch.

The word ' Asia ' in Roman usage—which, since it is also that of the New Testament, I shall follow in these lectures—means not Asia Minor, but one westerly pro-

---

[1] The power of 'binding and loosing' is still correctly interpreted of the *teaching* office (of the bishop) in the epistle of Clement to James (§ vi.) in the *Clementine Homilies*. Peter instructs Clement to keep himself free from all secular business : ' Now, if you were occupied with secular cares, you should deceive both yourself and your hearers. For not being able, on account of occupation, to point out things that are advantageous, both you should be punished, as not having taught what was profitable, and they, not having learned, should perish by reason of ignorance. Wherefore you preside over them, without (worldly) occupation, so as to send forth seasonably the words that are able to save them ; and so let them listen to you, knowing that whatever the ambassador of the truth shall bind upon earth is bound also in heaven, and what he shall loose is loose. But you shall bind what ought to be bound, and loose what ought to be loosed.'

The passage (Matt. xviii. 18) in which the power of binding and loosing is given to *all* the Apostles is obviously a doublet. If this is from Q, or from a Jerusalem source, the alternative version (xvi. 18 f.) conferring it on Peter will be from Antiochene oral tradition.

vince of Asia Minor. In strict legality the capital of this was Pergamum, but in practice Ephesus and Smyrna were the first and second cities—Ephesus enjoying a certain customary precedence.[1] The coast cities of Asia Minor had been Greek from immemorial times. Ionia was the birthplace both of the poems of Homer and of Greek philosophy. Ephesus had been ruled by Greeks, and its Anatolian population had been under Greek influence, centuries before Antioch was founded by one of Alexander's generals. There, as elsewhere, Paul had preached to the synagogue first, and doubtless with some slight success. But the Church of Ephesus was the most thoroughly Greek, or rather Hellenistic, of the churches so far mentioned, and it was the most Pauline. Here Paul had worked for three years, more than twice as long as in any other city. Ephesian Christianity, then, was the gospel of Paul—in so far as the religion of one reared in the discipline of Pharisaic Judaism *could* be assimilated and understood by any minds formed in an environment essentially Hellenistic. In the interpretation to the Greek world of a religion originally expressed in terms of Palestinian thought, Ephesus could play the leading part; from this church could come the Fourth Gospel—the culminating point in the New Testament of the effort to interpret Christianity to the Greek.

Rome in the first century of the Christian era was no longer, like the Rome that defeated Hannibal, an Italian city; it was international.[2] Its population was drawn from all parts of the Empire. Rome was the centre of the world's politics, administration, and commerce. But

[1] W. M. Ramsay, *The Letters to the Seven Churches of Asia*, p. 228. (Hodder, 1904.)

[2] Much fresh material bearing on this is contained in the important article by G. la Piana, 'Foreign Groups in Rome during the First Centuries of the Empire,' which forms the whole of an enlarged number of *The Harvard Theological Review*, Oct. 1927.

Rome derived the arts and luxuries of civilisation entirely
from its Hellenised population, which was thus far
larger and more important than is the foreign element in
any of the great capitals of the modern world. ' I cannot
stand Rome Greek,' spits the indignant citizen; 'but how
little in this sewer is even Greek! The drains of Antioch
have long discharged into the Tiber.'

> Non possum ferre, Quirites,
> Graecam urbem : quamvis quota portio faecis Achaei ?
> Iam pridem Syrus in Tiberim defluxit Orontes.[1]

That is why the Roman could be in a unique sense
the *representative* Church; it reflected the characteristics, not of Jew, Greek, Syrian, Egyptian, or Italian,
but of the Empire as a whole. At the same time it
entered into that heritage of practical sagacity and
administrative experience, and that capacity for taking
'a world view', which become part of the very atmosphere
of any imperial city.

The ' atmosphere ' of Rome proved stimulating to
the Church in another way. Under the later Republic
and earlier Emperors there was here a considerable output of literature of an historical and biographical character ; and supply is to some extent an evidence of
demand. At Rome, then, (so it would seem) the demand
for a Life of Christ first became effective ; the response
to it was the work of Mark, the oldest of the Gospels.
Here, probably, the Acts also—perhaps, too, the Gospel
of Luke, to which it is a sequel—was written, to meet
a demand for an account of the historical origins of
Christianity that was felt sooner in Rome than elsewhere.[2]

When Jerusalem was destroyed, it was inevitable that
Rome should sooner or later succeed to the vacant

---

[1] Juvenal, iii. 60-61. This satire was published c. A.D. 107.
[2] Cf. *The Four Gospels*, p. 531 ff.

primacy of the Church. Luke saw this happening, or about to happen. The Acts is the story of the progress of Christianity on the road from Jerusalem to Rome—with the concomitant acceptance of it by the Gentile and rejection by the Jew. The position of the Church of the capital of the world was further enhanced by its prestige as the church where Peter and Paul had met—or, what came to the same thing, were (at least as early as A.D. 170) generally believed to have met—a martyr's fate. The Roman claim to be in a special sense 'the see of Peter' is not heard of till the third century. That claim Antioch could and did make ; and Antioch could make out the better case. In the second century the Roman Church put forth what then seemed the larger claim—to be the Church of Peter *and* Paul.

As the conflict with Gnosticism and with Marcion (which raged most acutely in the half century after A.D. 144) became more and more a matter of appeal to public, as against secret, traditions of Apostolic doctrine, the public tradition of a Church which was believed to rest on the joint foundation of Peter and Paul became more and more a court of final appeal. What Rome accepted as apostolic, was guaranteed as such ; what Rome rejected, was new-fangled heresy. Irenaeus gives vigorous expression to this conviction.

The tradition, therefore, of the Apostles, made manifest in all the world, all in every church who wish to see the truth may study ; and we can enumerate those whom the Apostles appointed to be Bishops in the Churches, and their successors down to our own day ; who neither taught nor knew any such thing as the ravings of those [heretics]. . . . But because it were very long in such a work as this to reckon up the successions in *all* the churches ; there is one, very great and most ancient and known to all, the Church founded and established at Rome by the two most glorious Apostles, Peter and Paul, whose tradition which it hath from the

Apostles, and her faith proclaimed unto men, as by succession of Bishops it comes down even unto us, we point to ; thereby confounding all those, who in any way form unauthorised assemblies, on account either of self-pleasing ways, or of vainglory, or of blindness and wrong opinion. (*Adv. Haer.* iii. 1, 1-2.)

Accordingly we find Basilides from Syria, Valentinus and Carpocrates from Egypt, Marcion from Pontus, Montanists from Phrygia—anyone, in fact, who had some striking doctrine to propound, sooner or later making his way to Rome. The very number, diversity, and complexity of new views and systems, which were for ever knocking for admission at the doors of the Roman Church, necessitated circumspection—and thereby trained it.

The genius of Marcion confronted the loosely jointed system and the heterogeneous, undefined theology of the ' great Church ' with an opposition Church—well organised, with a clear-cut theology and a definite selection of sacred books in a *New* Testament. In reply, the 'great Church' strengthened its organisation, gave definition to its doctrines, delimited its Canon. It began that process of standardisation which went on in the Church Universal until the lasting schisms which followed on Chalcedon, A.D. 451, in the Latin Church until the Infallibility Decree of 1870—by which in the last resort all doctrines are subsumed under that of authority, and all duties under that of obedience.

The Christian Church of the present day is suffering, it may seem, from the inheritance of an organisation unduly hardened, and of a theology too much defined. In things spiritual, standardisation is less profitable than in things material. But in that age some measure of standardisation was a condition of survival. In that process the most important event was the delimitation of the Four Gospel Canon, the principal instrument was the monarchical episcopate.

By the year A.D. 180 we find both of these accepted throughout the Catholic Church. But in the hundred and fifty years between that date and the birthday of the Church there had been time for much to happen.

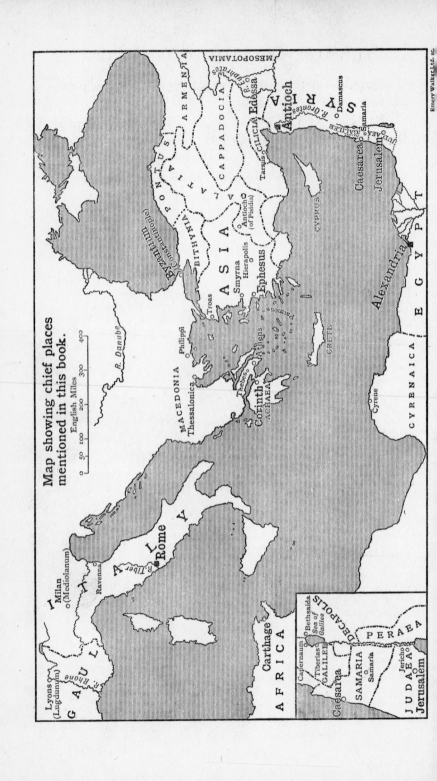

Map showing chief places mentioned in this book.

English Miles

III

THE EVOLUTION OF CHURCH ORDER IN THE NEW TESTAMENT

SYNOPSIS

HYPOTHESIS TO BE TESTED

To the first Christians the Last Day was at hand, and the outpouring of the Spirit a vivid experience. They were not interested either in the definition of doctrine or in the theory of Church Order.

Our hypothesis is that within the New Testament an evolution in the system of Church Order can be traced, comparable to that evolution in doctrinal reflection which has long been recognised by scholars. In both cases the movement was largely due to the genius of Paul ; and in both it culminates in the Johannine writings.

Harnack's theory that there were originally two distinct kinds of ministry—a universal (Apostles, Prophets, and Teachers), and a local (Presbyter-Bishops and Deacons)—briefly considered. The facts desiderate an explanation less cut and dried and more dynamic.

JERUSALEM

The unique position of James. Christians here would naturally organise themselves as a ' synagogue '—with the normal body of ' Presbyters '. At an early date certain individuals were appointed to do the work of almoners. The question whether the *name* ' Deacons ' was actually used of these. Owing to these exceptional circumstances something very like the later mon-episcopal system was *in Jerusalem* really primitive. It does not follow that things were the same elsewhere.

ANTIOCH

This the capital of Gentile Christianity, and the headquarters of the original mission of Paul and Barnabas. But it had been founded by Hellenistic Jews, refugees during the persecution in which Stephen fell ; and these (possibly deliberately) did not make the Jerusalem Church their model.

It would seem from Acts xiii. 1 ff. that the leading—and quite possibly the only—officers in this church were ' Prophets and Teachers '. Probability that the churches in its sphere of influence would be more or less organised on its model. The *Didache* shows that in parts of Syria this system still prevailed at the end of the first century.

CHURCHES FOUNDED BY ST. PAUL

The Acts states that Paul and Barnabas appointed Elders in every church. The evidence of the Epistles supports this statement, but with the important qualification that at first these officers seem to be persons of less weight than Prophets and Teachers. Gradually, however—probably because experience (especially at Corinth) showed the need of strengthening discipline—growing emphasis is laid by Paul on the importance of Episcopoi (or Shepherds).

Paul's farewell speech at Ephesus (Act xx. 17 ff.) occurs in a 'we' section, and has therefore value as evidence for Paul's views. Note here (1) that the terms 'Episcopoi' and 'Presbyters' are applied to the same persons ; (2) the great stress laid on their responsibility (which of course presumes authority) 'to feed the Church of God'.

THE EPISTLES OF ST. JOHN

Two questions are raised by these Epistles :

(1) Who is 'the Elder' who writes 2 and 3 John—and who, on stylistic grounds, appears also to be the author of 1 John ?

(2) What is the position held by the Diotrephes, 'who loveth to have the pre-eminence among them', whose defiance of the Elder is the subject of 3 John ?

The answer to the second question is clear : Diotrephes exercises the power, not only of a veto on visiting Christians who wish to address the church, but also of excommunicating members of the church over which he has 'the pre-eminence'. Evidently, then, he holds the position of monarchical bishop in that church. The Epistle is therefore conclusive evidence that at the time it was written a mon-episcopal system of Church government already existed in at least one (and probably several) of the churches in Asia.

'The Elder' is a person of admitted status. In 2 John he addresses a letter of exhortation to a church other than his own ; in 3 John he writes as if he was himself a person who held a position of greater dignity and prestige than Diotrephes the local bishop ; in 1 John he speaks as the spiritual father of a large community.

Objections to Harnack's theory as to the identity and position of the Elder. Alternative suggestion that the Elder was the Bishop of Ephesus and claimed, as such, an honourable precedency among the bishops of the local churches of Asia.

THE ELDER JOHN

Reasons for identifying the Elder who wrote 2 and 3 John with the Elder John mentioned by Papias as a ' disciple of the Lord ' ; presumably, that is, a person who had seen Christ in the flesh. If so, 3 John must have been written—and therefore mon-episcopacy was in being in some churches in Asia—not later than A.D. 100.

Discussion of the evidence of the *Apostolic Constitutions* and of the *Life of Polycarp* by Pionius, that Aristion was Bishop of Smyrna, and that at the close of the first century the Bishop of Ephesus was named John, and believed to be a disciple of the Apostle John.

III

THE EVOLUTION OF CHURCH ORDER IN THE NEW TESTAMENT

HYPOTHESIS TO BE TESTED

CHRISTIANS of the first generation troubled themselves little about the theory either of doctrine or of Church Order; 'the hammer of the world's clock was raised to strike the last hour '. In the meanwhile the most vivid fact of present experience was the outpouring of ' the Spirit '. To the individual Christian something had happened—something so obvious that it could be pointed to as evidence of something else. ' Received ye the Spirit (says St. Paul) by the works of the law or by the hearing of faith ? ' (Gal. iii. 2), as if the reception of the Spirit was something as definite and observable as, for example, an attack of influenza. Some such manifestation of the Spirit had been an expected precursor of the Last Day:

> Your sons and your daughters shall prophesy . . . and on my servants and on my handmaidens in those days will I pour forth of my Spirit . . . before the day of the Lord come, that great and notable day.

So quotes Peter, in a speech (Acts ii. 17) obviously regarded by Luke as giving his readers the key to the right understanding of the history of primitive Christianity. Inevitably in that generation the *Prophet*, the man or woman supremely inspired by the Spirit, was an outstanding figure in the Church.

To the prophetic type of mind, system, whether in thought or organisation, is normally uncongenial. The Apostle Paul belonged to this type ; but his was a genius of abnormal range. To him, it is generally conceded, must be credited the beginnings of that intellectual formulation of belief out of which was gradually developed the theology of the Church. To him also, I am about to argue, must be ascribed an importance hardly less in the introduction of system into the organisation of the Church. And in both cases what is begun by Paul reaches its climax, so far as the New Testament is concerned, in the Johannine literature. Nineteenth-century scholarship has traced the evolution of theology in the New Testament stage by stage, through the series of the epistles of Paul and that to the Hebrews, to its culmination in the Fourth Gospel. Taking these writings in their chronological sequence, we see conceptions, at first undefined, moving steadily (though all but insensibly) in the direction of an ever-increasing definiteness. Yet this process of development was not due to any desire to frame an abstract theology ; it was the result, simple but inevitable, of the application to new circumstances of first principles, originally vague and implicit, as problem after problem arose and demanded immediate practical solution.

Since Newman wrote his *Essay on Development* it has been generally recognised that, so far as the later period of Church history is concerned, organisation as well as doctrine developed in this way—as the reaction of the living organism to a changing environment. The purpose of this chapter is to marshal evidence which suggests that, within the period covered by the writings of the

New Testament itself, there is traceable an evolution in Church organisation parallel to the evolution in theology —and similarly explicable as the reaction of organism to environment. And this evolution also, curiously enough, reaches its culminating point in writings ascribed to St. John.

I ought perhaps to make clear the relation of this hypothesis to the theories, on the one hand of Harnack, on the other of Lightfoot. Harnack and Lightfoot share the distinction of being so eminent in this particular field of history that it is assumed—unless the contrary is explicitly affirmed—that ordinary persons will be to a greater or less degree disciples either of the one or of the other. It may be worth while, then, to insist that, although my debt to both of them is immeasurable, yet the general position I have reached is one which, whether admissible or not, is a third alternative to that maintained by either of them.

Lightfoot's *Dissertation on the Christian Ministry*, in his *Philippians*, is a standard classic; but Harnack's views, in England less familiar, I may here summarise. They were largely inspired by the discovery of the *Didache* (first published 1883), which led everywhere to a renewed study of the origins of the Christian ministry. Harnack's main contention is that in the earliest period there existed side by side what were really two distinct kinds of ministry—a universal and a local.[1] The first, comprising Apostles, Prophets, and Teachers, had a scope of activity theoretically co-extensive with the Church universal, and derived its authority from the Holy Spirit; the second consisted of Presbyter-bishops and Deacons, appointed by popular election in particular

---

[1] *The Constitution and Law of the Church in the First Two Centuries*, E.T. (Williams & Norgate, 1910.)

local churches—with functions limited to the church which had elected them.

To me this theory seems to postulate in the mind of the primitive Church an abstract and systematic way of looking at a concrete and ever-changing situation which I find it hard to accept as historical. I prefer, however, instead of criticising this or any other theory, to make a fresh start. I ask whether a re-examination of the evidence does not suggest that the actual course of events was of a more haphazard, and at the same time a more dynamic, character than students of the subject have hitherto suspected—an original diversity, a rapid evolution in response to urgent local needs, to be followed later by standardisation up to an efficient uniform model.

JERUSALEM

At Jerusalem, James the brother of the Lord, and those who regarded him as leader, observed, we have seen, not only the law of Moses, but the recognised scribal interpretation of it (Matt. xxiii. 1-3). They were, moreover, assiduous devotees of the Temple worship. It had long been the custom for groups of Jews resident in Jerusalem to have their own synagogues—we hear of synagogues of Freedmen, and of Jews of Cyrene, Alexandria, Cilicia, and Asia (Acts vi. 9). These were, so to speak, recognised conventicles—in no way regarding themselves, or regarded by others, as in any sense heretical. Nothing, then, would be more natural than for the Jewish Christians resident in Jerusalem to regard themselves, and sooner or later to organise themselves, as a ʻ synagogue ʼ of this kind. The place where Christians met for worship is actually called a synagogue in the epistle of James (ii. 2) and in Hermas (Mand. xi.

9. 13, 14). Some commentators have inferred that, when the epistle of James was written, Christians still met for worship in the same building as the Jewish synagogue ; the survival of the name ' synagogue ' at Rome as late as Hermas shows the error of this view.

Now, a Jewish synagogue normally had a board of Presbyters, who formed a kind of committee of management. In the Christian ' synagogue ' at Jerusalem this board was already in existence by about A.D. 46 ; for we note that ' the presbyters ' are specified (Acts xi. 30) as the persons to whom the delegates from Antioch handed over the funds collected for famine relief after the prophecy of Agabus. But the position of James, as eldest male of the Messianic House (p. 40), brought it about that in the Church of Jerusalem there was from the earliest times a single person credited with an unique authority, different in kind from that of the ordinary presbyter. From the first, then, the government of this church was of the type that it will be convenient to describe by the adjective ' mon-episcopal '—which I shall use to imply the presidency of an individual ' bishop ' whose status is confessedly much more than that of *primus inter pares* among the presbyters.

In another respect circumstances at Jerusalem were exceptional. The number of believers requiring charitable relief was there unusually large. Barnabas and Ananias, though with different motives, sell land to increase the funds available. The three ' pillars ' exhort Paul to ' remember the poor ' (Gal. ii. 10) ; and the epistles to the Romans and Corinthians (Rom. xv. 26 f. ; 1 Cor. xvi. 1 ff. ; 2 Cor. 1 ff.) and the Acts (xxiv. 17) attest his efforts to raise money among the Gentile churches for Jerusalem. Heart-burnings are an inevitable incident in any system of large-scale charity ; from this human weakness the Church of Jerusalem was not exempt. To meet the difficulties a body of seven were appointed (Acts vi. 1 ff.) to act as almoners to the community. The Seven are not actually spoken of as Deacons (διάκονοι) ; but since, by the time that Luke wrote, there existed in most churches an Order of Almoners who did bear this title, his use of the corresponding noun and verb (διακονία, διακονεῖν) is most naturally read to mean that he regards the appointment of the Seven as the institution of this Order. And to this view it is no valid objection that the actual proceedings of Stephen, as preacher and controversialist, have little to do with poor relief ; it is not the habit of enthusiasts to keep strictly to the routine of their official duties.

But the situation at Jerusalem was unique. We cannot safely deduce that in the Gentile churches the primitive form of government even roughly corresponded to a threefold hierarchy of Bishop, Presbyters, and Deacons.

ANTIOCH

If we seek to know the type of organisation characteristic of the Gentile Churches, our investigation will necessarily begin with Antioch—the city where first of all Christian preachers turn to Gentiles (Acts xi. 20), where the name ' Christian ' has its origin, the headquarters from which Paul and Barnabas start on their first and second missionary journeys, and to which they report on their return (Acts xiv. 26 ; xviii. 22 f.).

The Church of Antioch was founded by refugees from the persecution in which Stephen fell (Acts xi. 19) ; but, though we are told ' they were all scattered abroad ', there is added the remarkable qualification ' except the apostles ' (Acts viii. 1 f.).   Persecutors who wish to stamp out a movement always strike at the leaders first. If, then, the Apostles could remain unharmed in Jerusalem, it can only be because they were not regarded by the persecutors as being associated with that disparagement of the Law and the Temple which had caused the attack on Stephen and his supporters.   It has been surmised that the dispute about the administration of poor relief, which led to the appointment of the Seven, was concomitant with—and perhaps symptomatic of—a growing rift between those Christians who were converts from the partially Hellenised Jews of the Dispersion settled in Jerusalem, and the more conservative section made up of Palestinian Jews.   Be this as it may, the Church at Antioch was founded by members of a group whose general attitude towards the Law and the Temple was evidently not that of James and such of the Twelve as were then in Jerusalem.   This may be one reason why the constitution of the newly founded Church at Antioch was definitely *not* modelled on that of Jerusalem.   At any rate, the evidence shows that it was not so modelled.

There were at Antioch, in the church that was there, prophets and teachers, Barnabas, and Symeon that was called Niger, and Lucius of Cyrene, and Manaen the foster-brother of Herod the tetrarch, and Saul.   And as they ministered to the Lord, and fasted, the Holy Ghost said, Separate me Barnabas and Saul for the work whereunto I have called them.   Then, when they had fasted and prayed and laid their hands on them, they sent them away (Acts xiii. 1 ff.).

The five persons named are mentioned as if they were in charge of the church, and no other officers are mentioned.   The occasion was an important one ; the step taken is evidently conceived of as being a corporate

act of the church, and the representative agents in this
act are styled ' Prophets and Teachers '. Clearly, whatever other officers the Church at Antioch may have had,
Prophet and Teacher (διδάσκαλος) are the titles borne
by those of chief importance. The burden of proof
lies with those who would argue that already at the
time of Paul's first missionary journey the Church of
Antioch possessed Episcopoi, but omitted to make use
of their services on this historical occasion. For though
it might be argued that Prophets, being inspired persons,
might have been preferred to Episcopoi, this could
hardly hold good of Teachers.

The position of Antioch in the Province of Syria was
of so dominating a character that we should expect—on
the hypothesis that the original constitution of the church
of that city was such as I have inferred—to find traces of
a similar type of Church Order elsewhere in that area.
And this is precisely what we do find. It is clear from
the *Didache* (p. 145) that in Syria, at any rate in *some*
districts, there were still at the end of the first century
churches where Prophets and Teachers existed, but in
which there were as yet no Episcopoi or Deacons.

CHURCHES FOUNDED BY ST. PAUL

We are told (Acts xiv. 23) that Paul and Barnabas on
their first missionary journey—on the return visit, be it
noted—' appointed for them elders in every church '.
The actual word πρεσβύτερος does not occur in the ten
probably authentic letters of Paul, though frequent in the
Pastoral Epistles. Nevertheless, Luke's statement gains
some support from the allusion to those who are ' over
you in the Lord ', which occurs a few years later in Paul's
earliest extant epistle :

We beseech you, brethren, to know them that labour among you, and are over you in the Lord, and admonish you ; and to esteem them exceeding highly in love for their work's sake (1 Thess. v. 12-13).

The nucleus of the body of converts in the churches founded by Paul consisted of Jews and proselytes ; and since he regarded the Christian Church as being the authentic Israel, it would have been natural for him to view the newly founded local communities as synagogues—and to organise them accordingly. Nevertheless, from other epistles it is clear that these Presbyters—who perhaps already bore titles Episcopoi and Deacons—were, at any rate to begin with, regarded as persons of quite minor importance. This seems strange ; it is most easily explicable on the view that Prophets and Teachers were the recognised leaders of the Church of Antioch (from which Paul and Barnabas had themselves been sent out), and that, *so far as Gentile churches were concerned*, the appointment of Presbyters was an innovation.

Paul's earlier theory of the Christian ministry is clearly laid down in the letters to Corinth and Rome.

God hath set some in the church, first apostles, secondly prophets, thirdly teachers, then miracles, then gifts of healings, helps, governments, divers kinds of tongues (1 Cor. xii. 28).

Since Apostles obviously belong to a special class, it is evident that, even in Corinth, a church of Paul's own foundation, the terms Prophet and Teacher represent the two most important offices in what may be called the normal ministry in a local church. The notion that a Prophet was usually a person who led a wandering life is an entirely mistaken deduction from the *Didache* ; the fact that some Prophets led that kind of life is no evidence that all or even that a majority did so. After naming the three main offices of the Christian ministry, the passage quoted above runs on with a list of spiritual gifts, ' miracles ', ' gifts of healings ', ' helps ', ' governments ', ' divers kinds of tongues '. In this enumeration the term ' helps ' would well describe the gift of being a good almoner, while ' governments ' appears to mean administrative capacity. If so, the offices of Deacon and Episcopos would seem to have already existed at Corinth ; but their functions, we should surmise, were at this time and place analogous to those of the officers styled ' Deacons ' in the modern Congregationalist system. Nevertheless it is remarkable that the gifts required for the exercise of these offices should be, as it were, ' thrown in ' near the end of the list, as though these officers (even if they already had a specific name) were as yet persons of quite minor importance.

This passage in Corinthians should be compared with a similar one in Romans.

And having gifts differing according to the grace that was given to us, whether prophecy, let us prophesy according to the proportion of our faith ; or ministry, let us give ourselves to our ministry ; or he that teacheth, to his teaching ; or he that exhorteth, to his exhorting ; he that giveth, let him do it with liberality ; he that ruleth, with diligence ; he that sheweth mercy, with cheerfulness (Rom. xii. 6-8).

Here again the Prophet and the Teacher come high up in the list, while ' he that ruleth ' ($\acute{o}$ $\pi\rho o\ddot{i}\sigma\tau\acute{a}\mu\epsilon\nu o\varsigma$) comes towards the end. Yet he—or rather they, for the singular is generic as in the case of the other persons mentioned—is not mentioned actually last, which might have implied that he was of special importance. Curiously enough, both in Romans and Corinthians the gifts of a Deacon are mentioned before those of a person who rules. Evidently the word translated ' rule ' means ' lead ' rather than ' govern '.

The Church of Corinth exhibited over a period of years a turbulence which strained Paul's capacities, physical, moral, and intellectual, to the uttermost. The worst troubles broke out at intervals after he had left Corinth and was working at Ephesus—fortunately for posterity, since otherwise certain letters, which are among the world's classics of religion, would have been left unwritten. Live minds grow through conflict, and no one who turns from the epistles to the Thessalonians to those written to Corinth three to five years later can fail to see an enhancement of mental range and insight.[1] We can see how questions asked by the Church of Corinth compelled Paul to formulate more clearly than heretofore his conceptions of ' the spiritual body '—a *via media* between the Greek idea of the essential immortality of the reasoning principle only in man, and the Jewish notion of the resurrection of the flesh, which had evidently been found too crude by certain members of that church. We can study his reactions to a practical difficulty caused in this non-Jewish community by a too logical interpretation of his principle of the glorious freedom of the Christian from the Law. ' All things are lawful,' cry the antinomian party at Corinth.[2] ' All things are not congruous,' replies the Apostle ; and he then proceeds to build up a new ethic to replace the now obsolete code of Moses—in the form of a series of such moral principles and injunctions as are most evidently the external expression of the inward spirit of Christian love.

[1] This point holds good to a considerable extent, even if Burkitt's suggestion be accepted that the letters were drafted by Silas (whose name appears along with that of Paul in the salutation) and revised by Paul. Cf. F. C. Burkitt, *Christian Beginnings*, p. 131 ff. (Univ. London Press, 1924.)

[2] Cf. K. Lake, *The Earlier Epistles of St. Paul*, p. 225.

The suggestion I would make is that, in a similar way, it was the practical disorders at Corinth (with which his epistles are so largely concerned) that forced Paul to face more clearly than heretofore the need, if not of a new Church Order, at least of a new emphasis on the respect due to those who stood for discipline and coherence in the Church. That intention certainly seems to underlie the exhortation :

Now, I beseech you, brethren (ye know the house of Stephanas, that it is the first-fruits of Achaia, and that they have set themselves to minister unto the saints), that ye also be in subjection unto such, and to every one that helpeth in the work and laboureth (1 Cor. xvi. 15-16).

At any rate it is a notable fact that in his later epistles a growing importance is assigned to the regular ministry. Thus, in Philippians, the Episcopoi and Deacons are specially singled out in the salutation, in a way which would be unnatural unless he wished them to be recognised as persons of great importance in that church.

Paul and Timothy, servants of Christ Jesus, to all the saints in Christ Jesus which are at Philippi, with (the) bishops and deacons (Phil. i. 1).

The epistle to the Ephesians is of disputable authorship. On the whole I incline to think it genuine.[1] If not, it is a rewriting of Colossians—of very early date,

---

[1] Two of the greatest objections to its genuineness disappear if we follow the text of our oldest MSS. B ℵ, which (with other MS. support) omit ἐν Ἐφέσῳ in i. 1—and so remove the difficulty that the letter is addressed to persons who only knew Paul by hearsay (iii. 2) ; B also omits ἀποστόλοις in iii. 5. With this omission τοῖς ἁγίοις αὐτοῦ καὶ προφήταις will mean ' His saints (i.e. all Christians) and (contemporary Christian) prophets ', and Paul is not speaking of the ' Holy Apostles and (Old Testament) prophets '. ' Built upon the foundation of the apostles and prophets, Jesus Christ himself being the chief corner-stone ' (ii. 20), may thus mean that apostles and prophets (the words being used as in 1 Cor. xii. 28) were the ' founders ' of churches—being careful to make Christ the chief corner-stone in every building they founded.

for it seems to be known to all the Apostolic Fathers—
and is therefore evidence for the state of affairs in one of
the Pauline churches of Asia. The passage in Ephesians
which deals with the ministry should be carefully compared and contrasted with that quoted above (p. 77)
from 1 Cor. xii.

And he gave some to be apostles; and some, prophets; and
some, evangelists; and some, pastors and teachers; for the
perfecting of the saints, unto the work of ministering, unto the
building up of the body of Christ (Eph. iv. 11-12).

Two points are to be noted :

(1) The administrative officers, the Pastors (ποίμενες,
= shepherds),[1] are obviously the equivalent of Episcopoi;
but these are no longer nameless, as in the Corinthian
letter, but come between the Prophets and the Teachers.
And in the title ' shepherd ' there are wide-reaching
implications. In the Old Testament, more especially in
the Prophets and Psalms, ' shepherds of Israel ' is a
standing equivalent for *rulers*—and the Christian Church
regarded itself as the New Israel.

(2) The stress is no longer laid primarily on the
spiritual gifts required—which is an individual matter—
but on the *office as such* in relation to its function in the
corporate life.

The apostolic authorship of the epistles to Timothy
and Titus—commonly styled ' The Pastoral Epistles '—
as well as of the first epistle of Peter, is so widely ques-
tioned that I postpone discussion of them to the next
lecture. But it is appropriate to consider here the
evidence afforded by the farewell speech of Paul to the

---

[1] The only ' evangelists ' named in the New Testament are Philip, one of
the Seven (Acts xxi. 8) and Timothy (2 Tim. iv. 5). Possibly it was a title
given to persons of deutero-apostolic status.

G

Ephesian Elders (Acts xx. 17 ff.). This occurs in a 'we section' of the Acts. Probably, then, it is either based on actual reminiscence of what the Apostle actually said at the time, or it represents views which Luke, who was with Paul to the end, knew him to entertain towards the close of his life. We are justified, therefore, in treating this speech as being, at any rate, secondary evidence for Paul's own views.

We note first that the delegates from Ephesus are described by Luke as ' Presbyters ' or ' Elders ', but they are addressed by Paul as 'Episcopoi' or 'Bishops'. It is clear, then, that there were at this time in the Church of Ephesus several persons who bore the title Episcopos ; it is also clear that Episcopoi could be called 'Presbyters'. It does not, however, follow that all Presbyters could be called 'Episcopoi'. The main point of the speech is the immense responsibility which attaches to the office held by those addressed.

Take heed unto yourselves, and to all the flock, in the which the Holy Ghost hath made you bishops, to feed the Church of God, which he purchased with his own blood (Acts xx. 28).

The actual wording of such a speech may be open to the suspicion of some coloration by the views and needs of the time when Luke wrote. Nevertheless the mere fact that Paul sent for the Elders is an important piece of historical evidence of a growing desire on his part to enhance the prestige of, and foster a sense of responsibility in, officers charged with the direction of the church.

The total amount of evidence yielded up by the passages considered above is not large ; nor do I claim that it is always unambiguous. But it all points in the same direction ; and taken as a whole it suffices, if not to prove, at least to make probable, the fact of a slow but steady movement. And it is a movement away from the state of things implied in 1 Corinthians—where pre-eminence in the Church depends on the *personal* possession of some spiritual gift (of which ' government ' is one of the least esteemed)—and towards a state of things where importance is attached to the holding of *an office* invested with recognised authority.

THE EPISTLES OF ST. JOHN

The two little notes, known as the second and third epistles of John, are the shortest, and perhaps the most neglected, books of the New Testament. But to the historian they are of unique importance. The author describes himself simply as ' the Elder '. This in itself implies that he occupies a position of unique consideration; he is a personage so well known that there is no need for him to append his name. The second epistle is addressed ' Unto the elect Lady and her children, whom I love in truth '. The omission of the substantive ἐκκλησία (church) in the phrase ἡ ἐν Βαβυλῶνι συνεκλεκτή (she that is elect with you) in 1 Peter v. 13, and the absolute use of the feminine adjective ἐκλεκτή (elect) in Ignatius (Trall. i.), make it probable that the elect Lady is not a person but a church. This is further implied by the salutation in the last verse from ' the children of thine elect sister ', the ' elect sister ' being obviously the church in which the author writes. It is, then, a little surprising to find that he takes upon himself to say ' I rejoice greatly that I have found certain of thy children walking in the truth '. This, surely, is a very remarkable expression for an individual to use in writing to a church.

It is explicable only if the writer occupied a position of almost patriarchal prestige—and that not only in his own but in neighbouring churches.

We collect the same impression of the author's pre-eminent position from reading the third epistle. It is addressed to Gaius, evidently a Christian of some local prominence, and informs him that he had previously written to the church—observe again it is to a church—of which Gaius is a member. But a certain Diotrephes, 'who loveth to have the pre-eminence among them', had declined to receive his representations, indeed had publicly flouted him, 'prating against us with wicked words'. Diotrephes had refused to receive certain brethren whom the writer had evidently commended to the church, and had even gone to the length of excommunicating those members of the church who desired to receive the commended brethren. It may fairly be presumed that the brethren in question, like those mentioned just before (verse 7), were on a preaching mission, and that therefore the writer had commended them as persons qualified to address the church—a mere letter of introduction, asking for no more than hospitality, would hardly have aroused such opposition. The writer goes on to threaten that he may visit the church in person; and he implies that this will bring Diotrephes to his senses.

Who, then, is this ' Elder ' who so quietly takes for granted an almost apostolic authority over neighbouring churches ? Who, and what, we ask, is Diotrephes ? To the historian this, possibly trifling, local dispute may turn out to be of supreme interest for the light it throws on the status of the leading disputants.

Diotrephes, it is evident, not only loved the pre-eminence—many in all times and places have done that—

he had actually secured it. One cannot be a ' Jack in office ' unless the office is already there ; and Diotrephes holds a position which enables him not only to forbid Christians whose doctrines he suspects from addressing the church, but to ' cast out of the church ' those members of it who express sympathy with them. He not only has supreme control of public worship, but also (it would seem on his own sole authority) the power of excommunication. In other words, in this church Diotrephes held the office of Bishop, in the full monarchical sense of the term. Since, then, it is not disputed that the Johannine literature originated in Asia, it follows that, by the date when 3 John was written, the monarchical episcopate was established in at least one, more probably in several, of the churches of that province. This is a historical conclusion of immense interest.

And the Elder, who was he ? Clearly he was regarded by others, besides himself and his supporter Gaius, as a personage of special importance. Letters like 2 and 3 John—dealing with an obscure and uninteresting quarrel—would never have been preserved at all, let alone have crept into the Canon, unless they had been venerated as relics of a man whose person or position was highly revered in some very influential church.

If I may assume that the linguistic studies of Dr. Charles[1] have proved the first epistle of John, so called, to be by the same author as 2 and 3 John, there is further evidence as to the prestige which he enjoyed. The first epistle of John is miscalled an ' epistle '. It is not a letter at all. It has no introductory greeting, no closing salutation. It is either a pamphlet, or, as I think

---

[1] *Revelation*, i. p. xxxiv ff.   (T. & T. Clark.)

more probable, a sermon delivered on some important occasion. It is called an ' epistle ' simply because the compilers of the New Testament had no other way of classing it in the collection of sacred books. It reads like an address—by a very old man speaking to those whom, though adults, he can without offence call his ' little children '—summing up, in what he feels is perhaps his last message to them, in the simplest words he can command, the very core of what Christianity means to him, and giving them a last warning against the worst perils of the time.

This authoritative position, not so much asserted as taken for granted—in the first epistle to a whole community, in the second epistle in writing to another church, in the third in regard to a local bishop—would be perfectly explicable if the author was the Apostle John and could speak with the authority of an Apostle. Paul writes in much the same tone to the rebellious Corinthians. But, as every one knows, there are grave difficulties in the supposition that the Apostle John lived in Asia Minor and wrote the gospel and epistles that are called by his name. Yet the two shorter epistles are indubitably genuine letters of somebody. No motive for forgery can be discovered. They develop no doctrinal thesis, they contain hardly any moral or religious exhortation, they mainly consist in obscure allusions to a not specially creditable incident of local church history. Moreover, the hypothesis that they are pseudonymous is excluded by the mere fact that they are put forward *without* an author's name.

Harnack regards the dispute between the Elder and Diotrephes as ' an example of a flagrant collision between the general spiritual and missionary organisation, represented by the Elder, and the local organisation ' (*op. cit.*

p. 65).[1]   Personally, as I have already said, I see no sufficient evidence for the existence of these two clear-cut types of organisation.   Harnack is also disposed to identify the Elder with the author of the Apocalypse. Of this work he says :

> But the position of the writer, John, is important. He appears in point of fact as the superintendent of these communities (the Seven Churches), although he describes himself as a brother (1. 9).

Later on he remarks :

> The author of the three Epistles . . . who is probably identical with the John of the Apocalypse, appears in these likewise as a superintendent.

A fatal objection to this identification of the Elder with the author of the Apocalypse is the linguistic evidence that the shorter epistles of John are related far more nearly to the Gospel and first epistle than to the Apocalypse.[2]   I would also demur to the description of the John of the Apocalypse as a ' superintendent ', which implies a person in a position of *permanent* authority.   The writer of the Apocalypse describes himself, not only as ' a brother ', but also as ' a prophet ' (Rev. i. 3, 10 ; xxii. 10, 18 f.) ; but a prophet is a person whose authority is necessarily *intermittent*.   When ' in the Spirit ' he speaks with the voice of God ; on other occasions he is merely a ' brother ' or ordinary church member.[3]   The writer to the Seven Churches writes, not as a superintendent, but as a prophet (Rev. i. 9-11).   What he writes he expects to be taken, not as

---

[1] But on Harnack's general theory an ' elder ' is a *local* officer !

[2] R. H. Charles, *Revelation*, i. p. xxxiv ff.   (T. & T. Clark, 1920.)

[3] The reason, I take it, of the rubric in the *Didache* (x. 7) that a prophet is free to use extempore prayer at the Eucharist is, not that the prophet *as such* is a church official, but that the prayer he would offer was likely to be in a special sense prayer ' in the Spirit '.

a set of disciplinary exhortations of his own, but as an inspired message.

The true answer, then, to the question, What position did the Elder hold ? must be looked for in some other direction. We may find it, I suggest, by asking, What are the implications of the greeting, ' The children of thine elect sister salute thee ' (2 John 13) ? Surely it is likely that the church on whose behalf he sends this salutation is one of which he himself is the acknowledged head. Now the development of things in small towns usually lags behind that in large centres. If, then, at this date the church over which Diotrephes presided already had a monarchical bishop, it is probable that Ephesus had reached that stage of development some years before. But the Bishop of Ephesus would naturally claim a certain precedence among other bishops of the province. He would at least expect that persons bearing letters of commendation from him would be accepted by the smaller churches as orthodox. All the evidence, then, is satisfied by the hypothesis that the writer of 2 and 3 John is the Bishop of Ephesus, the mother church of Asian Christianity.

Partly as President of the mother church of Asia, partly, perhaps, in virtue of the personal influence he enjoyed, he assumes the same kind of responsibility for the smaller churches of the province as Clement's epistle shows the Roman Church exercising at about the same date over churches within its sphere of influence, or which Ignatius wields a little later in the region of Antioch (cf. p. 259). We note, however, an essential difference. Clement writes merely as the anonymous mouthpiece of the Church of Rome ; the Elder writes, like Ignatius, in his own name. Indeed, to describe his office, the title ' Archbishop ' would—of course without the formal implications of later canonical law and usage—be even more appropriate than that of ' Bishop '.

At any rate, my thesis stands that the evolution of Church Order in the New Testament culminates in the Johannine writings.

THE ELDER JOHN

There remains, however, to date this culminating point. For that it will be necessary to explore further the question of the identity of the, so far anonymous, Elder who wrote the epistles we have been discussing. I cannot without apology thrust once more upon the notice of such of my readers as are students of theology an ancient fragment on which they have so often been lectured. I mean the quotation by Eusebius from a work of Papias, Bishop of Hierapolis—a city of Asia, situated about 100 miles due east of Ephesus—written at some date between A.D. 130–160.

And again, on any occasion when anyone came in my way who had been a follower of the Elders, I would inquire about the discourse of the Elders—what was said by Andrew, or by Peter, or by Philip, or by Thomas or James, or by John, or Matthew or any other of the Lord's disciples, and what Aristion and the Elder John, the disciples of the Lord, say. For I did not think that I could get so much profit from the contents of books as from the utterance of a living and abiding voice.

Eusebius adds later:

Papias . . . confesses that he had received the words of the Apostles from those who had followed them, but says that he was himself a hearer of Aristion and the Elder John ; at all events he mentions them frequently by name, and besides, records their traditions in his writings.

The word Elder was until the third century used as a general title of respect for the great men of a previous generation. Clement of Alexandria calls Pantaenus 'the blessed Elder ', and Hippolytus of Rome does the same by his teacher Irenaeus.[1] Papias, at the beginning of the passage quoted, is obviously using the plural ' Elders' in this general sense, in order, I suggest, to cover *both* the Apostles mentioned *and* the two ' disciples of the Lord '. It has been argued by a few scholars, Provost Salmon and Dom Chapman among them, that Papias means the Apostle when he speaks of the Elder John. But though a group of venerable persons—including with Apostles men who were *not* Apostles—could be spoken of collectively as ' Elders ', it would be quite another matter to speak of an *individual* Apostle as an Elder. The view, therefore, that the Elder and the Apostle are the same person, seems to me impossible. But granted it were linguistically possible, what about Aristion ? He is mentioned as ' a disciple of the Lord ', on a par with, and actually *before*, the Elder John ; was Aristion, then, as an authority for the teaching of Christ, the equal, or even the superior, of the Apostle John ?

Another fragment of Papias quoted by Eusebius begins, ' And the Elder said this also . . . '. This use of the phrase ' the Elder ' without the name being added is for our immediate purpose significant ; for we at once recall the fact that the author of 2 and 3 John does not give his name, but calls himself ' the Elder '.

The letter of Irenaeus to Florinus (*ap.* Eus. *H.E.* v. 20) is usually quoted as evidence for the presence in Asia of the Apostle John. He relates how, when still a boy, he listened to the discourses of Polycarp, and remembered

how he would describe his intercourse with John, and with the rest who had seen the Lord, and how he would relate their words.

[1] Lightfoot, *Clement*, ii. p. 435 f.

The difficulties of supposing that the Apostle John resided in Asia are well known.[1] But if the Apostle did *not* live in Asia, Polycarp may well have used a phrase like ' John and the rest who had seen the Lord ' in speaking of Aristion and the Elder John.

There is thus good evidence of the existence of a personage known as the Elder John, who was held in special veneration as a ' disciple of the Lord ' (which must at least mean one who had himself seen the Lord), and was so notable that he could be spoken of simply as ' The Elder ', as one to whom that title belonged *par excellence*. Assuming this individual to be the author of the Johannine epistles, the personal authority which the writer takes for granted, the description of himself as ' The Elder ', and the attachment to the writings of the name John, are all satisfactorily explained. So also are the opening words of the first epistle :

That which was from the beginning, that which we have heard, that which we have seen with our eyes, that which we beheld and our hands handled.

We now have—what to the historian is supremely welcome—a means of approximately dating the epistles. John the Elder was ' a disciple of the Lord ', in some sense which made him an authority for authentic tradition second only to the original Apostles. At least he must have seen Christ in the flesh, and that at an age reputed to be outside the years of childhood. For certain purposes childhood was reckoned by Jews to last till the age of twelve. Supposing, then, the Elder had been just twelve years old at the time of the Crucifixion, by A.D. 100 he would be eighty-two. His controversy with

---

[1] They are conveniently summarised by Dr. Charles, *Revelation*, p. xlv ff.

Diotrephes can hardly have been carried on long after he had reached the age of eighty, and, since Diotrephes had the full powers of a bishop, it follows that in Asia the monarchical episcopate was established, at any rate in some cities, before the year A.D. 100.

An intensive study of the Johannine epistles has suggested the inference that their author was Bishop of Ephesus. We naturally ask whether there is any external evidence that John the Elder held that position. For the Churches of Rome, Antioch, Jerusalem, and Alexandria complete lists of the names of the early bishops are given by Eusebius. The Roman list has much the best attestation—it can be traced back to Hegesippus, who visited Rome c. A.D. 165—the Jerusalem list has the worst.[1] For Ephesus no such list has survived ; but it must have once existed. *The Apostolic Constitutions* (vii. 46),[2] however, gives the names of the bishops of all churches who were ordained in the lifetime of the Apostles—that is, before A.D. 100, the reputed date of the death of John.[3] The names given for Jerusalem, Antioch, Alexandria, and Rome correspond closely with Eusebius —that is only what we should expect. What we should like to know is, How far had the author access to genuine local tradition in the case of less important churches ? Fortunately there is a test case—the Church of Smyrna— which creates a presumption that, at any rate as regards

[1] Cf. C. H. Turner in *J.T.S.* i. p. 529 ff.

[2] Zahn thinks the *Apostolic Constitutions* is by Acacius of Caesarea, A.D. 340–366. It alludes to the observance of Christmas on December 25, a usage which came from the West and was, we know from Chrysostom, introduced at Antioch c. 376 ; but this may have been adopted earlier at Caesarea. The standard edition of the text is by F. X. Funk, *Didascalia et Constitutiones Apostolorum* (Pederbornae, 1905). There is an English translation in *The Library of Ante-Nicene Fathers* (T. & T. Clark).

[3] Jerome, *De Vir. Illustr.* 9, dates the death of John in the sixty-eighth year after the Passion A.D. 100, since Jerome dates Passion A.D. 32. Earlier tradition inclines to 29 A.D. for date of the Passion. Recent chronologists prefer A.D. 30. *J.T.S.* xii. 120 (Fotheringham); *Harvard Theol. Rev.* xxii. 157 *n.* (Bacon).

Asia, he had *some* evidence to go on. In regard to this church he states the succession as follows :

Ariston the first, after whom Strataeas the son of Lois, and the third Ariston.

The recurrence of the name Ariston twice is curious ; it may be that the presidency of the Church of Smyrna not yet being a life-office, the same person held it twice.[1] Or possibly in the list used a name had been duplicated by a scribal error ; this happened in the old editions to the list of early Roman bishops in Epiphanius in regard to the name Evaristus.[2] Later on I shall raise the question whether this Ariston may not be the Aristion whom Papias ranks along with the Elder John. Undoubtedly Ariston and Aristion are used in pagan writings as interchangeable forms of the same name ; and both occur on the coins of Smyrna.[3]

That this list goes back to an early tradition is shown by the flagrant contradiction between it and the statement of Irenaeus (*Adv. Haer.* iii. 3. 4) :

Polycarp was not only taught by Apostles, and held conversation with many who had seen Christ, but he was appointed by Apostles in Asia bishop of the church in Smyrna.

Tertullian gives the statement further precision :

For this is the manner in which apostolic churches transmit their registers ; as the church of Smyrna, which records that Polycarp was placed therein by John (*De Praescrip. Haer.* xxxii.).

Tertullian had read Irenaeus. Whenever I have had

---

[1] Cf. pp. 95 and 269.

[2] A similar slip, I think, is the reading of the Sinaitic Syriac in Matt. i. 16, 'Joseph begot Jesus'. Cf. *The Four Gospels*, p. 6.

[3] Cf. Lightfoot, *Ignatius*, i. p. 463. It is to be noted that the famous Armenian Codex at Etchmiadzin, in which F. C. Conybeare found Mark xvi. 9-20 headed by the rubric, ' Of Ariston the Presbyter '—presumably meaning the Aristion mentioned by Papias—spells it ' Ariston '.

occasion to compare their statements, I have noticed that the relation of Tertullian to Irenaeus, in the matter of all statements concerning the Apostles or their writings, is almost exactly comparable to that of Jerome to Eusebius. Each ' dots the " i's " and crosses the " t's " ' of his predecessor's statements. The two Latin writers have a fine style and a keen sense of the effective; the more dingy Greeks give the statement in a more original, if less embellished, form.

The early date and wide circulation of these writers, especially Irenaeus, whose statement about Polycarp was republished by Eusebius, must have familiarised the Church at large with the idea that Polycarp was ordained by the Apostle John; and it was an idea of considerable apologetic value in controversy with the Gnostics. But here we find a writer completely ignoring the famous martyr Polycarp, naming as the first bishops of Smyrna three persons quite unknown to fame, and—most notable of all—refraining from the assertion that any one of these was ordained by an Apostle. This certainly looks as if he had access to authentic tradition as regards the bishops of the Church of Smyrna.

This view receives some confirmation from comparison with the tradition, evidently quite independent, made use of in the *Life of Polycarp* by Pionius—a document which, in spite of Lightfoot's strictures, I believe to be of very considerable historical value (see Appendix A). This document suggests that Strataeas, son of Lois, was the first Bishop of Smyrna; and gives as the teacher and immediate predecessor of Polycarp an otherwise unknown Bucolus:

After the departure of the Apostle (*i.e.* Paul) Strataeas succeeded to his teaching, and certain of those after him, whose names, so far as it is possible to discover who and what manner

of men they were, I will set down. But for the present let us
proceed at once to Polycarp. One whose name was Bucolus
being bishop in Smyrna at that time, there was in those days
. . . a little lad named Polycarp.

Unfortunately the *Life of Polycarp* is incomplete, and
the promised list of the successors of Strataeas has (with
much other matter) fallen out of the text; but the
passage above quoted implies that Bucolus was *not* the
immediate successor, and he is never spoken of as if he
in any sense belonged to the age nearest to the Apostles.
Assuming the repetition of the name Ariston in the
Apostolic Constitutions to be due to dittography, the
original list may have run : Strataeas, Ariston, Bucolus,
Polycarp.

Neither the *Apostolic Constitutions* nor the *Life of
Polycarp* is an historical authority on which much reliance
can in general be placed; but just because they so little
scruple to prefer edification to fact, their concurrence in
dissociating Polycarp from any connection with the
Apostle John is worthy of note. It is also favoured
by chronological considerations. Polycarp, on his own
statement to the Roman magistrate,[1] was eighty-six
years old at the time of his death in A.D. 156. He would
therefore have only just attained his thirtieth year in
A.D. 100, the traditional date for the death of the John
who lived in Asia (whether we suppose him to be the
Apostle or his namesake the Elder). The canonical rule
that a bishop must not be under thirty derives ultimately
from the Jewish practice of making that the lower age-
limit for all posts of special responsibility. The ancients
had no belief in the wisdom of youth. The accident of
birth gave Alexander and Augustus the command of
armies before the age of twenty ; but in Roman, even

[1] *Martyrdom*, 9.

more than in Jewish, custom, young men must wait their turn for all high office. Polycarp, to judge from his surviving epistle, was a person of small ability ; and without ability, goodness and honesty rarely secure a man election as supreme governor of a community by the age of thirty. The statement of Irenaeus is therefore inherently less probable than that of these otherwise inferior authorities. Moreover, it is not the statement of an unbiased witness. To Irenaeus, Polycarp was the link between himself and apostolic tradition. It was very tempting to be able ' to place upon his own brow that crown of apostolic succession, at only one remove from the Apostle John, which Basilides had claimed through Glaukias from Peter, and Valentinus through Theodas from Paul '.[1] Polycarp, again, was the link between the Apostles themselves and the tradition of the churches of Asia, on which—along with that of the See of Rome—the main argument of Irenaeus' work against the Gnostics was based. Irenaeus is not the only person who, seeing in some statement ' a short way with dissenters ', has inclined to view the evidence for it with a perhaps too partial eye.

The *Apostolic Constitutions* is commonly dated *c.* A.D. 370 ; but it consists in the main of older material re-edited. Some of this material is very early ; it includes, for example, practically every sentence in the *Didache*, with ' corrections ' and amplifications meant to adapt it to fourth-century ideas.[2] If, then, its author had access to an authentic list of the bishops of Smyrna, there is some slight presumption that he had one for the neighbouring and more notable church of Ephesus. Now for

---

[1] B. W. Bacon, *Z.N.T.W.*, 1927, p. 190.

[2] The text of *Apos. Constit.* vii. 1-32 is printed in full, with the passages taken from the *Didache* in bold-face type, in Harnack's edition of the *Didache*, p. 178 ff.

Ephesus he gives ' Timothy ordained by Paul ; and John ordained by (the Apostle) John '. The author of the *Apostolic Constitutions* has no conscience at all about ascribing words or actions to Apostles ; no stress, therefore, can be laid on the part of his statement which avers that the Bishop John was ordained by the Apostle of that name. Nevertheless if, as I believe, the Beloved Disciple of the Fourth Gospel is the Apostle John, and the author of the Gospel had been in some sense a pupil of his in Palestine,[1] the statement that John the Elder was ' ordained ' by John the Apostle—in spite of the ' tendencious ' character of the document which states it— may have *some* basis in fact. But, quite apart from this possibility, our argument that the Elder was Bishop of Ephesus is, I think, strengthened by a piece of evidence that at the close of the first century the Bishop of Ephesus was named John.

It would seem, then, that we must make an addition to the names of those outstanding leaders in the great churches, commonly known as ' Apostolic Fathers ', whose epistles have come down to us and are our main authority for the history and doctrine of the Church at the turn of the first and second centuries. Along with, indeed in front of, Clement of Rome, Polycarp of Smyrna, and Ignatius of Antioch, we must place the Elder John.

[1] *The Four Gospels*, p. 432.

H

CONSPECTUS OF CHRISTIAN LITERATURE TO A.D. 230

ASIA.		SYRIA (including Palestine).		ROME.		ALEXANDRIA.	
Epistles and Gospel of John	85–100	Gospel of Matthew	85	Gospel of Mark	65	*Gospel according to Egyptians	78–120
Apocalypse of John	90	Didache	90	Hebrews	75	'Barnabas'	120–160
1 Peter	90	Epistle of Jude	105	Acts (? also Luke)	85	2 Clement	140
Sections of Ascension of Isaiah	90	?*Gospel according to Hebrews	105	James	90	?*Preaching of Peter	145
Pastoral Epistles	110	Ignatius	115	1 Clement	96	? Epistola Apostolorum	200
Polycarp of Smyrna	115	Original Clementine Romance	170	Hermas	97–110	Clement Alex.	till 231
*Papias of Hierapolis	145	*Hegesippus	175	Justin Martyr	155	Origen	
? 2 Peter	150	Theophilus of Antioch	180	Tatian	170		
?*Gospel and Apocalypse of Peter	150			Muratorianum	200		
Martyrdom of Polycarp	156	**ATHENS.**		Hippolytus	190–235		
Acts of John	165	Aristides	125 or 150			**AFRICA.**	
Acts of Paul	170	Athenagoras	177	**GAUL.**		Acts of Scillitan Martyrs	180
Melito of Sardis	175			*Letter of Churches of Lyons and Vienna	177	Tertullian	197–223
Acts of Peter	190			Irenaeus	185	Acts of Perpetua and Felicitas	203
*Polycrates of Ephesus	190					Minucius Felix	?

The Table does *not* include the Epistles of St. Paul, 50–62, nor (with a few exceptions, marked with asterisk) writers only extant in fragments. A varying degree of probability attaches to dates and localities assigned. The following are unlocated : Epistle to Diognetus, Protevangelium of James, Acts of Pilate, Infancy Gospel of Thomas.

IV

THE CHURCH IN ASIA

SYNOPSIS

The Pastoral Epistles

In the fourth century the genuine epistles of Ignatius were expanded, and five fresh ones were composed, by the author of the *Apostolic Constitutions*; in the second century the author of 2 Peter treated Jude in a similar way.

The epistles to Timothy and Titus present an analogous case, 2 Timothy and Titus being amplifications of genuine notes by Paul, 1 Timothy being a fresh composition by the same editor.

Reasons for believing they were composed in Ephesus—in which case they afford evidence in regard to the state of things in Asia at the date of writing—not later than A.D. 110.

Timothy may have settled in Ephesus after the death of Paul and inherited something of his authority; but there is evidence (Acts, Epistles, *Ascension of Isaiah*) of troublous times in Asia, due to the moral failure of church officers, so that Timothy's rule (if any) was of short duration. Suggestion that order was restored by John the Elder, supported by persons who remembered the benefits of individual rule under Timothy.

In any case, since the monarchical episcopate existed in Asia by A.D. 100, it antedates the Pastorals; and their purpose will be misunderstood if this fact is forgotten. That purpose is moral rather than ecclesiastical. It is with the character of the officers, not the form of church government, that the author is mainly concerned. The terms Episcopos and Presbyter are still, to some extent, interchangeable (assuming the two passages in which 'episcopos' occurs to be original), but the use of them is probably designedly ambiguous in order that the advice given may be appropriate to churches which had not, as well as those which had, adopted a monarchical rule.

The use of the Epistles in Pionius' *Life of Polycarp*, which may well represent a second-century interpretation of their main purport.

In general the advice given is more appropriate where the monarchical system prevails. Timothy and Titus are not actually described as Bishops (historic fact forbade this), but they are depicted as exercising the functions which, at the date of writing, were those of Bishops. Under these names is portrayed the Ideal Bishop—in the one case of a large city, in the other of a country district.

The First Epistle of St. Peter

The address is to the Church in the provinces of Asia Minor, north of the Taurus ; it ends with a salutation from the Church in Babylon.   There is no improbability in Peter visiting Babylonia, where there still existed a large Jewish population.   Nevertheless, here, as in Revelation, Babylon would seem to be a veiled name for Rome.

This raises considerable difficulties as to the authorship and character of the document.   The question of Petrine authorship and of inspiration not to be confused.

The external evidence in its favour is less strong than might have been expected.

From the side of internal evidence three main objections to Petrine authorship require careful weighing.

After fifty years of discussion no general agreement of scholars has been reached in regard to the historical situation implied by the epistle.   It is not, therefore, temerarious to propound a new solution—if that be avowedly of a tentative character.

Hypothesis that the epistle really consists of two documents : (1) a sermon given by the bishop to a group of newly baptized persons (i. 3-iv. 11); (2) a letter of encouragement (iv. 12-v. 11), written in time of persecution. The address and salutations (*i.e.* the first two and last three verses) of the epistle in that case are later additions.

Six considerations which suggest that (on the assumption that the epistle is not by Peter himself) it originated in Asia.

The addition, perhaps at the time of Pliny's persecution (A.D. 112), of the first two and last three verses secured admission to the Canon of a document of the highest religious value which otherwise might not have been preserved.

Aristion of Smyrna

Suggestion—put forward not as ' a result of criticism ', but as a reasonable guess—that the actual author of 1 Peter was the Aristion mentioned by Papias, and that he was Bishop of Smyrna at the time of the outburst of persecution in that Church mentioned in Revelation (ii. 10).

The Church Order Implied

The exhortation given to the Elders has meaning only if they stood to the people as a shepherd to his sheep, and were in a position to ' lord it over ' the flock.   In other ways also it is clear that the regular ministry had attained a position of authority far in advance of that implied in the epistles of Paul.

The identification of the writer with Aristion, Bishop of Smyrna, makes it easier to bridge the gulf between the rule by corporations of bishop-presbyters established by Paul in Asia, and the mon-episcopal system generally prevalent there in the time of Ignatius.   The position of John the Elder at Ephesus and of Aristion at Smyrna would lead to imitation in the smaller churches.

IV

THE CHURCH IN ASIA

THE PASTORAL EPISTLES

SOME much-debated questions in regard to the epistles to Timothy and Titus will become clearer if we first consider an analogous literary problem. Somewhere about the year A.D. 360 an unknown ecclesiastic—it would seem from his style that he is identical with the author of the *Apostolic Constitutions*—took upon himself to produce an enlarged and (in his own judgment) an improved edition of the epistles of Ignatius. The seven genuine letters he amplified with edifying matter, appropriate to the needs of his own time ; and he composed five additional letters. Fortunately there survives a single Greek manuscript (and a Latin translation) of the letters in their original form ; and as in the *Apostolic Constitutions* we have a quite other work in which to study the style and methods of this enterprising editor, we are in a position to ascertain the exact state of affairs in regard to the Ignatian letters.[1]

This re-editing of Ignatius was done in the fourth century ; but the same sort of thing could happen in the second. No one can read side by side the epistle of Jude and chapter ii. of the second epistle of Peter,

---

[1] In bks. i.-vi. he works over the *Didascalia* ; in bk. vii., the *Didache* ; in bk. viii., a work by Hippolytus, which (in something near its original form) is preserved in the *Egyptian Church Order*.

so-called, without perceiving that in these two documents the same things are being said in very much the same words.   There can be no reasonable doubt that the author of 2 Peter has, with slight verbal alterations, incorporated practically the whole of the older epistle of Jude.[1] What he found in Jude, along with what he added himself, seemed to comprise ' a tract for the times ' so vitally needed that—feeling sure Peter, if alive, would have taken that line—he deemed it justifiable to gain for it wide and immediate publicity by putting at the head of it the name of the Apostle.

It has long been thought that the epistles to Timothy and Titus, in the form in which we have them, are the result of a similar process of editing. If any doubt still remained, it has been removed by the brilliant study of Dr. P. N. Harrison.[2] It seems clear that 2 Timothy embodies several authentic letters of the Apostle—these being short notes, similar to many, only a few lines in length, that have been discovered among the papyrus finds in Egypt. Titus concludes with one such ; but 1 Timothy would seem to be entirely the composition of the editor. The epistles in their present form appear to have been known both to Polycarp in Smyrna and to Ignatius in Antioch[3] by A.D. 115 ; hence they can hardly be later than A.D. 110. The evidence, therefore, which they afford in regard to Church Order must be taken as evidence as to the state of things in the church in which they were produced

---

[1] The parallels are conveniently set out and discussed by J. Moffatt, *Introduction to the New Testament*, p. 348 ff.

[2] *The Problem of the Pastoral Epistles*, P. N. Harrison. (Oxford University Press, 1921.)   The analogy with the Ignatian letters I owe to Prof. K. Lake.

[3] The verbal echoes in Ignatius of phrases that occur in the Pastorals are just not sufficient to *prove* his knowledge of them.   But he tells the Ephesians (xii. 2) that Paul makes mention of them ' in *every* letter ' ; but if the Pastorals were not included in his collection of letters of Paul, 1 Corinthians would remain as the only letter in which Ephesus is even named.

at about that date, rather than as evidence for the
Apostolic Age.

That the church in and for which the editor worked
was in the province of Asia we may conjecture with
some confidence. Most probably he worked in Ephesus
itself.

(1) Two out of the three letters, and those the longest, purport to be addressed to Timothy while resident
at Ephesus; and the editor is concerned to make a
good deal of Timothy's connection with Ephesus. Thus
the first epistle opens with a reminder to Timothy of a
previous occasion in which he had been left by Paul
to take charge of this church; and as nothing is
said in this epistle about the Apostle being in prison,
while he twice expresses an intention of coming to
Ephesus in person, the author evidently intends the
epistle to be read as if written, either when Paul was
at liberty, or in the earlier stages of his imprisonment
when he still anticipated release. The second epistle
to Timothy, on the other hand, is represented as written
when the Apostle is in prison, and expecting death.
But Timothy is still at Ephesus—as appears from the
fact that salutations are sent to the house of Onesiphorus
(2 Tim. iv. 19), who earlier in the letter (2 Tim. i. 16-18) [1]
is identified as having come to Rome from Ephesus.

(2) The editor names certain persons whom he thinks
should be treated as especially dangerous heretics—
Hymenaeus, Alexander, and Philetus (1 Tim. i. 20;
2 Tim. ii. 17). We know the names of a large number

[1] Prisca and Aquila, who are also saluted, were settled in Ephesus and had a
church in their house a few years earlier (1 Cor. xvi. 19). They are also saluted
in Romans (Rom. xvi. 3). Personally, I accept the view that Rom. xvi. was
originally a separate letter addressed to the church at Ephesus, or else a post-
script appended to a copy of Romans sent by Paul himself to the Ephesians at
the time of writing. At any rate, they cannot have been in Rome when 2 Tim.
iv. 19 was penned, since Paul was writing this in Rome.

of early heretics; but of the above none is ever heard of elsewhere. Their importance, we infer, must have been purely local. Our editor would never have singled out these persons, and these only, for special execration unless he wrote in a locality where they were well known and had a considerable following. Since, then, they are represented as among the most serious enemies whom Timothy would have to face in Ephesus, it is a fair presumption that the epistles were written in, and primarily for, the Church in Asia.

If the editor wrote in Ephesus not later than A.D. 110, we may accept it as an historical fact, preserved by local tradition, that Timothy had been either left in Ephesus by Paul, or subsequently sent there by him. We know that he had been sent on analogous missions to Corinth and to Philippi.

For this cause have I sent unto you Timothy, who is my beloved and faithful child in the Lord, who shall put you in remembrance of my ways which be in Christ, even as I teach everywhere in every church (1 Cor. iv. 17 f.).

Our editor's representation of the character of Timothy, his relations with the Apostle, and the nature of his mission, has obviously been influenced by this passage, as well as by the similar notice in Philippians (ii. 19-24). The Apostle's repeated promise that he will follow up Timothy's visit with one by himself (1 Tim. iii. 14, 15 ; iv. 13) is clearly an echo of the similar promises in 1 Cor. iv. 19 and Phil. ii. 24. Similarly the injunction, 'Let no man despise thy youth' (1 Tim. iv. 12), is evidently an exegetical comment on 'Let no man therefore despise him' (1 Cor. xvi. 10, 11)—a mistaken exegesis, it should be noted, since Timothy cannot have been a very young man at this date.

It is possible that, after the death of Paul, Timothy

settled permanently in Ephesus. In that case the mantle
of Elijah would have descended upon Elisha, and Timothy
would have virtually stepped into the place of Paul, and
found himself in a position of acknowledged supremacy
over other officers of the local church. He would, in
fact if not in name, have at once become bishop, in the
monarchical sense, of that city — with, in addition, a
kind of patriarchal jurisdiction over all other churches
in the province. It is more probable that after a time
Timothy resumed the life of a wandering ' Evangelist ' ;
or possibly he did settle and become virtually Bishop of
Ephesus, but did not hold the position long. We hear
of him once at a later date as being in prison ; and on
his release he may have had to leave Asia (Heb. xiii. 23).

What happened to Timothy is a matter of conjecture ; but there is clear evidence that later on, precisely from the lack of wise and trustworthy leaders, the
Church at Ephesus passed through stormy times.

I know that after my departing, grievous wolves shall enter
in among you, not sparing the flock ; and from among your own
selves shall men arise, speaking perverse things, to draw away
the disciples after them. . . . I coveted no man's silver or gold,
or apparel. Ye yourselves know that these hands ministered
unto my necessities, and to them that were with me. In all
things I gave you an example (Acts xx. 29-30, 33-35).

How far these are the exact words spoken by the
Apostle to the Ephesian Episcopoi may be disputed
(about himself he says something very like this in
1 Thess. ii. 3-12) ; what is certain is that they would
never have appeared as the central point of emphasis in
Paul's farewell address, unless the author of Acts had
known that in after years this church had suffered, not
only from heretical teaching, but also from the venality
and domineering spirit of its officers. And the language

used is far more intelligible if the church was ruled by a group of officers of co-equal power, than by one single individual, who might have been held more or less responsible for what his subordinates taught and did. Other evidence points in the same direction. From Colossians we see that, even within the lifetime of St. Paul, Gnosticism, of an early type, was beginning to invade the Church in Asia. In 1 John we hear of ' many Antichrists ' who ' went out from us, but they were not of us ' ; such ' going out ' implies a previous struggle; 'many' implies heretics of more than one type. There is also the allusion to the teaching (probably of Cerinthus) that Christ did not really suffer on the Cross (1 John v. 6). I comment, later, on the hint in 1 Peter, coinciding with the passage quoted above from Acts, that there was serious moral failure in some of the church officials—otherwise what need to exhort the Presbyters to keep clear of ' filthy lucre ' and of ' lording it over ' the flock of Christ ? (1 Pet. v. 2 f.).

The iniquities of church officers are vigorously denounced in one of the ancient sources—believed to date from the first century—embodied in the *Ascension of Isaiah*.

In those days many will love office, though devoid of wisdom. And there will be many lawless elders, and shepherds dealing wrongly by their own sheep, and they will ravage (them) owing to their not having holy shepherds. . . . And there will not be in those days many prophets, nor those who speak trustworthy words, save one here and there in divers places. On account of the spirit of error and fornication and of vainglory, and of covetousness, which shall be in those who will be called servants of that One and in those who will receive that One. And there will be great hatred in the shepherds and elders towards each other (iii. 23-27).[1]

---

[1] *The Ascension of Isaiah*, p. 22 f., ed. R. H. Charles. (A. & C. Black, 1900.)

In the same document, but in another context, there
is an obscure phrase which seems to imply that at the
time of writing there were, though ' few ', still *some* alive,
who had seen the Lord in the flesh. We know that two
such, Aristion and the Elder John, survived in Asia till
late in the first century; and the evidence of Acts and
1 Peter suggests that in Asia the clergy earlier than
elsewhere acquired considerable power, and frequently
abused it. On the other hand, if the *Didache* be taken
as evidence for the state of affairs in Syria at this date,
it would seem that in that province the Episcopoi and
Deacons had too little authority (p. 144 ff). I infer that
the document represented by this section of the *Ascension
of Isaiah* probably originated in Asia.[1] If so, it casts a
flood of light on the situation there.

It would look as if in the Church of that date—as has
sometimes happened in the State, ancient and modern
—a situation was developing such that the autocratic
rule of an individual seemed the only alternative to
disintegration of the society. We may surmise that
in Ephesus the situation was saved by the Elder John.
In that case the memory of the period or periods in
which Timothy, as the accredited representative of the
Apostle, had kept the church true to the ideal of a
Christian community, would have been the precedent
everywhere quoted by the party who supported the
concentration of power in the hands of a single individual; so that, in effect, John (and other local bishops)
inherited in permanency the position once temporarily
held by Timothy.

But whatever may have been the history of the

---

[1] The fact that it was known to Ignatius at Antioch (Charles, *op. cit.* p. 77),
while evidence to the early date of the document, is no objection to the view
that it originated in Asia; he echoes phrases in other literature written in
Asia, *e.g.* the Pastorals and the Fourth Gospel.

emergence in Ephesus of the monarchical episcopate, the case of Diotrephes shows that it already existed in some churches of Asia by the end of the first century. In Asia, mon-episcopacy *antedates* the writing of the Pastoral Epistles. We shall, then, make nonsense of the evidence they afford as to Church Order, unless we study them with this fact in mind. It will then appear that what the author has in mind is, not advocacy of one type of church government rather than another, but the moral level of its personnel.

It was pointed out long ago by Jerome and by several of the Greek fathers, that there is no passage in the New Testament which compels the assumption that the terms ' Episcopos ' and ' Presbyter ' are the names of two different offices. We remember that the leaders of the Church at Ephesus summoned to Miletus (Acts xx. 17-28) are styled ' Presbyters ' but are addressed by Paul as ' Episcopoi '; while in the Pauline church of Philippi the officers saluted are Episcopoi and Deacons. And so far as the actual use of the word Episcopos is concerned, there is nothing in the Pastorals to show that this usage has changed. Titus is instructed

to appoint elders in every city . . . if any man is blameless . . . for the bishop must be blameless . . . (Tit. i. 5-7).

Again, when the duties and qualifications of particular offices are being defined (1 Tim. iii. 1-13) the Episcopos, Deacons and ' women ' (apparently Deaconesses) are mentioned, but not Presbyters. The word ' episcopos ' is in the singular ; but both passages read most naturally if this is taken as the generic singular, which is quite compatible with there being several officers bearing that name in each church.

Harnack and others argue that these passages—the

only two in which the word 'episcopos' occurs—are
early interpolations. But in neither case is the connection of thought in the context really improved if they
are struck out. Thus the paragraph 1 Tim. ii. 1-15 is
concerned with the conduct of public worship ; it is
immediately followed by the section 1 Tim. iii. 1-13,
which deals with the qualifications required in a person
to be appointed to the office of Bishop or Deacon. The
writer then goes on to say :

These things write I unto thee . . . that thou mayst know
how men ought to behave themselves in the house of God,
which is the church of the living God (1 Tim. iii. 14-15).

In the English version this reads like an injunction
as to decorum in public worship ; but in Greek the word
' house ' in this context would suggest the idea of
organisation and management. It is, therefore, more
appropriate after a paragraph dealing with Church
Order, than after one concerned with the conduct of
worship.

There is more to be said for the view that the passage
in Titus is an interpolation. The paragraph (Tit. i. 10),
' For there are many unruly men . . .', follows admir-
ably on the conclusion of i. 6, ' who are not accused of
riot or unruly ', if the intervening verses (in which the
word ' episcopos ' occurs) are struck out. But this also
makes quite good sense where it stands, and it is quite
in the style of the author of the rest of the epistle.

Even if these passages be regarded as genuine, there
is not much in the way of direct reference in the Pastorals
to church organisation *as such* ; and what little there
is seems ambiguous—designedly ambiguous, I suggest.
The reference to

the elders that rule well . . . especially those who labour in the
word and teaching (1 Tim. v. 17),

would be appropriate to a church ruled by a body of
Episcopoi who, as in the older usage, could be spoken of
under the generic name of Presbyters. But it would
equally have point in a church in which a single Episcopos
held a position superior to other Presbyters who yet
enjoyed subordinate powers of discipline. Again, the
allusion to the spiritual gift conferred by ' the laying on
of hands of the presbytery ' (1 Tim. iv. 14) would be
appropriate whichever way the church was governed ;
for even to the present day priests are associated with
the bishop in the laying on of hands at ordinations.

What more likely than that the author, writing for
a district where most—but not as yet all—churches had
a monarchical bishop, should preserve a studious am-
biguity. He could do so, since the discussion of church
organisation is *not* the main purpose of his epistles.
Controversy about primitive Church Order has largely
raged round the interpretation of the Pastoral Epistles ;
again, the only two passages which name ' the bishop '
do so as ' the husband of one wife '—and this lends them
to modern ears a faint absurdity and picturesqueness
which makes them stick in the memory. Thus it has
come about that among scholars and divines it is
more or less taken for granted that the Pastoral
Epistles as a whole are primarily concerned with church
organisation. But if they are read apart from these
two sections, there results a very different impression of
the author's main aim. His purpose is then seen to be,
not so much ecclesiastical, as moral ; that is to say, he
is not primarily concerned with advocating a particular
type of Church Order, but with exhorting the persons who
actually hold office to live worthily of their high responsibilities. He is not concerned to make out that the
monarchical episcopate existed in Ephesus in the lifetime

of the Apostles ; he was doubtless aware that it did not.
What he is concerned to do is to urge the rulers of the
churches of his own time—in Ephesus and elsewhere—to
exercise their office with the diligence, tact, and sense of
a sacred responsibility, that persons like Timothy and
Titus displayed in the exercise of analogous, though not
quite identical, functions in the Apostolic Age. It was
not the form of church government, but the character
of those who held office, which was disquieting the
Church at this period.

The moral problems of any church differ from age to
age much less than the theological. Hence it will not be
entirely irrelevant to cite the Pionian *Life of Polycarp* as
evidence of the way in which the moral emphasis in these
epistles struck the early Church. The passage to be cited
is also relevant as evidence, if not of the primitive
method of appointing a bishop, yet of that practised in
Asia, perhaps already in the second century.

And on the Sabbath, when prayer had been made long time
on bended knee [Polycarp], as was his custom, got up to read ;
and every eye was fixed upon him. Now the lesson was the
Epistles of Paul to Timothy and to Titus, in which he says what
manner of man a bishop ought to be. And he was so well fitted
for the office that the hearers said one to another that he lacked
none of those qualities which Paul requires in one who has the
care of a church. When, then (after the reading, and the instruction of the bishops and the discourses of the presbyters), the
deacons were sent to the laity to enquire whom they would have,
they said with one accord, ' Let Polycarp be our pastor and
teacher'. The whole priesthood then having assented, they
appointed him, notwithstanding his earnest entreaties and his
desire to decline.

Accordingly the deacons led him up for ordination by the
hands of the bishops according to custom. And being placed in
his chair by them, he moistened and anointed first with tears of
piety and humility the place where in the spirit he saw standing

the feet of Christ, who was present with him for the anointing to the priestly office. For where the ministers are—the priests and Levites—there in the midst is also the High-priest arrayed in the great flowing robe. Then the company present urged him, since this was the custom, to address them. For they said that this work of teaching was the most important part of the communion (*Life of Polycarp*, § 22-23).

Then follows a brief sermon, in the course of which, it is interesting to note, the Pastoral Epistles are again alluded to.

This office exceeds my powers ; for I well know that no man could fulfil it well, except that he hath just received it from the Lord from heaven, as the blessed Paul has shown in his epistles, showing in a single word the whole life of one who is appointed to office, when he speaks of it as ' blameless '.

Of the practical advice given to Timothy in the Pastorals the larger part is pointless except as given to persons in a position to exercise a virtually supreme authority. Timothy and Titus are historical individuals, and are represented as having such authority delegated to them by the Apostle who writes the letters ; but the actual letters are the work of one who wrote years after these two distinguished personages were dead. The question, then, which the historian must ask himself is, What was the motive of the editor of the Pastorals in developing all this elaborate advice as to how an individual in supreme charge of a church was to order his own life and that of the community? Clearly, such advice would have point only if at the time of writing (at any rate in some churches) individuals existed who were in a position to carry it out.

The author of the Pastorals, we infer, takes the monarchical episcopate for granted. To him the figures of Timothy and Titus are of interest, not as historical personages, but as affording him an opportunity of portraying two different types of the ideal bishop. Timothy is the ideal bishop in his relation to his own church in a province like Ephesus, where organised churches already existed in all the principal towns. Titus, on the other hand, is the ideal of the Missionary Bishop—the bishop of some outlying province, where the churches outside the bishop's own headquarters are weak and disorganised. That is why in the epistle to Titus rather more stress is laid on church organisation as such. But, though mentioned first, this subject is still treated as one of which the actual details may be taken as a matter of established tradition.

Clement of Alexandria quotes a story about the Apostle John and a convert who became a robber chief and was reconverted.[1] He may have got this from the *Acts of John*; but Clement tells us he had lived in Ionia —the ancient name for the coast cities of Asia—and he implies that he got it from oral tradition; and his incidental remark, 'a certain city . . . whose very name is told by some', seems to imply divergencies in the tradition unlikely to be found in a written source. If so, the story stands on a different footing from the narratives derived by various fathers from the *Acts of John*. But if we may take leave to assume that the story is in the main historical, but should be told, not of the Apostle John but of the Elder, we get a picture of his activities on a more extended scale.

He went also, when invited,[2] from Ephesus to the neighbouring regions of the Gentiles : in some to appoint bishops, in some

---

[1] *Quis Dives*, xliii., also Eus. *H.E.* iii. 23.

[2] Euseb. *H.E.* iii. 23. The phrase 'when invited' has a primitive look. It is not an attitude which a later writer would attribute to churches in dealing with an Apostle. Another evidence of antiquity is the fact that the same person is first spoken of as 'the Bishop' and then as 'the Presbyter'. Cf. § 7-8 in Eusebius' version.

to institute entire new churches, and in others to appoint to the ministry some one of those that were pointed out by the Holy Ghost.

Now the procedure here attributed to John is exactly that ascribed to Titus in the epistle addressed to him.

But why, we ask, are not similar duties in regard to the smaller cities of the province assigned to Timothy, whose headquarters is Ephesus ?   Timothy and Titus are character sketches of the ideal bishop.   But by the time the Pastorals were written mon-episcopacy would seem to have been established in all or most of the cities of Asia. And these bishops may have been a trifle jealous of their rights as against the See of Ephesus.   Even John the Elder may have found it more difficult than he had anticipated to bring Diotrephes to heel.   In the days of John's successor, who necessarily lacked the prestige of being a disciple of the Lord, it was more tactful not to raise this question.   Timothy and Titus are painted as models of the ideal bishop ; but it was perhaps safer not to suggest that the one of them who was stationed at Ephesus exercised in regard to neighbouring cities duties and authority which pertained to the bishops of provincial capitals in more backward provinces.

But, it may be objected, the Timothy of the Pastorals is not permanently at Ephesus ; his residence there is temporary, ' Till I come ' (1 Tim. iv. 13).   To this I reply that the facts about Timothy's stay in Ephesus were well known and could not be otherwise represented. But if we examine the instructions given him, it is clear that they are not at all of an emergency character ; they are appropriate only if given to a person who has both the responsibilities and the difficulties of a man in supreme charge of a great church *over a period of years*.   He is told that the example of a good life is to be relied on, quite

as much as steady sound teaching, to counteract heresy
(1 Tim. iv. 12) ; that a body of 'faithful men' is to
be trained up to hand on to others the true doctrine
(2 Tim. ii.), and so on.   The epistles might be entitled,
"Advices to those who are, or who aspire to become,
Bishops'.   And the advice is exactly what we should
expect of an author who wrote *after* the monarchical
episcopate had been established in Ephesus and the
principal towns of the neighbourhood.   He wrote to
supply what the time needed ; and what the time needed
was, not a defence of episcopacy, but good bishops.

The First Epistle of St. Peter

The first epistle of Peter is addressed to the Church in
certain provinces of Asia Minor.   It ends with a salutation from the Church in Babylon.   Does this mean the
famous city on the Euphrates, or is it a veiled name for
Rome ?

That Peter should have conceived the idea of preaching in Babylon is highly probable.   Paul, born a Roman
citizen and conscious of a call to evangelise the Gentiles,
naturally turned his eyes towards the West—ultimately
towards Spain.   Just as naturally a Palestinian Jew,
convinced as Peter was that God's call for him was to
preach to the 'circumcision', would look East, towards
Babylonia.   We moderns, with 2000 years of European
religion behind us, think as Paul thought ; but to a
Palestinian Jew, Babylon must have seemed a far more
important, and a far more promising, field for missionary
endeavour.   It was the best of the Jews who had been
taken into exile ; and if anyone was inclined to forget
that fact, there were there to remind him the prophecies
of Jeremiah (xxiv. 1 ff.) about the good and 'very evil

figs ', not to mention the evident fact that the religious reforms of Ezra and Nehemiah were forced upon the Palestinian Jews by men from Babylon. The purest stock and the strictest orthodoxy still had its centre in Mesopotamia. The Christians of Jerusalem did not forget this. In the tradition which had reached Luke about the day of Pentecost, the list of persons whom Peter addressed is headed, not by the Greek-speaking Jews of the Dispersion in the West, but by ' Parthians, Medes, Elamites, and dwellers in Mesopotamia '. The first place outside Palestine where we hear of Christianity is Damascus—on the high road to the Euphrates. If a Hellenised courtier like Josephus thought it worth while to write the first edition of his book on the Jewish war in Aramaic, for the benefit of his fellow countrymen in Mesopotamia, how much more would a missionary like Peter desire to bring the message of salvation to his people in their second home ' before the great and terrible day of the Lord come '.

But if Peter did go to Babylon, it is unlikely that he was well received there. Babylon, the home of Ezra, practically untouched by Hellenistic culture, would be rocky ground on which to sow the seed. In all ages there has been a wide gulf between orthodox and liberal Judaism ; and the difference between the Judaism of Antioch and that of Babylon would be comparable to the difference to-day between the Judaism of New York and of Damascus. At any rate, Peter did not succeed in laying in Babylon the foundations of a church which preserved the memory of his work and of his name.

But though Peter may well have gone to Babylon, we should not have expected to find there in his company both Silvanus (=Silas) and Mark, who had been such useful and successful fellow-workers of Paul in the

Gentile West. Still less should we expect Peter, if he did go to Babylon, from that city to write a letter addressed expressly to the churches of Northern Asia Minor—the special sphere of Paul's activity. Accordingly, the view that in this epistle, as in the book of Revelation, the name Babylon should be understood to mean Rome, has the balance of probability in its favour.

Yet it is surely very strange that anyone writing an actual letter from Rome itself should date it as from Babylon. To call Rome ' Babylon ' is entirely consonant with the fiery symbolism of the Apocalypse ; it is appropriate in a work like the *Sibylline Oracles*, which is not only apocalyptic in spirit but metrical in form. But in the sober prose of a letter it seems out of place, and quite extraordinarily so in this particular letter.

Not only the style of 1 Peter, but its whole attitude towards the Roman power, is the very antithesis of that of the author of Revelation, awaiting with exultation the fall of

the great city, the woman on whose forehead a name is written, MYSTERY, BABYLON THE GREAT, THE MOTHER OF THE HARLOTS AND OF THE ABOMINATIONS OF THE EARTH . . . drunken with the blood of the saints, and with the blood of the martyrs of Jesus (Rev. xvii. 5 ff.).

How absolute a contrast is Peter's exhortation :

Be subject to every ordinance of man for the Lord's sake, whether it be to the king as supreme; or unto governors, as sent by him for vengeance on evil doers and for praise to them that do well. . . . (1 Peter ii. 13 ff.).

He goes on to put side by side the precepts, ' Fear God; honour the king '. Could one who speaks in this way of the sacred duty of obedience towards the Emperor and the provincial governors who are his representatives, proceed in cold blood to name the seat of Empire, ' Babylon ' ?

Perforce we must raise the question, Is this epistle so called really a letter at all, and with that the consequential question, Is it an authentic work of Peter ?

The first epistle of Peter is one of the finest things in the New Testament ; and were plenary inspiration and apostolic authorship identical—as was supposed when the Canon of the New Testament was settled—we could only affirm it to be the work of an Apostle. But once we have made up our minds that such marvellous pieces as the epistle to the Hebrews and the Fourth Gospel are not by Apostles, we have recognised the fact that inspiration in the fullest sense was in no way limited to St. Paul and the Twelve. Frankly I confess the pang it costs me to surrender the Petrine authorship ; but the loss I feel is in our knowledge of Peter himself, not in the value which the epistle has for me. We are free, then, to consider the problem of this epistle apart from any *a priori* prejudice in favour of apostolic authorship derived from its high religious quality.

The external evidence in favour of the epistle is not quite so strong as we should have expected.

(1) Eusebius classes it among the books concerning which there has never been any doubt in the Church. We cannot, however, accept this without examination ; for among the undisputed books he includes the Gospel of John, concerning which there was at Rome in the middle of the second century considerable hesitation even in orthodox circles.[1] Moreover, in regard to 1 Peter and 1 John, Eusebius is careful to quote evidences of use by ancient writers—a thing which he does *not* do in regard

---

[1] See my *The Four Gospels*, p. 436 ff. Since the publication of that book I have learnt that in Barsalibi's Commentary it is stated on the authority of Hippolytus that Gaius (whom Eusebius elsewhere (ii. 25. 6) calls ' a churchman ') attributed both the Gospel and the Apocalypse to Cerinthus.

to the thirteen epistles of Paul which, with the Gospels,
Acts, 1 John, and 1 Peter, make up the list which he
classes as undisputed. He tells us it was used by Papias
and Polycarp; but the possibility that Polycarp knew it,
but not as Peter's (p. 126), cannot be ruled out.

(2) Westcott remarks :

The actual traces of the early use of 1 Peter in the Latin
churches are very scanty. There is not the least evidence to
show that its authority was ever disputed, but, on the other hand,
it does not seem to have been much read. . . . Tertullian quotes
it only twice, and that too in writings which are more or less
open to suspicion.[1]

But if Peter both wrote the epistle and died in Rome,
it is precisely in the Latin churches that we should
expect to find it most quoted. True, it is cited by
Irenaeus, A.D. 185. But in the matter of the Canon he
represents Asian, more strictly than typically Western,
opinion.

(3) It is not included in the *Muratorianum*, which gives
the list of canonical books accepted at Rome A.D. 200,
or perhaps earlier. Its omission there *may* be accidental,
for the only surviving copy of that document has a very
corrupt text ; yet none of the conjectures, as to the
precise place in which an allusion to 1 Peter might have
originally stood, is satisfactory. Moreover, corrobora-
tive evidence of the absence of 1 Peter from the Roman
Canon in A.D. 170 may be deduced from its absence from
that of the Syriac-speaking church in Mesopotamia as
late as Aphraates (*c.* A.D. 350) and Ephraim (died A.D.
373). This shows that it was *not* among the books which
Tatian brought with him from Rome when he founded
the Church of Edessa (*c.* A.D. 172).

On grounds of internal evidence various objections

[1] *Canon of the New Testament*, p. 263. (Macmillan, 1896.)

have been raised to the epistle being the work of Peter
—of which three are weighty.

(1) It would seem that the author had read, and
that his language and thoughts have been influenced
by, epistles of Paul—more especially by Romans and
Ephesians. He also exhibits a mastery of the Greek
tongue greater than we should have expected of the
Apostle Peter. This objection has been countered by
the hypothesis that the letter was as much the work
of Paul's old comrade Silvanus, who is mentioned as
the scribe, as of Peter himself. It is also suggested
that there are points of contact—they do not amount
to very much—between the epistle and the speeches
attributed to Peter in the early chapters of Acts.
It is, however, improbable that these speeches rest on
records, or even authentic memories, of what Peter
actually said. In the exhilaration of those first days of
the ' outpouring of the Spirit ' it was on the present
and on the future, not on the past, that the minds of
all were turned. It is more likely that these speeches
represent the average apologetic of certain circles uninfluenced by Pauline thought with which Luke was
in contact. Moreover, the fact that certain passages in
1 Peter are most naturally explained by a *literary*
dependence on epistles of Paul, makes it not unlikely
that the author had read Acts as well; indeed, the exhortation, ' tend the flock of Christ ' (1 Pet. v. 2), is much
nearer to the speech attributed to *Paul* in Acts xx. 28
than are any passages in the epistle to speeches of *Peter*
in that book.

(2) We should not have expected Peter himself to
have said :

The elders, therefore, among you I exhort, who am a fellow-
elder, and a witness of the sufferings of Christ.

Not that Peter would have been too proud to call himself a Presbyter ; but in the apostolic age the titles ' Apostle ' and ' Presbyter ' were applied to persons who exercised functions of a wholly different character. The one was a wandering missionary, the other was a local official. An admiral might properly address a group of midshipmen as ' fellow officers ', but not as ' fellow soldiers ' ; the words ascribed to Peter would, *if* written *before* A.D. 70, have a similar inappropriateness.

Again, strictly speaking, Peter was not ' a *witness* of the sufferings of Christ '. Neither he nor any of the Twelve were present at the Crucifixion. This point may at first sound niggling ; and it would be so but for the fact that in the Acts, in *six* different speeches, Peter goes out of his way to call himself a ' *witness* ' of *the Resurrection*—which of course he truly was.

(3) The epistle was written at a time when the profession of Christianity was a crime punishable by death ; for it is implied (iv. 15-16) that for being a Christian a man might suffer the same penalty as for being a murderer. Liability to the death-penalty for the mere profession of ' the name ' may have followed automatically from the action taken by Nero—though this is a point of Roman jurisprudence disputed by eminent scholars. It certainly cannot have existed earlier than Nero. If, then, the epistle was written by Peter in Rome, it must have been written *after* the spectacular display in the gardens of Nero on the Vatican.[1] It is possible that Peter came to Rome shortly

[1] Prof. Bartlet suggests to me a view, partially based on that of Hort. If Paul was condemned to death by Nero A.D. 62, the profession of ' the name ' would have at once become *in law* a penal offence. Shortly *after* this, but *before* the great outrage of A.D. 64, Peter might have written from Rome to Asia, in *expectation* that the local authorities in the provinces would enforce the law— the use of Babylon for Rome being a precautionary disguise. If the epistle be regarded as being as much the work of Silas as of Peter, this would be a possible occasion. But the other difficulties discussed in this Lecture still remain.

after this event ; and if Paul was dead there would be nothing remarkable in Peter writing to a group of Pauline churches a word of exhortation, in view of the probability that a persecution begun in Rome would shortly extend to Asia. But in these circumstances it *is* remarkable that he should say not a word either about their founder Paul or about the recent horrors in Rome. More remarkable is what he *does* say. I find it hard to believe that anyone (pagan or Christian) with any sense of realities at all, however strongly impressed with the duty of civic obedience in general, in that mad *crescendo* of futility, debauchery, and crime with which the reign of Nero ended—while living in Rome itself in the very midst of it all—could write of such a government, without any hint of reserve or qualification, that it was sent by God

for vengeance on evil doers and for praise to those that do well. . . . Fear God ; honour the Emperor.

For fifty years the ingenuity of scholars has been taxed by the attempt to envisage the actual historical situation presupposed by the epistle. So small a measure of agreement has been reached that to venture a new solution will hardly be deemed temerarious. But if I do this, it is with full consciousness of its precarious character. The hypothesis I am about to put forward is one which would explain the facts, and that in a way which is, to my mind, less unsatisfactory than any other I have come across ; but I should be the last to maintain that it is the only hypothesis which will explain them, or that it is one which admits of verification of a convincing character.

I will begin, then, by allowing myself to make the tentative assumption—which I owe to a suggestion put

out by Harnack many years ago—that the address and
salutations (which form the first two and last three
verses) are additions by a later editor, who hoped thereby
to turn a document already old and valued into an
'epistle'—which could then find a place in the public
estimation of the Church alongside the epistles of Paul.
Apart from these verses, the document falls into two
clearly marked portions, the longer of which (i. 3–iv. 11)
reads, not like a letter, but like a *sermon*. H. Gunkel
in his Introduction to the epistle [1] mentions a recent
conjecture of Perdelwitz (a writer to whose works I have
not direct access) that this section of the epistle was
originally an address given by the bishop to a group of
newly baptized persons—presumably at some great
festival.

In the days of Noah, while the ark was a-preparing, wherein
few, that is eight souls, were saved through water : which also
after a true likeness doth now save you, even baptism—not
the putting away of the filth of the flesh, but the interrogation
of a good conscience toward God, through the resurrection of
Jesus Christ (iii. 20 f.).

In the early Church, candidates for baptism were
normally adults converted from heathenism, and would
include persons of very different classes—slaves, married
women, fathers of families (ii. 18–iii. 7). Read as an
address given on such an occasion the exhortations are
extraordinarily appropriate—an inspiring description of
the new life into which they have been reborn, followed
by encouragement to face alike the responsibilities
involved and the hostility of the outside world.

On any view the doxology and ' Amen ' (iv. 11) is
a note of conclusion which detaches the latter part of

[1] *Die Schriften des Neuen Testaments*, iii. p. 250. I owe the reference to
Dr. A. E. J. Rawlinson.

the epistle from what goes before. A fresh start is then made. This might be explained by supposing that the preacher now turns from the group of the newly baptized to address the larger congregation present— including presbyters who have come in from the adjacent villages. But there is a change both in tone and in substance at this point, which makes it more probable that this latter section (iv. 12–v. 11) really is a pastoral *letter*, written perhaps two or three years later by the same author as the sermon—no doubt the bishop of some important city—to be circulated in the smaller towns of the district. The difference between i. 3–iv. 11 and iv. 12–v. 11 is comparable to that between the first epistle of John and the second. Instead of discourse on the general principles of the Christian life (eminently suitable in an address to those just entering upon it), we find advice directed to a definite historical situation. In the first part of the epistle Christians are warned in a general way that they may expect trials (i. 6-7); but only when the preacher is specifically addressing slaves—who in antiquity might at any moment be put to the torture by their masters—does he dwell on the right attitude towards suffering. In the second a ' fiery trial ' has to be faced—of an *unexpected* character (' think it not strange . . .'). Clearly there has just occurred an outbreak of persecution, which threatens to become worse. Christians need the warning to stand firm—but first let each make quite sure that his own life is such as never to give the magistrate just cause for penal action. There are, it is implied, some Christians who require to be so exhorted : ' The time is come for judgment to begin at the house of God '.

In this hour of crisis the persons on whom rests the gravest responsibility are the presbyters (v. 2-3). Here again we come across indications of venality and arrogance among the ministers. This we have seen, from the Acts (xx. 24 ff.) and from other evidence (p. 105 f.), had become an acute problem for the Church in Asia after A.D. 80. We should not have expected to see it already within the lifetime of Peter. Again, the Apocalypse affords evidence of an outbreak of persecution in Asia near the end of the reign of Domitian (A.D. 90–95), possibly due to his attempted enforcement of Emperor-worship, which seems to have been carried out with exceptional vigour in that province.

These facts lead us on to the reflection that, if once we decide that the balance of evidence is against Petrine authorship, the case for the document having any connection at all with Rome simply disappears. On the other hand, a number of considerations point to Asia as the place where it was originally written, and where subsequently the opening and concluding salutations were added.

(1) Babylon as a name for Rome occurs in the Apocalypse of John, undoubtedly an Asian document. We know, therefore, that in Asia Rome was spoken of under that figure ; that the figure would be used by anyone living in Rome itself, is less probable.

(2) The list of provinces to which the epistle is addressed has caused puzzlement to scholars. It is neither addressed to a single church, like most of the epistles of Paul ; nor to the Church at large, like James or the pseudonymous 2 Peter. It purports to be sent to Christians in five different provinces of Asia Minor. Various theories have been put forth to explain by what possible complication of routes a messenger coming either from Rome or Babylon would be able to deliver such a letter to the persons addressed on his way through the

provinces named. But a glance at the map reveals the perfectly simple fact that the epistle is addressed to all Asia Minor north of the natural boundary formed by the range of mountains of which Taurus is the core.[1] Cilicia (and the smaller provinces south of the mountains) fell within the sphere of influence of Antioch (cf. Gal. i. 21 ; Acts xv. 23, 41).[2]

The curious order in which the various provinces are named is explained by Hort on the theory that the bearer of the letter would land at Sinope, or some other port in Pontus, and, traversing a circular route, would return to the same place—thus reaching Bithynia, which adjoins Pontus, last. I would offer the alternative explanation that the opening verses were first prefixed to the document in Sinope, at the time when Pliny (A.D. 112), then Governor of Pontus and Bithynia, had begun to persecute Christians, and when it was doubtless anticipated that his alacrity would be imitated by governors of neighbouring provinces. In such a crisis the message of the latter part of 1 Peter would be one to which church leaders might well desire to give fresh currency.

(3) The epistle is first quoted in Asia. Polycarp's frequent quotation of it implies that it was highly valued in Smyrna—although, as Harnack pointed out, we are not entitled to assume that, when Polycarp read it, the opening and closing paragraphs, which assert Petrine authorship, were as yet appended. It is noticeable, too, that whereas Polycarp names Paul twice, he never mentions Peter. Nor, I may add, does Polycarp's use of it imply that he regarded it as Apostolic ; for he

---

[1] I assume the correctness of Prof. Ramsay's view as to the borders of the Roman province of Galatia at this period.

[2] Cf. F. J. A. Hort, *The First Epistle of St. Peter*, p. 175 ff. (Macmillan, 1898.)

treats Clement in the same way ; while Clement makes
a similar use of Hebrews.

(4) Apart from the affinities which 1 Peter has with
Romans and Ephesians—which were circulated all over
Christendom—its literary contacts are with literature
definitely connected with Asia :

(a) The usage which speaks of a church as ' she that
is elect ' is paralleled in 2 John 13.

(b) ' Whom not having seen ye love ' recalls the words
of the Fourth Gospel, ' Blessed are those who
have not seen, and yet have believed '.

(c) The exhortation (1 Pet. v. 2), ' Tend the flock of
Christ ', echoes the tradition which lies behind
the ' Feed my lambs ' of John xxi. 16 ff. ; or
the farewell speech of Paul to the Ephesian
elders (Acts xx. 28).

(5) Prof. Goodspeed makes the interesting suggestion
that the emphasis on the Pauline principle that Christians were to honour the Emperor and his representatives
—as persons wielding, each in his own sphere, an authority Divine in origin—was directly called forth by the
necessity of doing something to counteract a dangerous
movement among Christians of Asia who had been too
powerfully affected by the identification of Rome with
the Power of Evil, preached by the author of the
Apocalypse.[1] This is an attractive suggestion ; but, if
it be accepted, surely an attempt to recall the churches
of Asia to the traditional attitude of their founder, Paul,
is more likely to have been made by one who lived on
the spot and knew the actual situation, rather than by
a writer in far-away Rome.

[1] *New Solutions of New Testament Problems*, E. J. Goodspeed, p. 32. (University of Chicago Press, 1927.)

(6) Some critics hold the epistle to have been written at Rome pseudonymously in the name of Peter, in order to be sent to Asia Minor to encourage Christians in face of some particular outbreak of persecution. I find such a conception difficult. In the time of Pipin the Frank it was possible for a Pope to write a letter in the name of Peter dealing with a present crisis ; it was not possible in the first century. A letter coming straight from Rome about A.D. 90 would not have been accepted in Asia Minor as the genuine work of Peter ; in order to be so accepted there, it must have been produced as a work of Peter which had reached the churches addressed in it long ago, and which had recently been rediscovered in Asia itself.

The epistle, then, I suggest, is made up of two writings by the same author, about the year A.D. 90—a sermon and a letter. These having been originally copied, one immediately after the other, on the same papyrus roll, were afterwards supposed to be a single piece. Twenty years or more later—the name of the author being lost, as so often happened in antiquity—its supreme religious quality led to the conjecture that it was the work of an Apostle. This conjecture proving to be generally accept- able, the existing address and salutation (i. 1-2 ; v. 12-14) were added—possibly in Sinope in Pliny's time— in order the better to secure for it the authority of an Apostolic name. It thus became possible to justify its inclusion alongside the epistles of Paul in the Canon of New Testament writings recognised by the churches of Asia—and on the guarantee of Asia it was rapidly accepted by the Church at large.

The battle with Gnosticism was largely fought on the appeal to Apostolic tradition ; hence Apostolic authorship became a *sine qua non* for the inclusion in the Canon of any document, save the Gospels of Mark and Luke—which were brought in under the wing, so to speak, of Peter and Paul.[1] The most notable instance is the epistle to the Hebrews. This was so highly valued at Rome A.D. 96 that it has largely determined the theology of the epistle of Clement. But at Rome it was evidently known not to be by Paul ; it was, therefore, not even considered for admission into the Canon in that church—in the *Muratorianum* it is not even mentioned. But at Alexandria a tradition had arisen, old enough for Pantaenus, the master of Clement of Alexandria, to take for granted, that it was the work of Paul. Thus the Alexandrians, though much troubled by the difference in style between this and the other Pauline letters, were able to accept it as Apostolic. Ultimately Rome, probably urged by Athanasius, re-accepted it on the authentication of the East as a genuine epistle of Paul.

The name of Paul was never inserted into the actual text of Hebrews. But in Asia there was less diffidence in re-editing ancient texts. The phenomenon of the Pastoral Epistles proves this. But there is no need to suggest a consciously fraudulent intention. It was becoming an axiom that an early document of high religious merit *must* be Apostolic ; for only to Apostles was supreme inspiration given. Since, then, the style of 1 Peter would not allow it to be ascribed to Paul, it was natural to conjecture that it was the work of Peter, the only other Apostle who had anything to do with the Gentiles. Peter was already connected in Asian tradition with the Gospel of Mark ; and in that tradition, as

---

[1] Cf. Tertullian, *Adv. Marc.* iv. 5 : ' (The Gospel) which was published by Mark may also be maintained to be Peter's, whose interpreter Mark was ; for the narrative of Luke also is generally ascribed to Paul ; since it is allowable that that which pupils publish should be regarded as their master's work '.

K

expressed by the Elder John, Mark had been Peter's
' interpreter ' ; but this epistle not being in the style of
Mark, conjecture supplied another interpreter in Silvanus.
The transition from hypothesis to definite assertion is
not a difficult one—even to modern critics. But in those
days an assertion, if made often enough to become a
' tradition ', could be more readily transmuted by some
ingenious pen into an address and a closing salutation,
modelled on those of the epistles of Paul—thereby, perhaps, saving the epistle from oblivion. Copies without
the editorial additions would doubtless still be in circulation. But in another fifty years these would be regarded
as mutilated—and there would be then no textual critic
to defend their originality. Their owners would ' correct '
them by the fuller text ; and any clean copies made
from these would show no traces of the fact of such
correction.

ARISTION OF SMYRNA

But, granted the epistle be not by Peter, is it still
possible to make a reasonable guess at the name of the
actual author ?

I am bold to hazard such, offering it, I would emphasise, not as ' a result of criticism ', but frankly as a
guess—but, I hope, a ' scientific ' guess. Let us re-
examine a sentence already quoted :

> The elders, therefore, among you I exhort, who am a fellow-
> elder, and a witness of the sufferings of Christ (v. 1).

The phrase ' fellow-elder ' clearly belongs to the original
document. If it is not easy to envisage Peter speaking of himself thus, it is far more difficult to imagine a
pseudonymous writer making an Apostle so speak. Such
writers invariably over-emphasise the status of the great

men in whose name they write. We proceed to ask whether the words ' a witness of the sufferings of Christ ' also belong to the original document, or whether they are an interpolation by the editor.

Obviously, if the original document did contain these words, they would readily suggest, and then be used to justify, the conjecture that it was the work of an Apostle. Let us, then, assume for the moment that the words are original, and see what conclusions that assumption would entail. First, that the original document was written by a person who had been present at the Crucifixion, if only as a mere boy. Now the passage of Papias quoted above (p. 89) shows that there were two persons who were reckoned in Asia to rank next after the Apostles as authorities for the authentic teaching of Christ, and were styled ' Disciples of the Lord ', namely, the Elder John and Aristion. I have given reasons (p. 90 f.) for supposing that it was this John whom Polycarp of Smyrna meant when he spoke of his contact ' with John and others who had seen the Lord '.[1] Now, in the context in Papias, the mention of this John required the addition of the title ' Elder ' to distinguish him from the Apostle John, previously named in the same sentence; but doubtless Aristion also bore the title Elder.[2] Hence it would be perfectly natural for Aristion to say in a letter :

The elders among you I exhort, who am a fellow-elder, and a witness of the sufferings of Christ.

We next notice a special connection between the epistle, the name Aristion, and the city of Smyrna. In the *Apostolic Constitutions* the name of the first Bishop of

---

[1] Cf. Irenaeus' Letter to Florinus (*ap.* Eus. *H.E.* v. 20).
[2] He is styled ' Elder ' in the colophon in the Armenian MS., which attributes to him the longer ending of the Gospel of Mark (p. 93, *n.*).

Smyrna is given as Ariston. The reasons for ascribing considerable historical value to this notice I have already discussed ; and I have noted the fact that in pagan writers Ariston and Aristion are interchangeable forms of the same name (p. 93). Now Polycarp was Bishop of Smyrna ; Irenaeus could remember his speaking of his connection not only with John (I will assume the John he spoke of was really the Elder, not the Apostle) but with ' others who had seen the Lord '. The ancients habitually exaggerate ; but the existence of at least *one* such person besides John is required to justify the plural ' others '. Further, Polycarp is the earliest writer to use 1 Peter ; and he echoes it more often than he does any other book in the New Testament. In Smyrna, therefore, it was a religious classic—though probably not yet attributed to Peter. Much the simplest explanation of all these facts would be that the baptismal sermon (1 Pet. i. 3–iv. 11), and the letter concerning persecution (1 Pet. iv. 12–v. 11), which together make up the epistle, are by Aristion, Bishop of Smyrna.

Turn now to the letters to the Seven Churches of Asia in the Apocalypse. The Church of Smyrna is mentioned second—naturally, next to Ephesus, Smyrna was the most important city of the province. But the message of the Seer to this church is shorter than that delivered to any other of the Seven. The core of it is this :

Fear not the things which thou art about to suffer ; behold the devil is about to cast some of you into prison, that ye may be tried ; and ye shall have tribulation ten days. Be thou faithful unto death, and I will give thee the crown of life (Rev. ii. 10).

This surely is the very same situation as that which has called forth the latter part of 1 Peter. The ' fiery trial ' ; ' suffering for the name ' at the hand of the magistrate ; and the devil—conceived not in his more usual rôle of tempter, but as the agent in persecution—

whom withstand, knowing that the same sufferings are accomplished by your brethren who are in the world (v. 9).

The writer of the Apocalypse views from outside an impending persecution by the civil power centring in Smyrna ; and to him that civil power is on the side of Satan. In 1 Peter iv. 12–v. 11 we have the reaction from within of the man responsible for the church, both in Smyrna and in the country towns dependent on it. He knows that it is dangerous to teach that kind of thing in a Levantine slum. Like Paul, he recognises in the Roman Empire, with all its faults, a power that upholds law, order, and civil justice. He had himself, perhaps only a year or two earlier, urged his people to look on rulers as sent by God ' for vengeance on evil-doers and for praise to them that do well '. It is no longer possible for him to speak so. But he will still urge the Christians not to lose their heads (iv. 12 f.) ; and, above all, not to come into conflict with the authorities in so far as they do function legitimately as the upholders of law and order.

He writes like a man entitled by his position, not merely to indite letters of exhortation in the face of an emergency, but to speak to the presbyters of the district in a tone of paternal admonition bordering on rebuke. Few men would be so entitled. But Aristion having the prestige, not only of Bishop of Smyrna, but still more of one who had ' seen the Lord ', would have title enough and to spare. He could afford to say, ' I, who am a fellow-elder '. And such writings by such a personage *would* be cherished at Smyrna as a religious classic.

The Church Order Implied

So far this discussion of the authorship of 1 Peter may have seemed pure digression, having little or no bearing on the question of the evolution of Church Order. That is not so; for supposing the identification of the author of 1 Peter with Aristion of Smyrna—the evidence for which I am quite aware falls a long way short of demonstration —to be provisionally accepted, we have a document which *we can date*. It is contemporary with the Apocalypse, *i.e.* A.D. 90–95. But, whoever was its author or whatever be its date, we have in 1 Peter evidence of a stage in the evolution of the importance of the regular ministry, considerably in advance of anything in the epistles of Paul.

The elders, therefore, among you I exhort. . . . Tend the flock of God which is among you [exercising the oversight], not of constraint, but willingly, according unto God; nor yet for filthy lucre, but of a ready mind; neither as lording it over the charge allotted to you, but making yourselves ensamples to the flock. And when the Chief Shepherd shall be manifested, ye shall receive the crown of glory that fadeth not away (1 Peter v. 1-4).

It is here taken for granted—as in Acts xx. 28 and Ephesians iv. 11—that Presbyters stand to the people in a relation comparable to that of a shepherd to his flock, and even, in a sense, to that of Christ Himself to the believers. More than that, it is implied that some Presbyters need to be exhorted not to ' lord it over ' the flock. But this would be a real temptation only to men whose status or office was one that made ' lording it ' a practical procedure.

It follows that we must read a passage in the first part of the epistle in the light of that discussed above.

For ye were going astray like sheep ; but are now returned to the Shepherd and Bishop of your souls (ii. 25).

This application to Christ Himself of the titles Pastor and Bishop, which *used thus in collocation with one another* are clearly meant to recall their use of the Christian ministry, is rather startling. It would have been impossible except it were addressed to a church where the powers, prestige, and responsibility of the regular ministry had for years been a matter of general accept- ance. If I am right in regarding the first part of the epistle as a sermon, this is primarily evidence for Smyrna itself. The warnings against venality and overbearing conduct occur in the latter part of the epistle, which is addressed to other churches—perhaps less fortunate in their rulers.

The identification of the writer with Aristion would also ease the solution of one of the most difficult problems of early Church history. How can we bridge the gulf between the original, more or less ' presbyterian ', organisation of the Pauline churches in Asia, and the monarchical episcopate which we find established there by the time of Ignatius and Polycarp (*c*. A.D. 115) ? So far as the Church of Ephesus is concerned, I have called in the personality of John the Elder to explain the development. Obviously a similar explanation holds good of Smyrna, *if* that was the church of Aristion. Like John the Elder, he could speak with authority as one who had seen the Lord ; if he was also a man of the character and religious insight shown by 1 Peter, it would not have been long before in his own church he attained a position of unique leadership. In periods of transition, names of offices matter little ; personalities count for much. Whether he enjoyed the title ' Bishop ' in any exclusive sense would matter little. In actual fact he would occupy the position of a bishop. Now if, round about A.D. 96, both in Ephesus and in Smyrna (the two largest cities of Asia, and intellectually the most alive) the church had, possibly for fifteen or twenty years, been directed by two outstanding individuals, who to all intents and purposes were bishops in the later sense, and if the system (as doubtless was the case under men of this calibre) had proved a great success, the experiment would inevitably be imitated in neighbouring churches. The personality of John the Elder, operating from his strategic position in Ephesus, the chief city of the province, might alone suffice to explain the rapid transition from the older system to the new. But how much easier to explain it if, besides a John in Ephesus, capable of the Fourth Gospel, there was an Aristion in Smyrna, equal to the writing of the Petrine epistle. Two men together can do more than twice as much as one.

V

THE CHURCH IN SYRIA

SYNOPSIS

The 'Didache' versus Ignatius

The difficult historical problem posed by the fact that documents implying the most opposite types of Church Order, viz. the *Didache* and the Letters of Ignatius, both seem to represent Syria. The *Didache* the document mainly relied on by champions of the view that 'Independency' was primitive, the Ignatian letters by the defenders of 'Episcopalianism'.

The *Didache*, 1 Clement, and the Pastorals should be regarded as three, more or less contemporary but independent, efforts to deal with the problem of Church Order in three different localities. If however, the *Didache* emanates from Syria, can the gulf between it and the Letters of Ignatius be bridged ?

Syria

The New Testament evidence (discussed in the last two Lectures) for an advanced development of Church Order along the lines originated by Paul is confined to Asia. But at Antioch there were at work in the first century anti-Pauline influences ; moreover, the Paul who had worked at Antioch as a young convert was not the developed personality known to us through the epistles written in later life.

Accordingly, to envisage the historical situation at Antioch we must ignore the developments attested by the epistles of Paul and John, and return to our original starting-point—the statement (Acts xiii. 1), ' There were in the Church of Antioch Prophets and Teachers '. Starting from this point, the *Didache* is clearly the next step forward.

Hypothesis propounded—the *Didache* was composed in Antioch c. A.D. 95 with the object of bringing the organisation of the smaller churches in Syria up to a standard already reached at Antioch, and of protecting them from exploitation by bogus ' prophets '.

Church Order in the 'Didache'

Presumption that the type of Church Order recommended in the *Didache* was that already established in the church where it was written.

Already, then, this church had Bishops and Deacons who were regarded as officials deserving high respect. The smaller churches are advised to follow this example.

The injunctions about wandering Apostles and Prophets—the mention of Apostles is possibly an archaism—deal with a problem which, towards the end of the first century, was becoming acute all over the Christian world. The words of a true prophet, admittedly, are the voice of God which it is blasphemy to disregard ; but how are the churches to know the difference between a true prophet and an impostor ? The same problem is felt in Rome by Hermas, in Asia by the author of 1 John, and in Syria as early as the Gospel of Matthew. The test proposed, an ethical one.

The *Didache* marks the stage when the system in which Prophets and Teachers were the natural leaders of the churches is breaking down, and gradually being replaced by a ' regular ' ministry of Bishops and Deacons.

The importance (hitherto overlooked) of the injunction that a prophet who settles in a church has a claim to ' first fruits ', if taken in connection with the rubric which implies that a prophet when present celebrates the Eucharist. A person who controls the offerings, and is the regular leader in the worship of a local church, has become *de facto* something very like a monarchical bishop.

Ignatius, monarchical bishop of Antioch, was a Prophet.

CLEMENT AND THE EAST

Evidence that the epistle of Clement to the Corinthians (A.D. 96)—doubtless because the claim it makes to inspiration was taken seriously—exercised enormous influence on the East, more especially in Syria. This the more explicable if we suppose that, owing to its insistence on discipline and its doctrine of apostolical succession, it became, from the time of Ignatius onward, the Magna Charta of the hierarchy in Syria.

To the eye of the modern critic the epistle of Clement implies that monepiscopacy was not yet established at Rome and Corinth. But it could easily be read as implying a threefold hierarchy—the writer Clement being the Bishop (=High Priest). The fact that such a letter emanated from the Roman Church explains Ignatius' salutation of the Roman Christians as ' the instructors of others '.

THE ACTS AND THE CORPUS PAULINUM

The publication of Acts brought the Church at large to a new recognition of the real greatness of Paul and of his life's work. Goodspeed's suggestion that this led to the completion of the collection of his letters. These were known *as a collection* to the authors of the Pastorals and (probably) of the Apocalypse. If the collection reached Antioch along with the Acts about A.D. 90, the Pauline theology would have begun to take root there before Ignatius—this fact bridges the gulf between the *theology* of the *Didache* and that of the Ignatian letters.

IGNATIUS

His letters, besides constituting a difficult historical problem, are fascinating as a vivid 'human document'. The historical difficulties disappear if two points are recognised. First, the hierarchical system championed was *at Antioch* of recent origin, and not yet securely established. Secondly, Ignatius is a man of genius who, psychologically regarded, is of ' the neurotic temper '; and he was writing under circumstances of great nervous strain. Inevitably his language, at a time when he felt that he was striking the last blow for the consolidation of his life's work, strikes a note of consistent exaggeration.

Two facts which support the view that the system defended by Ignatius was a recent development at Antioch. But the conflict envisaged is not for the supremacy of the Bishop as against the Presbyters, but of the clerical order as such as against the laity.

Five considerations indicating the bearing on the historical problem of the psychological idiosyncrasy of Ignatius himself.

Summary statement. The language of Ignatius about the position of the Bishop.

The question, whether the gulf between the *Didache* and the Ignatian letters can be bridged, is satisfactorily answered.

Additional Note

Possibility that the epistle of Jude emanates from Syria. A conjecture as to its authorship.

V

THE CHURCH IN SYRIA

THE 'DIDACHE' VERSUS IGNATIUS

TYPES of Church Order at the furthest possible remove from one another are represented respectively, on the one hand by the ancient Christian handbook known as the *Didache* or *Teaching of the Twelve Apostles*, on the other by the Epistles of Ignatius. The *Didache* is the stronghold of those who think that the Church Order of the Primitive Church closely resembled what we know now as Independency; the Letters of Ignatius have always been the embattled fortress of the defenders of Episcopalianism. And the curious thing is that on one point every one is agreed: both these writings emanate from Syria.

It is not surprising that the historical problem thus raised should have overtaxed the patience of many scholars. Many have been the attempts to cut the Gordian knot by assigning either to the one or to the other of these two authorities an origin or a date which would justify the historian in completely discounting its evidence. One set of scholars have, in this way or in that, tried to discredit the *Didache*; the other side in the controversy has impugned the genuineness of the Letters of Ignatius, or else the correctness of the date assigned to his martyrdom. But these attempts have succeeded only in raising commemorative monuments to the gift for special pleading possessed by their several authors. I propose, therefore, to relegate to Appendices the discussion of the genuineness and the dating of the documents ; and to ask whether it is not possible—accepting provisionally for the *Didache* the obvious date *c.* A.D. 90, and for Ignatius A.D. 115—to reconcile the apparently conflicting evidence by approaching the historical situation from a new angle.

Once among the most influential and popular of Christian writings, the *Didache* (cf. Appendix C) has left a mark upon the work of Eastern writers on Church Order as great as, if not greater than, that left by the New Testament itself. Yet after the fifth century it gradually went out of fashion, and at length completely disappeared. As lately as 1875 it was rediscovered, and is now known from a single MS.—a strange fate for a book of which the prestige was once so great that it was a candidate for inclusion in the New Testament.

If we allow ourselves provisionally to assume that the *Didache* was produced in Syria at a date not later than A.D. 100, we are led to an interesting reflection. Just about this time in the churches all round the Mediterranean there is an outcrop of literature arising from the need of strengthening the leadership, and consolidating the organisation, of the churches. In the West there is Clement's letter to the Corinthians, in Asia Minor there are the Pastoral Epistles, in the East we have the *Didache*. It would be highly illuminating if we could view these three documents as parallel expressions of a single tendency, and see the *Didache*, the Pastoral Epistles, and 1 Clement as three independent, but more or less contemporary, attempts—emanating from the three main foci of Christian activity in the first century—to achieve, in circumstances which varied very greatly in their respective localities, what is fundamentally the same end.

But can the view that the Church Order implied in the *Didache* is at all representative of Syria at this date, be maintained in face of the entirely different picture guaranteed by the Letters of Ignatius of Antioch. Can the gulf between these be bridged ? That is the main problem which this lecture will discuss.

SYRIA

If the conclusions of my last two lectures are sound, the evidence for the more advanced developments in Church Order discoverable in the New Testament is confined to the province of Asia. Indeed practically all the writings examined were either Epistles of Paul or, like the Pastorals and 3 John, stand still further on in a line of development originated by Paul. But Syrian Christianity came under influences antithetic to St. Paul. The fact that the *Clementine Homilies*, even if Elkesaite in origin, were circulated in the Church, shows that in Syria well on into the third century there were still those who would have liked to believe that Peter was a champion of legalism, and to set James above Peter himself. Emissaries from James had driven Peter to the act of backsliding, in the matter of eating and drinking with Gentiles, for which Paul denounced him (Gal. ii. 11 ff.). Even if, from the way Paul speaks of Peter in 1 Corinthians, we think the inference legitimate that Peter subsequently came round to Paul's view, it is clear that, in that case, a vigorous section of the Judaising party refused to follow him. The population of Antioch was so largely Jewish that it is probable that

the Judaistic view of Christianity would long continue
to have there many adherents. And since Jewish Christians fled to Antioch in the persecution in which Stephen
died (Acts xi. 19), much more would they do so in the
far severer persecution, in which James was martyred
A.D. 62, and which went on all through the Jewish war.
But these refugees, unlike the former, would be a re-
inforcement of the Judaistic strain at Antioch. Doubtless, especially among Gentile converts, there were some
to whom the name of Paul was a venerated memory.
On the whole the Syrian Church seems to have followed
the *via media* of Peter, and did not absolutely reject
Paul. It is the probably Syrian Gospel of Matthew, not
the Roman Gospel of Mark, that quotes the word of
Christ conferring on Peter ' the Keys ', and whatever
Jesus Himself actually said, and meant, we may surmise
that the author of the gospel quotes them quite as much
against the extreme followers of James as against those
of Paul.

To suppose, therefore, that, so far as the first century
A.D. is concerned, any large section of the Church of
Syria looked up to Paul as the great leader is probably
the reverse of the truth. We must remember that,
though Paul had worked in Antioch, it was *before* he
began his missionary journeys ; and this was not the
Paul of the great epistles. Capacity to profit by experience is one of the hall-marks of genius. Before the age
of fifty the minds of most men become fixed ; they may
go on doing good, and even creative, work, but they no
longer strike out new lines. But Paul was one of those
exceptional men who remain capable of continuous
mental growth. Between the epistles to the Thessalonians
and the epistle to the Romans, though they are only
separated in time by about five years, there is an ex-

pansion of mental stature which cannot be accounted for merely by differences in the theme treated or in the audience addressed. The epistle to the Colossians (Ephesians, too, if that be genuine) exhibits a still further growth. The question is forced upon us, If we possessed a letter by Paul prior to the great experience of the first missionary journey, should we not find a similar gulf between this and the Thessalonian letters, the earliest that survive ? The Paul who had lived and worked in Antioch was not yet the Paul we know. The Church of Antioch was not his foundation ; and it never felt the impact of his developed personality or the benefit of his later experience.

If, then, we would study the development of Church Order in Syria we must return to our original starting point—the statement in Acts (xiii. 1), ' There were in the Church of Antioch *prophets and teachers* '. Begin again at this point, and it is pellucidly clear that the state of things implied in the *Didache* marks *the next step forward*.

I propose, then, to test the hypothesis that the *Didache* is a manual drawn up at Antioch, approximately A.D. 90, and circulated by the mother-church of Syria, with the object of standardising the organisation of the churches in the smaller towns and villages of Syria, and of encouraging them to establish a permanent ministry— largely with a view to saving them from exploitation by wandering impostors professing to be prophets or ' apostles '.

Church Order in the *Didache*

In whatever church the *Didache* was produced, it was not intended merely or mainly for home consumption.

On the contrary, it reads like ' advices ' sent out from a larger and more settled church to assist the less developed congregations within its ' sphere of influence '. This is a consideration of great importance ; and failure to give due weight to it has unnecessarily complicated the historical problem presented by the contrast between the Church Order implied in the *Didache* and that known to exist elsewhere at the end of the first century. There occurs, for example, in the *Didache* the injunction :

> Appoint for yourselves, therefore, bishops and deacons . . . despise them not, for they are your honourable men along with the prophets and teachers (xv. 1).

From this we must infer that in the church from which the *Didache* emanated, bishops and deacons were *already* an established institution ; and the holders of these offices were in that church *already* regarded as persons of an importance comparable with that assigned at an earlier period only to prophets and teachers. The argument of those who maintain that the *Didache* must have been produced in an out-of-the-way and backward church has this amount of truth in it. It was *addressed* to backward and out-of-the-way churches ; but the church from which it came must have already, perhaps for some years, adopted the advice which it gives to others. If the *Didache* is to be treated as evidence for Antioch this point is obviously vital.

The opening words of the *Didache* are striking :

> There are two ways, one of life and one of death, and there is a great difference between the two ways. The way of life is this. First of all, thou shalt love the God that made thee ; secondly, thy neighbour as thyself. And all things whatsoever thou wouldest not have befall thyself, neither do thou unto another.

The first half of the work consists of impressive moral

L

exhortation, working out the teaching of these *Two Ways* in its detailed application—ending :

But concerning eating, bear that which thou art able ; yet abstain by all means from meat sacrificed to idols ; for it is the worship of dead gods (vi. 3).[1]

The *Two Ways* are followed by instructions as to Baptism, Fasting, and Prayers to be used at the Eucharistic thanksgiving. Then come the sections which make the *Didache* a primary document for the historian of Church Order.

But concerning the apostles and prophets, so do ye according to the ordinance of the Gospel. Let every apostle, when he cometh to you, be received as the Lord ; but he shall not abide more than a single day, or if there be need, a second ; but if he abide three days, he is a false prophet (xi. 3 ff.).

The title ' apostle ' in the first generation was given to many besides the Twelve. Thus Paul salutes two persons, Andronicus and Junias, whose names are never mentioned elsewhere, as being actually ' *of note* among the apostles ', ἐπίσημοι ἐν τοῖς ἀποστόλοις (Rom. xvi. 7). Nevertheless, it is a little surprising, as late as A.D. 90, to find ' apostles ' alluded to as if they were a class sufficiently numerous to make the problem, whether they be true or false, one of practical import. The

---

[1] There must be some connection between the *Didache* and the form in which the Apostolic Decree (Acts xv. 28-29) appeared in the Western text as it was read by Irenaeus in Gaul, Cyprian in Africa, and Eusebius in Caesarea. ' For it seemed good to the Holy Ghost, and to us, to lay upon you no greater burden than these necessary things ; that ye abstain from things sacrificed to idols and from blood and from fornication. And whatsoever ye would not have befall yourselves, do not unto another.' The title of the *Didache*, ' The teaching of the Lord to the Gentiles by the twelve Apostles ', seems also to reflect the Apostolic Decree, ' It seemed good unto the Holy Ghost and to us '; for, where prophecy was in question, the distinction between the Spirit and the Lord did not exist in the first century. In the *Didascalia*, a third-century amplification of the *Didache*, the connection with Acts xv. is made quite clear ; Prof. Turner reminds me that this document explicitly claims to represent the Acts of the Council of Jerusalem.

Hebrew equivalent of the name 'apostle'—perhaps best translated 'commissioner'—was a title of persons sent out officially from Jerusalem, often, though not always, with a commission to collect money. The Church of Jerusalem may have imitated this practice; and it is not unlikely that some of the Judaistic emissaries who caused such trouble in the churches founded by St. Paul bore the title 'apostle' in this sense. It is possible that after A.D. 70 the restored Church in Jerusalem tried for a while to revive this practice.

It is, however, in my opinion more likely that the only contemporaries whom the author of the *Didache* has in mind are wandering prophets; but that their manner of life, and therefore their right to entertainment by a local church, was regarded as governed by the 'ordinance of the Gospel'—that is, the injunctions of Christ concerning 'apostles' on a preaching tour recorded 'in the Gospel' (Matt. x. 9-16), to which he expressly refers (xi. 3). The use of the word 'apostle' may also be in part an intentional archaism. The *Didache* claims to be a message to the Gentiles from the Twelve; but in a document purporting to emanate from the Twelve it would be appropriate so to phrase their injunctions as to make them seem to cover the circumstances of the Apostolic Age, as well as those of the latter part of the century. At any rate the equation, apostle = prophet, is twice repeated where the case is that of a false prophet; no difference between their respective functions can be discerned; and in the greater part of these advices prophets only are named.

All over the Christian world at this time the gift of prophecy was a cause of acute difficulty. On the one hand, if a person was a true prophet, to reject him involved the gravest peril.

Any prophet speaking in the Spirit, ye shall not test, neither pass judgment on ; for every sin shall be forgiven, but this sin shall not be forgiven (*Did.* xi. 7).[1]

On the other hand, experience had shown that both impostors and self-deluded egotists frequently claimed to be prophets. Everywhere there was urgent need of some means of 'testing the spirits'. We find John in Asia (1 John iv. 1-2), and Hermas in Rome (*Mand.* xi.), giving advice about this same difficulty. And in the Gospel of Matthew there are two passages which suggest that the problem had arisen in Syria at an even earlier date. Matthew inserts, into a context otherwise all but verbally identical with Mark xiii., the warning :

Many false prophets shall arise, and lead many astray. And because ἀνομία (*i.e.* moral antinomianism) shall be multiplied, the love of the many shall wax cold (Matt. xxiv. 11 f.).

Again, in the version of the Great Sermon in that gospel, a whole section (Matt. vii. 15-23) is devoted to this question of the false prophet.

Beware of false prophets, which come to you in sheep's clothing, but inwardly are ravening wolves.

And the test of such, ' By their fruits ye shall know them ', is twice repeated. If, however, we compare the parallel passage in Luke's Sermon on the Plain (Luke vi. 43-45), or again the doublet in Matthew (xii. 33-35), there is no mention of false prophets, and the moral, ' by their fruits ye shall know them ', though perhaps intended, is not explicitly drawn. It would look as if Matthew has taken the words of his source (Q, or perhaps

---

[1] This interpretation of the sin of ' blasphemy against the Holy Ghost ' shows that the author of the *Didache* knew our Gospel of Matthew. For there only is such blasphemy connected with the saying about judging a tree by its fruits (Matt. xii. 31-35)—a saying which in turn is interpreted of false prophets in Matt. vii. 15-20, but is *not* so interpreted in the parallel in Luke (vi. 43 ff.).

it stood both in Q and M) and amplified them slightly in order to bring out their application to what was becoming a practical difficulty acutely felt as such by the church for which he wrote.

The tests which the *Didache* puts forward, like those laid down by Matthew, John, and Hermas, are primarily ethical; both the moral teaching and the personal conduct of the prophet must be in accordance with righteousness.

Whosoever therefore shall come and teach you all these things that have been said before [*i.e.* in the *Two Ways*], receive him; but if the teacher himself be perverted, and teach a different doctrine to the destruction thereof, hear him not; but if to the increase of righteousness and the knowledge of the Lord, receive him as the Lord (xi. 1).

The Church Order implied in the *Didache* is that of an era of transition. The older system of dependence on Prophets and Teachers is breaking down; but the Bishops and Deacons have not yet quite taken their place. As at Antioch in the Apostolic Age (Acts xiii. 1), the Prophets and the Teachers are the officers in highest repute; but the Bishops and Deacons are recognised as also 'performing the service of the Prophets and Teachers', and they are to be held in similar esteem (*Did.* xiii. 1; xv. 2). A prophet who settles permanently in a community is accorded the highest measure of respect; but the institution of the wandering prophet, though still existing, is obsolescent. In fact, the attitude of the *Didache* towards prophecy is comparable to that of Paul towards speaking with tongues. Paul entirely allows that speaking with tongues is a gift of the Spirit; but for the sake of edification and good order in the church he prefers coherent prophecy. Just so the author of the *Didache* allows the supreme

value and unique prestige of a true prophet; but
experience has by this time proved that self-authenticated
wandering prophets are a doubtful blessing.

> Not every one that speaketh in the Spirit is a prophet, but
> only if he have the ways of the Lord. . . . No prophet when
> he ordereth a table in the Spirit shall eat of it; otherwise he is
> a false prophet. . . . Whosoever shall say in the Spirit, ' Give
> me silver ' or anything else, ye shall not listen to him; but if he
> tell you to give on behalf of others that are in want, let no man
> judge him (xi. 8).

The aim, therefore, of the author of the *Didache* is
to create, wherever it did not yet exist, a *resident
ministry of episcopoi and deacons*. Where this already
exists, he tries to raise its status; congregations are
bidden to regard these as their ' honourable men along
with the prophets and teachers '. Evidently one main
object of the *Didache* is to secure that the resident
ministers shall *no longer be treated as of subordinate
importance*. That is to say, the *Didache* attempts to do
in Syria what Paul a whole generation earlier had seen
to be necessary in the churches which he controlled.

There is one injunction in the *Didache* of which the
full historical significance has (so far as I am aware)
escaped the notice of scholars—that which encourages a
prophet to settle permanently in a local church. It is clear
that whenever a person recognised as a true prophet
accepted an invitation so to settle, his position would
at once become one of outstanding influence—quite
apart from the fact that, when actually ' in the spirit ',
he necessarily spoke with divine authority. First, the
liturgical prayer prescribed as the eucharistic thanksgiving is followed by a rubric, ' But permit the prophets
to offer thanksgiving as much as they desire '. This
implies that a prophet, as such, has a special claim to

celebrate the Eucharist. Secondly, the faithful are exhorted to give first-fruits of wine, corn, and cattle to the prophets, ' For these are your chief priests '. There follows, quite inevitably, this conclusion : in any church where one, and only one, prophet had permanently settled on these terms, that prophet would have become, to all intents and purposes, a monarchical bishop.[1] He would be the regular celebrant of the Eucharist ; he would have control of the offerings from which clergy would be supported and the poor relieved ; while in addition he would, on occasion, be able to speak as the mouthpiece of the Holy Ghost. It has been suggested that the injunction (Is it the origin of church tithe ?), that the prophets receive the first-fruits due to the chief priests, was prompted by the desire to prescribe, in the case of Christians, a use and destination for religious offerings of a kind which had become customary, analogous to, but different from, the Jewish use. However this may be, it is certain that, as soon as a prophet settled down in any important city and became practically a monarchical bishop, this analogy between him and the Jewish chief priest was one which had in it the seed of great future developments.

I have already pointed out that the instructions given in the *Didache* to congregations in general imply that somewhere a standard existed towards which they ought to aspire. We infer, then, that the *Didache* emanated

---

[1] Outside Syria also there seems to have been at first a tendency to prefer as bishop a person having the prophetic gift. Polycarp is described as ' an apostolic and prophetic teacher in our own time, a bishop of the holy church which is in Smyrna ' (*Martyrdom of Polycarp*, xvi. 2) ; and there is reason to believe that the author of the Fourth Gospel (cf. my *The Four Gospels*, p. 367 f.) was a prophet, and is to be identified with the Elder John whom I have argued above was Bishop of Ephesus. Possibly the claim to inspiration made in 1 Clement (lix. 1 ; lxiii. 2) implies that the writer of that letter was a prophet ; or it may be that the letter is regarded as the corporate voice of the spirit-indwelt community.

from some important church where Episcopoi and Deacons *already* enjoyed the status and high degree of respect which it enjoins. And what, we must ask, happened to an ' approved ' prophet, if one permanently settled in that church ? He surely in that provincial capital (whether Antioch or elsewhere) would not enjoy less powers and privileges than those which the *Didache* demands for prophets when settled in a smaller church. There, too, he would become *de facto* Bishop.

Suppose, then, that in the Church of Antioch a time came when there was only one such resident prophet, and he a man of ambition and possessed of administrative ability—in a single generation the Church Order which the *Didache* implies would, *ipso facto*, and as it were automatically, harden into a threefold ministry of Bishop, Presbyters, and Deacons.[1]

Tradition names one Bishop of Antioch before Ignatius—Euodius. Whether he was a prophet or not is not recorded ; but of Ignatius we know for certain that he *was* regarded as a prophet.

Clement and the East

There are writings which have made history. These should be studied, not merely nor mainly as evidence for the historical situation at the time of writing, but also and more especially as efficient causes of the situation which followed next. The document commonly cited as the first epistle of Clement is, I suggest, one of these. Considered as evidence for an actual situation, the epistle relates to the Church of Rome from which it emanated in

---

[1] It is not impossible that in some churches the President was called *the* Episcopos; in others, *the* Elder. If in a particular case one of the Episcopoi developed the gift of prophecy, that might easily determine a local usage.

A.D. 96, and that of Corinth, to which it was addressed. A discussion of its importance in that regard will be more appropriate in the next lecture, which will deal with the Church of Rome. What I propose here to examine is the influence exercised by this epistle on the future development of the Church in Syria.

The epistle is written, not in the name of Clement, but of the Roman Church ; it therefore came to the East backed by the prestige of that church. More than that, it makes a definite claim to be directly inspired :

If certain persons should be disobedient unto the words spoken by Him [the Holy Spirit] through us . . . (lix. 1).

And again :

If ye render obedience unto the things written by us through the Holy Spirit (lxiii. 2).

In an age which took inspiration seriously, as a contemporary phenomenon, we should expect a document thus guaranteed by the testimony of a great Church to have world-wide acceptance as the voice of God. And that in point of fact it was so received, we have abundant evidence. Clement's letter was circulated, almost at once, throughout the East. The verbal parallelisms between 1 Clement and the Pastoral Epistles are just not striking enough to *prove* a literary connection ; but they are enough to make it probable. Since, then, 1 Clement is the earlier document, it will be the editor of the Pastorals who is the borrower, of ideas as well as words.[1] In Smyrna, by A.D. 115, Polycarp is more influenced by the language of Clement than by any book of the New Testament, except perhaps 1 Peter.[2] Fifty years later

[1] Cf. the table of parallel passages in Harrison, *The Problem of the Pastoral Epistles*, p. 176.

[2] The parallels are set out in Gebhardt and Harnack, *Patres Apostolici*, i. p. xxiv ff.

the Church of Smyrna, having occasion to write to the Church of Philomelium the letter which we style the *Martyrdom of Polycarp*, turns to 1 Clement as the model of the way in which one church addressing another should open and conclude a letter.[1] Dionysius of Corinth, A.D. 170, tells us it was read there at the Sunday services (Eus. *H.E.* iv. 23). Clement of Alexandria calls him 'the Apostle Clement' (*Strom.* iv. 17). But it was in Syria, to judge from subsequent literature, that the epistle made most impression. Here Clement came to be regarded as the mouthpiece and successor of Peter; and he became either the hero, or the pseudonymous author, of an immense amount of literature, beginning in the second century with an early recension of the story in the *Clementine Recognitions*. The epistles of Clement are frankly and unreservedly included in the Canon of the New Testament in the undoubtedly Syrian *Apostolic Constitutions*—which itself purports to be a work of Clement. And these epistles appear as an appendix to the New Testament in the early fifth-century Codex A, which probably represents not an Alexandrian, but a Syrian, textual tradition.[2]

But for our immediate purpose the thing to note is the association of the name of Clement with the idea of sound Church Order. The pseudonymous letter of Clement to James the Lord's brother, which formerly stood as a preface to the *Clementine Recognitions*, was one (says Rufinus) 'in which the whole subject of Church Order is treated'; and Church Order is the main theme of the (clearly identical) letter of Clement to James still extant in the *Clementine Homilies*. The *Didascalia*, a book of Church Order of the third century, is in the Syriac version entitled *The Third Book of Clement*, while the *Apostolic*

---

[1] Cf. Lightfoot, *Ignatius*, i. p. 626 f.   [2] Cf. *The Four Gospels*, p. 119 ff.

Constitutions, the most elaborate work on that subject in the first six centuries, is directly ascribed to him. In Rome there originated a book of Church Order ; but this is ascribed to the actual author Hippolytus. But in Syria regulations on this subject are uniformly ascribed to Clement, or to apostles using him as their mouthpiece.[1]

What, we ask, is the reason of this special association in Syrian tradition of the name of Clement with the idea of sound Church Order ? Lightfoot called attention to the striking contrast between the reputation of Clement and wide circulation of his writings, genuine or otherwise, in the East, and the exiguous mention of him in the West,[2] but he offered no explanation. The hypothesis I advance is that Clement's genuine epistle was one of the chief weapons wielded by the dominating personality of Ignatius in a lifelong battle for ecclesiastical discipline ; and that it thus exercised a creative influence in the development of the powers of the hierarchy in Syria. In that case it would have remained the *magna charta* of episcopal authority in Syria for the next two generations —indeed until that authority had been consolidated to the point of being no longer open to challenge. We have seen reason to believe that, before the time of Ignatius, the Church in Syria in this respect was less advanced than in other provinces. But if so, the dominant position of the episcopate implied in the letters of Ignatius can only have come into existence after a period of acute struggle.

[1] The name of Clement occurs also in the MS. title of *The Apostolic Church Ordinances*. But as it does not occur in the actual text it probably derives from some scribe who knew Clement as the reputed author of most other works on Church Order. Another work ascribed to Clement is the *Testamentum Domini*.

[2] When Lightfoot wrote, no Latin translation of his letter existed, and none is referred to by any Latin Father. But a single copy of a Latin translation of the two Letters attributed to Clement has since turned up. Since the translator found the second epistle already ascribed to Clement, I should suppose his date to be of the fourth or fifth century, when the translation of Greek theological classics into Latin was the vogue. Published 1894; G. Morin, *Anecdota Maredsolana*, ii.

Once that is granted, it is obvious how valuable to the
' High Church ' party of that day Clement's letter would
have been—with its exhortation to Christians to imitate
the notable discipline of the Roman army, and its
derivation of the authority of the regular ministry from
' Apostolical Succession '.

Higher critics sometimes miss the mark through for-
getting that the ancients did not share their art.   To
ascertain, for instance, the influence of any book of the
Old Testament upon the New, we must ask, not the real
meaning of the Hebrew writer, but what the Christian
thought he meant.   The same holds good in the present
case.   To the sharp eye of the modern critic, as we shall
see in the next lecture, Clement seems to imply that at
Corinth (and presumably at Rome) church government
was nearer to the Presbyterian type than to the Episcopalian.   So far as I am aware, no scholar hitherto has
pointed out how easy it would be for Ignatius to read
into Clement's language a totally different meaning.   In
the course of working out an analogy between the officers
of the Christian and the Jewish Church, Clement writes :

For unto the High Priest his proper services have been
assigned, and to the Priests their proper office is appointed, and
upon the Levites their proper ministrations are laid.   The layman is bound by the layman's ordinances (1 Clem. xl. 5).

What Clement had in mind when writing thus, was the
analogy between the function of Christ and that of the
High Priest worked out in the epistle to the Hebrews—
a writing by which Clement has been profoundly influenced.   This analogy he had already drawn in the
near context (xxxvi.) in language suggested by Hebrews,
and doubtless intended to recall his readers to the argument elaborated in that epistle.   But Hebrews was probably unknown at Antioch at this date ;   and, without

the key to Clement's meaning which that document
affords, the passage quoted above positively invites misinterpretation. Nor does it follow, even if Hebrews were
known at Antioch, that anyone would turn to it for light
on the exegesis of Clement in a passage which, on the
surface, presents no obscurity. Ignatius is familiar with
the idea of Christ as High Priest (Philad. ix. 1). But in
Syria, Clement would be read by men brought up on the
Didache, whose minds, therefore, would be preoccupied
with the injunction (*Did.* xii.) concerning prophets who
had settled permanently in a church : ' They are your
chief-priests '. In a church where the *Didache* was a
religious classic, and where already a single resident
prophet was established as the most important person
in the community, the natural and obvious reading of
Clement's words would make the point of his remark to
be the correspondence between the three Old Testament
orders of High Priest, Priest, and Levite, and the
Christian offices of Bishop, Presbyter, and Deacon ;
more especially as the orders of Bishops and Presbyters
were clearly distinguished both in Asia and in Jerusalem,
that is, in the churches of the provinces which marched
with Syria on either side.

The writer of the letter—there is no reason to doubt
that his name was Clement—would at least be the presbyter normally chosen to represent the Roman Church
in its dealings with other churches, and was very likely
in other respects the leading personage in the church.
What would be more natural for a Syrian Christian than
to assume that Clement held at Rome a position of
formally recognised supremacy, similar to that which in
the Church of Jerusalem had descended in the family of
James, and which John the Elder had occupied in Asia ?
In the light of the practice of these churches, the passage

of Clement I have quoted would naturally be read as implying that he, Clement, occupied at Rome a position analogous to that of the Jewish High Priest—that is, belonged to an order hierarchically distinct from the other presbyters. So interpreted, the moral of his letter would appear to be that the monarchical episcopate was the one right and apostolic system.

This view at once explains an otherwise very difficult passage in Ignatius : ' Ye were the instructors of others ' (Rom. iii. 1). When and how, we ask, had the Roman Church instructed other churches ? The answer of this question will appear, if we ask another. What was the kind of instruction Ignatius thought the church of his time most needed ? Submission to the Bishop and Presbyters, as representing Christ (or God), and His Apostles, is the main theme of *all* his letters—*except that addressed to Rome.* Why the exception? Obviously, when Ignatius speaks of the instruction which Rome had given other churches, he is thinking primarily of that letter of Clement which he found so valuable in consolidating his own position at Antioch, for its inculcation of obedience to the local hierarchy.[1] That was the kind of instruction which, in view of the exigencies of the times, Ignatius deemed of all things the most necessary ; and it was a kind which his own temperament, instinct with ' the will to power ', disposed him enthusiastically to accept.

I shall argue later that the high satisfaction expressed by Ignatius at the election of his successor shows that the hierarchical party had definitely triumphed at Antioch (p. 175 f.). That being so, Clement, as the author of the epistle which was their charter, would inevitably become, after the Apostles, their greatest saint. Soon

---

[1] Lightfoot in his note *ad loc.* thinks Ignatius *may* be referring here to 1 Clement, but prefers another (I think inferior) interpretation.

legend makes him the chosen companion of Peter—the
special Apostle of Antioch.   And while Roman tradition
put Linus and Cletus between Clement and the Apostles,
Syrian romance makes Peter consecrate Clement as the
first Bishop of Rome.   Henceforth Clement of Rome
becomes—not, be it observed, in Rome itself, but in
Syria—the mouthpiece of Peter, and thus the pseudonymous guarantor of any views for which Apostolic
sanction was desired.

THE ACTS AND THE CORPUS PAULINUM

Another document which, as Prof. Goodspeed has
recently pointed out,[1] undoubtedly ' made history ' is
the Acts of the Apostles.   It made history by compelling
churches in which he had not himself worked to recognise
the real greatness of Paul ; and by providing his epistles
with a background in biography, which made them the
living message of a vividly conceived personality, rather
than a number of disconnected memoranda in which
inspiring exhortation and ' things hard to be understood '
alternate in almost equal proportions.   Without the Acts
as a background, it would require the skill of a trained
literary critic clearly to envisage the personality of the
Apostle.   Of course, in his own churches there would
have been memories handed down in local tradition.   But
these would, in the main, relate only to his impact on the
local church in which they were preserved.   Of his career
as a whole, of the magnitude of the task he accomplished,
of the variety of his adventures and of the intensity of
his endurances, till Acts was written, no one, even in the
churches which he had himself founded, could have any
adequate appreciation.

[1] E. J. Goodspeed, *New Solutions of New Testament Problems*. (University
of Chicago, 1927.)

Prof. Goodspeed makes the further suggestion that it was the revived interest in Paul, due to the publication of the Acts, that caused search to be made in the churches round the Aegean for letters by him, which hitherto had been hardly known outside the particular church to which they had been originally addressed. He points out, what we are apt to forget, how enormously these letters gain in weight from the fact that they are read *as a collection* ; and how important an event, therefore, for the history of the Church the formation of that collection must have been. And in the Pauline Church of Ephesus, where probably it was first made, it would attain at once an all but canonical authority.

Certainly it is hard to believe that Luke himself, when he wrote the Acts *c.* A.D. 85, had access to the complete collection of epistles of Paul ; and if Luke did not possess them all, who else would ? I think he knew Romans[1] and 1 Corinthians ; and those two epistles circulated widely from a very early date. But, asks Prof. Goodspeed, where did the author of *Revelation* get the idea— a very strange idea, when one comes to think of it—of prefacing an apocalyptic writing with a collection of seven letters to churches ? He brilliantly suggests the explanation that John the Seer was familiar in Ephesus with *letters to churches* by another whom he regarded as an inspired prophet—these being already formed into a *definite collection*.[2] At any rate, the author of the Pastorals—who wrote, we have seen, in Asia—knew the Ten Epistles as a collection already venerated in the Church[3] ; while the frequent reminiscences of the

---

[1] Cf. *The Four Gospels*, p. 555.

[2] For evidence that the author of Revelation was familiar with several of the epistles of Paul, cf. R. H. Charles, *Revelations*, i. p. lxxxiii ff. (T. & T. Clark, 1920.)

[3] The evidence for this important conclusion is forcibly marshalled by P. N. Harrison (*op. cit.* p. 87 ff.). The fact that the Prefaces to the Epistles found in

Pauline Epistles in Ignatius and Polycarp make it certain that, some time before A.D. 115, both Antioch and Smyrna possessed a collection of Pauline Epistles—and reasonably certain that this was our present collection of thirteen, including the Pastorals. Polycarp, again, had formed a collection of letters of Ignatius within a few weeks of their being written, and he sent copies thereof to at least one church, that of Philippi, at its request. The existence of this demand for a collection of the letters of Ignatius is explicable only if the Pauline corpus had familiarised that church with the idea of, and created the demand for, collected letters by Christian saints.

It is interesting to note that, whereas traces of a use of the *Gospel* of Luke are both scanty and doubtful, there appear to be clear reminiscences of the *Acts* in Clement, Polycarp, and Ignatius. It would look as if Mark and Matthew (or Q) had become established in the affections of these several writers and the churches they represent; so that they welcomed the Acts, which broke entirely fresh ground, with more enthusiasm than a new Gospel, which largely covered the same field. Luke also, we remember, often gives sayings of Christ in a different, and usually slightly Hellenised, form, which until they became familiar might grate on many, in the same way as a new translation does to-day on those brought up on the Authorised Version.

The deep impression made by Acts is further shown by the body of secondary literature which it called into existence—the original Ebionite romance of the adventures of Peter and Simon Magus, the orthodox *Preaching of Peter*, and then the series of Apocryphal Acts.

some Latin MSS. are evidently Marcionite in origin has suggested the theory that the first complete collection was made by Marcion ; but if this holds, the similar Prologues in some MSS. of the gospels would be evidence that the Four Gospel canon was of Monarchian origin !

M

For the moment, however, let us concentrate our attention on the probable effect on the Church of Antioch of the arrival there, perhaps c. A.D. 90, of the Acts and the collection of Pauline Epistles. By this time the church had become more Gentile than Jewish; and, Jerusalem having fallen, the Jewish element, in so far as it did not in a spirit of despairing nationalism revert to Pharisaism, would inevitably become more liberal. Paul then, as portrayed in the narrative of Luke, came to them, no longer as the rebel antinomian pictured to them by the Judaisers of an earlier generation, but as the Apostle—the continuator of the policy of Peter— who had verily ' laboured more abundantly than they all ', and who through his epistles, now heard at Antioch for the first time, still spoke to them voicing a passionate call to righteousness. Inevitably there would be a strong pro-Pauline reaction. Ignatius no doubt belonged to the party most profoundly influenced by this movement ; he may indeed have lived for a while in some Pauline church in Asia, for at times he seems to echo the Fourth Gospel. But he could hardly have written as he does, unless something very like the post-Pauline interpretation of Christianity was already regarded in Antioch as orthodox.[1]

Between the *Didache* and Ignatius there is as great a gulf theologically as there is in the matter of Church Order. But the Acts and the Epistles of Paul had ten years longer in which to do for the theology of Antioch what Clement's epistle, if I am correct in my view of its influence, had begun to do for its conception of Church Order.

---

[1] An historical analogy to this impact on Antioch of the Pauline theology, would be the impact of Alexandrian thought on Syria after Origen made Caesarea his base of operations.

IGNATIUS

Next to the epistles of Paul, the letters of Ignatius, Bishop of Antioch, written on his way to martyrdom in the Colosseum at Rome, *c.* A.D. 115—four from Smyrna, three when he had reached Troas—are, considered simply as ' a human document ', the most vivid piece of literature that has survived from the early Church. They also, by reason of the developed system of episcopal Church Order which they imply, pose a question which is one of the most controverted in early Church history.

The historical problem, however, becomes far less difficult of solution if sufficient weight be given to two considerations which heretofore have been commonly ignored.

First, there is evidence that the hierarchical system championed by Ignatius was, so far as Antioch is concerned, of recent origin, and not yet securely established. Secondly, Ignatius, like some other men of genius, exhibits certain characteristics of the ' neurotic temper ' ; and he is writing under circumstances of great nervous strain. Hence whatever he writes is instinct with excitement and exaggeration, and must be interpreted with due allowance made for the mentality of the writer.

The view that at Antioch the monarchical episcopate was an institution of relatively recent origin is borne out by two facts.

(1) In the traditional lists of Bishops of the great Sees only one name is given between Ignatius and the Apostles ; whereas Xystus, who, in the accepted chronology, was Bishop of Rome at the time of Ignatius' martyrdom, is reckoned the sixth after the Apostles in

that church. It is significant also that, in spite of his insistence on the importance of the Bishop, Ignatius (to quote the words of Prof. C. H. Turner) ' has no thought of a " succession " at all '.[1]

(2) Six of the seven letters are filled with exaggerated and passionate exaltation of the authority and importance of the bishop's office. What nobody questions, nobody defends ; over-enthusiastic defence implies the existence of strong opposition. The principle which Ignatius is so concerned to uphold is evidently one by no means universally recognised. More than that, we cannot but suspect that it is one for which he himself has had to fight long and hard. The language and tone of Ignatius on the subject of the episcopate is that of a man who had become Bishop of Antioch at a time when the mon- archical status and authority of that office was as yet not sufficiently ancient to be secure. He is fighting a battle which is not yet won.

Conflict is the note of the Ignatian correspondence. But we shall entirely misunderstand the nature of the conflict if we think of it as a struggle between Ignatius and the body of Presbyters. Ignatius is not fighting for the supremacy of the Bishop as against the Presbyters ; he is fighting for the supremacy of the regular church officers as a body. In this respect he is at one with Clement ; and he is carrying a stage further forward the process of strengthening their authority which the *Didache* already shows at work. He always speaks as if it could be taken for granted that the Presbyters and Deacons were in complete harmony with the Bishop, and will in all things act with him—an assumption which in some ages might seem precarious. But it frequently

---

[1] *Essays on the Early History of the Church and Ministry*, ed. H. B. Swete, p. 113. (Macmillan, 1918.)

happens that a governing class regards the concentration
of power in an individual as essential to their own predominance. That is the attitude of regimental officers
towards the commander, of Fascist leaders towards
Mussolini, and was that of the Prussian aristocracy
to the Hohenzollern. It is of the laity that Ignatius is
thinking in his reiteration of the demand for obedience;
and he urges this as a remedy both against the counter
attractions of heretical teachers and against the tendency
to form independent groups. It may be that Ignatius
had chanced on a body of presbyters whom he could
easily dominate; it may be he had succeeded in getting
rid of a recalcitrant minority. Be that as it may, the
Bishop to him is the keystone of the arch of authority;
he assumes that the other stones will be in place.

Let us now, giving due weight to these considerations,
examine the personal idiosyncrasy of Ignatius himself in
the light of modern psychological theory. The historical
difficulties, we shall find, begin to disappear.

Ignatius, like many who have achieved high fame,
was clearly of the ' neurotic temper '. His letters on
every page reveal a high-minded personality keyed up
to that peculiar intensity which is a symptom of that
temper. Genius is often a concomitant of the neurotic
constitution. Not that genius is the result of the
neurosis; but that same hypersensitiveness to im-
pressions, which makes the genius quick to perceive
what other men ignore, exposes him in early life to
injury from experiences which would leave unscathed
persons of more ordinary clay. A piece of grit that will
derange a watch will not affect a traction engine.

(1) The most obvious evidence that Ignatius was
a man of abnormal psychology is the prophetic seizure
he alludes to in writing to the Philadelphians:

For even though certain persons desired to deceive me after the flesh, yet the Spirit is not deceived, being from God ; for it knoweth whence it cometh and whither it goeth, and it searcheth out the hidden things. I cried out, when I was among you ; I spake with a loud voice, with God's own voice. . . . (Philad. vii. 1).

It is evident that he—like other ' prophets ' of his time—had an overwhelming conviction of possession by a personality other than his own. From the purely psychological point of view such an experience has obvious analogies to that of the medium in modern times. Ignatius believed himself to be under a control which made use of his voice, he himself being merely a passive instrument. That control he is convinced is the Holy Spirit. To discuss the question whether or no certain individuals—the Prophets of the Old Testament, for example [1]—may at certain moments be in some special sense susceptible to influences from the Divine Spirit (working, perhaps, through the ' subconscious ' region of the self) would be outside the purpose of this chapter ; but few, I think, would wish to maintain that Ignatius was one of these. In any case, psychologically considered, such an experience implies a state of ' temporary dissociation ', during which the vocal organs are directed by forces acting below the level of conscious volition. All I am here concerned to point out is, that the incident is evidence of a psychological disposition other than the normal.

The evidence is the more important since it is clear that such experiences were not unusual with him. He tells the Ephesians he purposes to write again to them, ' especially if the Lord should reveal aught to me '

---

[1] I have put together some facts and reflections bearing on this subject in an Appendix to my book *Reality*.

(Eph. xx. 2). This shows that the prophetic seizure was with him a matter of frequent occurrence.

(2) Another trait suggestive of psychological abnormality stands out in another passage of which the great editors have missed the real meaning.

Am I not able to write to you of heavenly things ? But I fear lest I should cause you harm, being babes. So bear with me, lest not being able to take them in, ye should be choked. For I myself also, albeit I am in bonds and can comprehend heavenly things and the arrays of the angels and the musterings of the principalities, things visible and things invisible—I myself am not yet by reason of this a disciple (Trall. v.).

The passage is a conscious echo of Paul's epistles to the Corinthians.[1]

I, like Paul [he means], am in bonds for the Gospel; like Paul, I have had visions and revelations; I have been caught up into the third heaven, and heard unspeakable words—but (like Paul) I do not pride myself thereon; I merely ask you ' to bear with me ', if, speaking as to babes in Christ, I withhold a wisdom fit only for the perfect, and veil the glory of my vision.

With an unhappy mixture of pride and humility Ignatius at once boasts of, yet declines to reveal the content of, his mystic visions. How sharp the contrast with the real reluctance of the Apostle—forced in self-defence to speak of high experiences—' I am become foolish, ye compelled me '. Ignatius conceived that it had been given him to share the Apostle's spiritual vision. To us, all that it shows is that he was addicted to trance-practice. Truly *spiritual* vision depends on the quality of soul of him who sees, not on the psychological mechanism of the moment of intuition.[2]

Theosophy has familiarised the modern world with the claim that certain ' Adepts ' can in the ecstasy of trance attain ' clairvoyant ' information about the

---

[1] Cf. esp. 1 Cor. iii. 1-2 ; 2 Cor. xi. 1, xii. 1-7.   [2] Cf. *Reality*, p. 327.

mysteries of the heavenly ' spheres '. That there were
Christians in the first century who claimed similar
knowledge of high things clairvoyantly ' seen ', is the
most natural interpretation of Paul's allusion in Colossians to ' worshipping of angels, taking his stand on
things which he hath seen '; especially if we accept
the brilliant conjecture, favoured by Lightfoot, ἃ ἑώρακε
κενεμβατεύων, ' making empty boasts of visions he has
seen ' (Col. ii. 18). The whole series of Apocalypses
points in the same direction. Some, at any rate, of
these visions of the Apocalyptists, even if subsequently
a good deal edited, must have been actually *seen*. The
notion that by the method of trance-practice the
individual can attain actual vision of things unutterable
opens wide the door to self-delusion and inflated self-
esteem. That result by no means always follows ; it
all depends on the moral quality of the visionary.
Ignatius ought not to be depreciated simply because he
had and valued such experiences ; but it must be recognised that the psychological make-up of the person who
enjoys them is not that of the ordinary man.

(3) Any one familiar with the literature of modern
psychology will incline to see in Ignatius an example
of that neurotic variety of ' the will to power ' which is
often found along with great ability, and not infrequently
with high ideals. In a man of the idealist temper ' the
will to power ' is usually to be explained as being the
result of a ' psychic over-compensation for an inferiority
complex ', that is, of a subconscious sense of inferiority
due to some humiliating experience or experiences in
early life. This phenomenon has been most elaborately
studied by Prof. A. Adler of Vienna,[1] who makes it the

---

[1] A. Adler, *The Neurotic Constitution* (E. T. Kegan Paul, 1917), and the more
recent *Individual Psychologie*.

foundation of his system. But the main facts—and the light they throw on the character of Ignatius—hold good, even if the system of psychology which Adler builds upon them be regarded as somewhat one-sided.[1]

Christianity, just because it has made humility a virtue, has made it a virtue the more difficult of attainment by persons of this temper. Self-deception can take many and subtle forms, but none more subtle than the self-esteem which prides itself on not being proud. Ignatius, like many religious leaders since, painfully and conscientiously *wills* to be humble ; but his subconscious mind is continually in revolt.

A prisoner for the faith, about to die for Christ's sake, writing letters of exhortation to the churches—with that ' repressed ' instinct of self-assertion, how can the thought not surge up that once a great Apostle was in that same position ? But no; let others, if they will—and the repressed self hopes they will—make that comparison ; he will disclaim it.

The Church in Tralles he salutes ' in the Divine plenitude ' in the apostolic fashion ; he speaks as one having authority :

Seeing that I love you, I thus spare you, though I might write more sharply on His [Christ's] behalf.

And at once comes the disclaimer :

I thought not myself competent for this, that being a convict, I should order you as though I were an Apostle (Trall. iii. 3).

---

[1] Cf. C. G. Jung, *Two Essays on Analytical Psychology*, E.T., p. 62 (Baillière, Tindall & Cox, 1928). ' The views of Adler and Freud are therefore in contradiction only if there be such a theory. . . . In the neurosis of a youthful introvert, the psychological theory of Adler seldom fails ; and in the treatment of the young extravert it is always advisable, indispensable indeed, to take account of the Freudian standpoint.' Ignatius, I would remark, clearly belongs to the ' introverted ' type.

Similarly he writes to the Romans :

I do not command you as though I were Peter and Paul ; they were Apostles, I am a convict (Rom. iv. 3).[1]

' I am a convict.' If we accept the tradition that Peter and Paul died for their faith in Rome, they too were 'convicts' in precisely the same sense as Ignatius ; if we reject that tradition, then an unconscious self-esteem half hints at a glory which belonged to him, but which the Apostles did not share. On this Lightfoot comments : ' His judicial condemnation by the Roman power was a type of his unworthiness, his conviction, in the sight of God ; his δικαίωσις was yet to come ' ; and he compares his remark to the Ephesians :

I know who I am, and to whom I write. I am a convict ; ye have obtained mercy, I am in peril ; ye are established (xii. 1).

Thus to assure the rank and file of an average church that they are more surely in the way of salvation than a martyr on his road to death, is not real humility. Lightfoot perhaps gives what Ignatius thought he *ought* to feel; and what (echoing 1 Cor. iv.) he meant to say. But there is often a gap between what the conscious self wills to *say*, and what the subconscious allows it to *convey*.

In most societies, whether secular or religious, there are persons deemed by their admirers to be ' indispensable '. There are more who deem themselves to be so. Sometimes it is on good grounds ; but few would state the fact as naïvely as Ignatius.

Remember in your prayers the church which is in Syria, which hath God for its shepherd in my stead (Rom. ix. 1).

---

[1] The words ὡς Πέτρος καὶ Παῦλος are commonly mistranslated ' as Peter and Paul did '. But Ignatius three times makes the same disclaimer of the right to command (διατάσσεσθαι). To the Trallians he writes, ' as though I were an Apostle '; to the Ephesians, ' as though I were somewhat '; to the Romans, ' as though I were Peter and Paul ' ; ὡς must mean the same in each case.

That this self-exaltation is merely the obverse side of an
' inferiority complex ' is seen when we contrast with it
expressions of humility—no less extravagant, and no less
sincere.   In as many as five of the seven letters he speaks
of himself as ' the very last of the faithful ', or as ' not
worthy to be a member ' of the church of Syria.[1]

That was a genuine humility which cried :

> And last of all, as unto one born out of due time, he appeared
> to me also.   For I am the least of the apostles, that am not meet
> to be called an apostle, because I persecuted the Church of God
> (1 Cor. xv. 8-9).

It is not humility, it is egoism repressed, that, consciously
echoing these classic words, can say of the converted
slum dwellers, who formed the rank and file of the Church
of Antioch :

> But for myself, I am ashamed to be called one of them ;
> neither am I worthy, being the very last of them and one born
> out of due time (Rom. ix. 2).

At times Ignatius himself, to do him justice, seems
to catch a glimpse of this inner contradiction.

> I have many deep thoughts in God ; but I take the measure
> of myself, lest I perish in my boasting.   For I ought now to be
> the more afraid and ought not to give heed to them that would
> puff me up . . . for though I desire to suffer, I know not whether
> I am worthy (Trall. iv.).

But even here—and the more so if this be read with
what follows in the context—we still seem to be listening
to a man who publicly disclaims a virtue expecting that
his hearers will repudiate the disclaimer.

(4) With Ignatius the desire for martyrdom has risen
to the height of passion.

> Why do I desire to fight with wild beasts ? (Trall. x.)

---

[1] Eph. xxi. 2; Rom. ix. 2; Magn. xiv.; Trall. xiii. 1; Smyrn. xi. 1.

> Pray ye . . . that I may be vouchsafed the lot which I am
> eager to attain (Trall. xii. 3).

This is not, I think, as with some of the later ascetics,
an indication of the neurotic desire to suffer, known as
' masochism '. It is rather an expression of the contradiction in his character—the heroic resolve by the imitation of Christ to serve God in a way worthy of his high
calling, combined with a desire to attain the glory of
martyrdom, which was the highest personal distinction
in the contemporary Church. He begs the Roman
Christians to forbear any attempt to procure for him a
reprieve.

> If ye be silent and leave me alone, I am a word of God ; but
> if ye desire my flesh, then shall I be again a mere cry (Rom. ii. 1).
> Let me be given to the wild beasts, for through them I can
> attain unto God. I am God's wheat, and I am ground by the
> teeth of wild beasts, that I may be found pure bread of Christ.
> Rather entice the wild beasts that they may become my sepulchre
> and may leave no part of my body behind (Rom. iv. 1 f.).

A note is here struck that compels both sympathy and
respect—but it contrasts rather curiously with another
cry : ' Father, if it be possible, let this cup pass '.

(5) Ignatius was a man used to deference and obedience, accustomed also to that reverential admiration
always in his own circle accorded to an outstanding
religious leader—a form of flattery the more insidious
because it is usually sincere. Brutality to prisoners condemned to the arena was the rule. Given guards with a
taste for prisoner-baiting, his was just the temperament
which would incite to that amusement. To his highly
strung, sensitive nature, the long road to Italy was itself
a martyrdom.

> From Syria to Rome I fight with wild beasts, by land and
> sea, by day and night, being bound amidst ten leopards, a

company of soldiers who only wax worse when they are kindly treated. Howbeit through their injuries I am becoming more of a disciple—yet am I not hereby justified (Rom. v. 1).

Inevitably such an experience would intensify, and force to find expression, psycho-neurotic tendencies latent in his mental constitution which in easier circumstances might never have developed. In that respect the portrait painted in his letters misrepresents the real Ignatius. The tension of a soul sorely overstrained rings in every sentence of this pathetic, yet still heroic, figure. We cannot but note the unconscious egoism in many a sentence; yet it is the egoism of a noble mind unstrung.

The psychological idiosyncrasy of Ignatius must be borne in mind when we approach the consideration of those passages in his epistles which bear on Church government. First, the commonest symptom of nervous overstrain is a loss of the sense of proportion, with the consequential resort to exaggeration of statement. Secondly, the neurotic temperament is frequently characterised by an obsessive concentration on certain dominant ideas. To Ignatius the monarchical episcopate is literally an *idée fixe*. It may easily happen that an *idée fixe* is an idea *intrinsically* valuable. In the circumstances of the time it probably was true statesmanship to strengthen the authority of the episcopate. A policy may in itself be sound, and yet in a particular individual become neurotically an obsession; and to Ignatius the importance of the Bishop had become a real obsession. His language in regard to that office is beyond measure extravagant.

Plainly, therefore, we ought to have respect to the bishop as to the Lord Himself (Eph. vi. 1).

The bishop presiding after the likeness of God and the presbyters after the likeness of the council of the Apostles (Magn. vi. 1).

The bishop as being a type of the Father and the presbyters as the council of God and as the college of the Apostles. Apart from these a church does not deserve to be called a church (Trall. iii. 1).

Wheresoever the bishop shall appear, there let the people be ; even as where Jesus may be, there is the Catholic Church. It is not lawful apart from the bishop either to baptize or to hold a love feast ; but whatsoever he shall approve, this is well pleasing also to God. . . . It is good to recognise God and the bishop. He that honoureth the bishop is honoured of God ; he that doth aught without the knowledge of the bishop rendereth service to the devil (Smyrn. viii. 2–ix. 1).

Sentiments like these are often reiterated several times in the same letter ; and they occur more than once in every letter, except that addressed to Rome. The exception is significant ; and I have already suggested the reason for it. To Ignatius the Church of Rome is the ideal church,

worthy of God, worthy of honour, worthy of felicitations, worthy of praise, worthy of success, worthy in purity and having the presidency in love, walking in the law of Christ.

It is the church which teaches other churches, ' Ye were the instructors of others '. The instruction given by the Church of Rome to other churches was, as we have already seen (p. 155 f.), the letter sent out some twenty years before—written in the name of the whole Church, though probably penned by Clement—the teaching of which seemed so supremely valuable to Ignatius and the party who supported him in his stand for discipline. Naturally Ignatius took it for granted that the church which had itself produced the epistle of Clement did not need his good advice ; he assumed—possibly on inadequate information as to the contemporary situation—that it was a model of episcopal discipline as well as of all other Christian virtues.

A still more tell-tale fact is the recurrence of this same topic when, on the occasion already alluded to, he was speaking under the control of the prophetic spirit.

> I cried out when I was among you ; I spoke with a loud voice, with God's own voice, Give ye heed to the bishop and the presbytery and the deacons. . . . He in whom I am bound is my witness that I learned it not from flesh of man ; it was the preaching of the Spirit who spake in this wise ; Do nothing without the bishop (Philad. vii. 1).

Utterances during the kind of prophetic seizure here described reveal the working of the subconscious mind— which is always the citadel of the *idée fixe*.

When a man on his road to death is seen using every opportunity to impress one idea with all the prestige that martyrdom would give him ; when he enforces it in language neurotically extravagant ; and when there is evidence that his subconscious as well as his conscious mind is dominated by the same idea, we may well conclude that it stood to him as the summation of his life's work. But if the consolidation of an ecclesiastical discipline centred in the monarchical bishop was the ideal for which Ignatius had lived, and which he hoped by a martyr's death firmly to rivet on the Church at large, it is a fair presumption that it was a thing which he had had to fight for in his own Church of Antioch.

Again, what is the meaning of the extreme anxiety in regard to the election of his successor voiced in the three earlier letters which he despatched from Smyrna ? Did he know that the party he had vanquished had raised their heads, and were intriguing to prevent the supreme power ever again being concentrated in the hands of a single person ? Till the new bishop was

seated in his chair, Ignatius' life's work was in peril.
After reaching Troas he heard satisfactory news on this
point ; thereupon he adjures the four churches to which
he then writes to send special deputations to congratu-
late the Church of Antioch on having acquired a bishop.
We may think it odd that he should expect them to
display such enthusiasm about a routine matter of that
sort ; then we reflect that the election of the right man
as successor meant to Ignatius the final victory of his
policy. With the self-centredness of the neurotic temper,
he takes it for granted that the churches of Asia will
share his delight. Whether they obeyed his behest we
shall never know. To us the point of interest is to note
that, alike in his anxiety and in his joy, there speaks a
man whose life work has just been saved.

I ask once more the question with which this Lecture
opened : Is it possible to bridge the gulf between the
Church Order—not to mention the theology—of the
Didache and that of the letters of Ignatius ? So far
as the theology is concerned, the impingement on the
Church of Antioch, soon after the writing of the *Didache*,
of the collection of Pauline Epistles would suffice. As
regards Church Order, the gulf, I have shown, is nothing
like so wide as it at first sight appears. On the one
hand, already in the church in which the *Didache* was
written, episcopoi and deacons were officials enjoying
high repute ; and the aim of the document is to increase
their prestige in the smaller churches. On the other
hand, it has become clear that the position claimed by
Ignatius for the hierarchy was, at Antioch, a thing
recently developed and, indeed, as yet by no means
secure. But between the *Didache* and the letters of
Ignatius three influences had operated concurrently to

strengthen that position—the epistle of Clement, with
its stress on the necessity of discipline under a ministry
deriving authority from Apostolic succession; the
obvious value of mon-episcopacy at a time when unity
in the local church was seriously threatened (Smyrn. vi.
and viii.) ; the lifework of Ignatius himself.

Throughout his struggle he would have been able to
quote the example of other famous churches. His
allusion to ' bishops settled in the farthest parts of the
earth ' may be a rhetorical exaggeration ; but at Jerusalem a monarchical episcopate was primitive ; in the
larger churches of Asia, as we have seen, it was established perhaps twenty years before Ignatius wrote.
Clement's letter was, I have shown, capable of being
interpreted as if mon-episcopacy had been immemorial
at Rome. In State as well as Church, the current of
the times was towards absolute personal rule. An able,
energetic man, concentrated on one object, wholly un-
sparing of himself, can in any circumstances effect much ;
but Ignatius held all the cards. Why, then, had it cost
him the effort, which unless our interpretation of his
letters is entirely amiss, it must have cost, to establish
at Antioch what elsewhere had come by easy stages ?
All is explained on the view that in this matter Syria
was behind the times ; that at Antioch the entrusting
of monarchical authority to the bishop was comparatively
recent ; so that Ignatius had had a long fight and a hard
one to bring his church into line with other churches.
Tradition knows of one predecessor only in the office ;
and Euodius may well have been little more than chairman of the local board of presbyters. Like many an
Anglican vicar in England in the last three-quarters of
a century, Ignatius during his tenure of office changed
his church from ' Low ' to ' High ', and so brought it

into conformity with what he sincerely believed to be the mind of Christ—and what, beyond doubt, was the fashion of the age.

ADDITIONAL NOTE

THE EPISTLE OF ST. JUDE

IF this epistle be ascribed to Jude, the brother of the Lord, we should naturally—in default of evidence to the contrary—assign its place of origin either to Palestine or, at any rate, to some locality in that part of the Roman Empire. In that case it is a document bearing on the early history of the Church in Syria. It is relevant, therefore, to the subject of this Lecture to consider briefly the question of its authorship and provenance.

The epistle opens with the words, ' Judas, a servant of Jesus Christ, and brother of James '. That a feeling of humility should have made Jude describe himself as the ' servant ', rather than as the ' brother ', of the Lord, is not unnatural. What surprises us is the addition, ' and brother of James '. Jude and his family were, we should gather from Hegesippus, well known in Palestine ; besides, in the early Church, letters were carried by hand by friends of the writer, so that there could be no doubt in the minds of the first readers as to the identity of the Judas named in the address. We suspect, therefore, that the identification, ' brother of James ', is an addition—perhaps originating in a marginal note in some early MS.—made at a later date, when the identity of the Judas who wrote it was open to debate.

But if the identification of the Judas who wrote the letter with the brother of James is a conjecture, it may possibly be a mistaken one. This possibility turns into a probability when we read the exhortation (verse 17), ' Remember ye the words which have been spoken aforetime by the apostles of our Lord Jesus Christ ; how that they said to you, In the last time there shall be mockers, walking after their own ungodly lusts '. This seems to imply that the writer of the epistle lived in what he believed to be ' the last time ', but a time related to that in which the Apostles lived as the time of fulfilment to the time of prophecy —the prophecy having been uttered by the great men of the past.

The persons denounced in the epistle are a group who, so far from condemning sexual immorality, defend it as the expression of the liberty justified by a higher spirituality. We know that Carpocrates, c. A.D. 125, taught this. But the Gnostic doctrine that the spirit and the flesh were completely separable lent itself from the first, either to extreme asceticism, or to extreme anti-nomianism. Hence this kind of teaching is likely to have appeared in some quarters very soon after the first infiltration of the Gnostic outlook into Christianity—i.e. before the end of the first century. It looks as if this conscientious immoralism was something of a novelty in the particular church to which the letter was addressed. At any rate, the impression left by the epistle is that the teaching in question was something which had only recently crept in ; the mere discovery of its existence had come to the author as something of a shock. It is the moral turpitude of the teaching, rather than any doctrinal theory, which stirs him to indignant denunciation. In so far, however, as the theoretical basis of Gnostic immoralism was a distinction between the ultimate Good God and the more or less evil Creator of the material universe, including our flesh, Judas appeals to his hearers to keep ' the faith once delivered to the saints '. But here, as in James, the typical article of faith, on its intellectual side, is ' thou believest that God is One '—which for all who accepted the Old Testament as Scripture needs not to be argued about.

So far as external evidence is concerned, Jude is one of the best authenticated of the catholic epistles. It alone, in addition to the Johannine epistles, is mentioned in the *Muratorianum*, which represents Rome ; Clement of Alexandria wrote a commentary on it ; and the author of 2 Peter—who probably wrote either in Asia or in Syria, c. A.D. 140—valued it so highly that he incorporated it practically whole in a work which he wished to be accepted as Peter's. This is against a date much later than A.D. 100.

But though not the work of Jude, the brother of the Lord, the epistle ought by no means to be treated as a specimen of early Christian pseudonymous writing. Jude is a person so obscure that no one, desiring to give weight to his own views by publishing them under an authoritative name, would ever have thought of him, until and unless he had used up all the greater figures of the Apostolic Age. The epistle must therefore be the authentic work of a Christian leader actually named Judas.

Prof. B. W. Bacon (*Journal of Biblical Lit.*, 1928, p. 230 f.) detects a connection between the aim and spirit of Jude and ' Matthew's attempt to counteract the antinomian laxity of the times ', depicting the historic Jesus ' as a second Moses, laying down commandments for a higher righteousness enforced by rewards and penalties of the world to come '. ' Luke ', he says, ' stands closer to James '. My own feeling as to the ' atmosphere ' of the documents coincides with his ; and while I would place Luke and James in Rome (or, at any rate, the West), I should conjecture Jude, like Matthew, to be a Syrian work.

Who was this Judas ? Though not an Apostle, he writes as one from whom written pronouncements on Church matters were expected (Jude 3). Can he have been the Bishop of an important See ?

The *Apostolic Constitutions*, in the passage already quoted (p. 92), gives the third Bishop of Jerusalem (following Symeon, the successor to James, the Lord's brother) as ' Judas of James '. As its author probably lived in Caesarea, he would be familiar with Jerusalem tradition. We have lists of Jerusalem bishops by two other persons who could have had access to that tradition, viz. Eusebius and Epiphanius. Their lists are nearly, but not quite, identical. Eusebius used a written authority, which did not give dates (*H.E.* iv. 5). Prof. Turner (*J.T.S.* i. p. 540) argues that Epiphanius used this same source—doubtless a list drawn up by the authorities at Jerusalem. Now, whereas in Eusebius' list the third name is *Justus*, Epiphanius gives it as *Judas*. There exist four later lists ; these vary, giving either Judas or Justus, or a combination of the two names. Epiphanius, I suggest, copied the original correctly as *Judas* ; the *Apostolic Constitutions* more accurately as *Judas of James*.

The conjecture lies ready to hand that the Epistle originally opened ' Judas of James, a servant of Jesus Christ '. The addition of the word ' brother ' would make ' of James ' no longer a kind of surname, but a description ; and for reverential reasons this would be transposed so as to follow ' servant of Jesus Christ '.

On that hypothesis the author of the epistle was Bishop of Jerusalem early in the reign of Trajan.

VI

THE CHURCH OF ROME

SYNOPSIS

THE EARLY POPES

THE lists of the early Bishops of Rome in Irenaeus and Epiphanius probably go back to one drawn up by Hegesippus, who visited Rome *c.* A.D. 165.

As regards the earliest names, Tertullian contradicts Irenaeus; but, though Irenaeus is the better authority, he too is capable of substituting inference for information.

Strictly speaking, neither Peter nor Paul 'founded' the Church in Rome.

The statement that Peter and Paul appointed the first monarchical Bishop of Rome is not borne out by the evidence of documents undoubtedly emanating from the Roman Church.

Documents undoubtedly Roman are 1 Clement and *The Shepherd* of Hermas; so possibly are the epistle to the Hebrews and that of James.

HEBREWS AND JAMES

Both these were known and valued at Rome at an early date, but were not there accepted as Apostolic. It was in Alexandria that Hebrews was earliest attributed to Paul; James is first mentioned by Origen, and first quoted by Dionysius of Alexandria.

Points of contact between Hebrews, James, and the Lucan writings.

Reasons for connecting Hebrews with Rome.

The situation presupposed in James is equally appropriate to Rome— though this is not generally realised.

The Church Order of Hebrews and James comparable to that implied in the farewell speech of Paul to the Elders of Ephesus. Mon-episcopacy would seem not yet to have been developed, but the disciplinary powers and pastoral responsibility of the regular ministry are strongly emphasised.

THE EPISTLE OF CLEMENT

Written in the name of the Church of Rome to the Church of Corinth.

Its date can be determined as immediately after the assassination of Domitian, A.D. 96.

'THE SHEPHERD' OF HERMAS

The Shepherd of Hermas and the Apocalypse of John the main literary survivals of the outbreak of prophetism which was a notable feature of early Christianity. *The Shepherd* a work of very mediocre quality ; but it enjoyed great popularity in the second and third centuries and reflects the mentality of the average church member of the time.

Internal evidence favours the view that it was written by a contemporary of Clement ; but the *Muratorianum* states that it was written by Hermas, ' while his brother Pius, the Bishop, was sitting in the Chair of the Church of the city of Rome ', *i.e.* A.D. 139-154.

This statement cannot be considered apart from evidence that *c.* A.D. 200 the question of the exact degree of authority to be ascribed to Hermas was a matter of acute controversy. Hippolytus and Tertullian (and certain synods) would dislike the book for theological reasons. Origen—here following Irenaeus and Clement of Alexandria—affirms it to be inspired. Origen ascribed it to the Hermas mentioned by Paul—which he could not have done unless it had been a religious classic in Alexandria long before the time of Pope Pius.

Four other objections to the Muratorian date.

Probability that only the first four *Visions* of Hermas date from the lifetime of Clement (*c.* A.D. 100). The composition of the latter and longer part of the book was probably spread over another dozen years or so.

CHURCH ORDER AT ROME

The epistle of Clement affords evidence as to Church Order at Rome as well as at Corinth—especially as it is supported by the evidence of Hermas.

The officers are named Episcopoi and Deacons ; and these terms are used in contexts which exclude the possibility that Presbyters was the name of a third order of intermediate rank. The term Presbyter appears to imply status rather than office, and to be somewhat wider than that of Episcopos.

Polycarp's letter to the Philippians shows that in this church also, as late as A.D. 115, mon-episcopacy did not yet exist.

The new and important thing contributed by Clement's letter is, not the names of the church officers, but the conception of the nature and source of their authority. The principle of *apostolic succession* as the basis of authority is affirmed—though the succession is a collegiate, not an individual mon-episcopal, succession.

Immense stress is laid on discipline and the duty of obedience. This is enforced by the analogies, on the one hand of the Roman army, on the other of the Old-Testament priesthood.

It is notable that at Rome—though apparently not yet at Corinth—the prophet is definitely subordinate to the regular ministry. With this contrast the situation implied in the *Didache*.

Mon-Episcopacy at Rome

Can the evidence that in the time of Clement and Hermas the Church of Rome was governed by a college of presbyter-bishops be reconciled with the monarchical form of government implied by Hegesippus' list of bishops ? Probability that the Roman Church was originally organised like a Jewish Synagogue, in which one of the Elders, known as $\dot{a}\rho\chi\iota\sigma\upsilon\nu\dot{a}\gamma\omega\gamma\sigma\varsigma$ or 'ruler of the synagogue', was in charge of the conduct of divine worship. The special sanctity of the Eucharistic service would enhance the import- ance among Christians of such an officer.   Personal character, and the inconveniences in time of crisis of committee-rule, might easily make him a kind of 'Managing Director' of the Board of Presbyters.   Evidence that as late as Irenaeus the Bishop of Rome was still entitled ' presbyter '.

Evidence, under three heads, that by A.D. 115 the position of the President of the Elders had grown in importance.

The Quartodeciman controversy ; Asian Christians at Rome ; and the *fermentum*.   Hypothesis that the episcopate of Xystus marked a turning- point in the development of mon-episcopacy at Rome.

The impingement of the arrival of Ignatius, with his impassioned advocacy of the predominance of the bishop, upon the local situation at Rome.

Some reflections on the mutual interaction of Rome and Antioch.

VI

THE CHURCH OF ROME

Early Popes

WERE it certain that the account of the origin of the Roman episcopate given by Irenaeus (A.D. 185) is as accurate as it is precise, our investigation so far as it concerns the Church of Rome would be ended.

We confound all [the heretics] by pointing to the tradition, derived from the Apostles, of the great, ancient and famous church founded and organised at Rome by the two most notable apostles, Peter and Paul, and the faith proclaimed to mankind, which has come down even to ourselves through its succession of bishops. . . . So having founded and built up the Church, the blessed Apostles entrusted the ministration of the bishopric to Linus (*Adv. Haer.* iii. 3. 2 f.).

Irenaeus then gives a list of the first twelve Bishops of Rome, from the Linus just mentioned to Eleutherus who was bishop at the time he wrote.[1]

1. Linus.	[64]	7. Telesphorus.	[125]
2. Anencletus.	[76]	8. Hyginus.	[136]
3. Clement.	[88]	9. Pius.	[140]
4. Evaristus.	[97]	10. Anicetus.	[155]
5. Alexander.	[105]	11. Soter.	[166]
6. Xystus.	[115]	12. Eleutherus.	[174]

A list containing the first ten of these names (save that Anencletus appears in the shortened form Cletus, as in the Canon of the Mass) is given by Epiphanius

---

[1] I add dates, as restored from the 'term numbers' in the *Chronica* of Hippolytus by H. J. Lawlor in his *Eusebius*, ii. p. 44.

(*Pan.* xxvii. 6) ; and Lightfoot showed that the list was derived by him from Hegesippus, a Palestinian Christian who visited Rome in the time of Anicetus, *i.e.* about A.D. 165. A fragment of Hegesippus is preserved, in which he says :

But when I came to Rome, I made for myself a succession-list (διαδοχὴν ἐποιησάμην) as far as Anicetus (Eus. *H.E.* iv. 22).

From this the most natural inference is that the list of the Roman succession was made out then for the first time, and is due to the researches of Hegesippus.[1]

The names Linus, Cletus, Clement occur (after those of the Apostles) in the Canon of the Mass, and are followed by that of Xystus. Liturgiologists believe this to be Xystus II. (martyred A.D. 258)—the first three being the remains of a list which originally enumerated all the Bishops of Rome. Parts of the Canon are of great antiquity, but it seems to have been modified considerably in the fourth century ; and there is no evidence at all as to the origin of the two diptychs, or lists of names. It is, however, not improbable that Hegesippus may have found a list of names already traditional in the eucharistic commemoration, and have drawn upon it on the assumption that, unless the contrary was clear, all names occurring in it were those of bishops.

The list of Irenaeus is derived, I shall try to prove later (p. 288 ff.), directly from that made out by Hegesippus. The historical value of such a list will for the later names be very high ; but its value, of course, will decrease the nearer we get back to the beginning. For the purpose, however, of our present investigation it is precisely the beginning that matters most—and it is just here that other evidence conflicts with that of Irenaeus.

[1] Cf. Lightfoot, *Clement*, i. p. 327 ff. ; also, for a defence of Lightfoot's views from criticisms by Harnack and Zahn, H. J. Lawlor, *Eusebiana*, p. 65 ff.

Rhetorical exaggeration is all but universal in ancient writers—an inevitable result of an education mainly conducted in the School of Rhetoric.[1] To this weakness the Fathers are not more subject than their pagan contemporaries; on the whole they are less so. But the historian who is not constantly on his guard against its influence will make grave mistakes in his estimate of evidence.

Tertullian contradicts the statement of Irenaeus that Clement was ' in the third place from the Apostles '; he affirms definitely that Clement was appointed first Bishop of Rome, and that, not by Peter and Paul, but by Peter. Tertullian had read Irenaeus ; but it would seem that he was attracted by the more vivid and picturesque narrative of the spurious letter of Clement to James (now in the *Clementine Homilies*) which describes the actual ceremony of Clement's consecration by Peter (p. 9). Of the rival statements, that of Irenaeus (and Hegesippus) has clearly the prior claim to consideration; but the fact that Tertullian, having alternative sources of information to choose from, prefers the one which is obviously the less authentic is significant for the mentality of church writers of the period. It compels us to adopt an attitude of caution in regard to the evidence of Irenaeus also—especially as it is not easy to reconcile with that of earlier documents emanating from the Church of Rome itself. Moreover, Irenaeus (in the chapter next following that quoted above), when tracing the episcopal succession in Asia, makes the almost certainly erroneous statement that Polycarp ' was appointed bishop of the Church in Smyrna by apostles in Asia '.

---

[1] Cf. C. Bigg, *The Church's Task under the Roman Empire*, p. 6 ff. (Clarendon Press, 1905.)

To the statement of Irenaeus that the Church of
Rome was 'founded' by Peter and Paul, St. Paul himself would probably have demurred. Some years before
he visited Rome there was in existence in that city a
church sufficiently important to elicit from him the
longest of his epistles—in effect a considered *apologia* for
his whole attitude towards Judaism and Jewish Christianity. And in that epistle he gives as one reason why
he had not been to Rome before, that he had made it
his aim not to preach ' where Christ was already named,
that I might not build on another man's foundation '
(Rom. xv. 20 ff.). Nor can it be said in extenuation
of Irenaeus' language that he used the word 'found'
loosely of Paul, but strictly of Peter—in the belief that
Peter first went to Rome in pursuit of Simon Magus
(p. 10 ff.) (and so may be said to have 'founded' the
Church there) in A.D. 42, seventeen years before the
arrival of Paul. For a few chapters earlier, in the well-
known passage on the origin of the Gospels, Irenaeus
uses the same word ' found ' ; and he there makes it
clear that he thought of Peter and Paul as being engaged
on this ' founding ' *at the same time.*

Matthew published his written Gospel among the Hebrews
in their own language, while Peter and Paul were preaching and
founding the church in Rome.

It is not irrelevant to remark that our confidence in
Irenaeus' accurate knowledge of the facts is not increased
by finding the statement that Peter and Paul founded
the Church of Rome coupled with the assertion that
Matthew wrote his Gospel in Hebrew. This is certainly
incorrect, being incompatible with the admitted dependence of our first Gospel on the Greek Gospel of Mark,
which is the one certain result of Synoptic criticism.
But it can be explained as a *mistaken inference* by

Irenaeus from the saying of Papias about τὰ λόγια. His statement that Linus was appointed Bishop of Rome, in the monarchical sense of that office, by Peter and Paul, *may* also rest on inference. If so, as will appear shortly, it would seem (whether first made by himself, or by Hegesippus) to be similarly a mistaken one.

Though Paul did not ' found ' the Church in Rome, his influence on its thought must have been considerable. And this influence *may* also have been determinative of the type of Church Order which it came to adopt. In that case we should antecedently have expected him to promote an organisation similar to that of the churches which he himself had founded. We have already seen that at Ephesus and at Philippi, the two churches about which we have clear evidence, the government was in the hands, not of a single monarchical bishop, but of a body of episcopoi. The tradition that Peter came to Rome has been recently subjected to formidable scrutiny by Prof. E. T. Merrill, of Chicago.[1] But of those scholars who think the evidence adequate, the majority hold that Peter did not reach Rome till *after* the two years' imprisonment of Paul with which the story of the Acts concludes.[2] Now if Peter was in Rome after Paul's death, it is *theoretically* possible that he then introduced a *new form* of church government. That possibility, however, shrinks to the point of invisibility when we study the evidence available as to the state of affairs at Rome during the ensuing fifty years.

Of documents indisputably emanating from the early Roman Church there survive two—the epistle of the

---

[1] *Essays in Early Christian History.* (Macmillan, 1924.)
[2] Even Monsignor Duchesne writes : ' He had, perhaps, been there before ; this is possible, but it cannot be proved '. *Early History of the Christian Church*, E.T., p. 45. (Murray, 1910.)

Roman Church to that of Corinth, known as the first epistle of Clement ; and the quaint collection of visions and revelations known as *The Shepherd* of Hermas. The epistle of Clement is usually, and I believe correctly, dated A.D. 96. The date of Hermas is disputed ; I shall argue later that his book was published in instalments between A.D. 97-114. But there are in the New Testament itself two documents of a date earlier than these, which can with some degree of probability be connected with Rome, viz. the epistle to the Hebrews and that of James. The case, then, for connecting them with Rome —and the light they throw on Church Order—must be briefly considered before we proceed to scrutinise the evidence of the other, and undoubtedly Roman, documents.

HEBREWS AND JAMES

There is a remarkable analogy between these two epistles—in other respects so different—so far as concerns the history of their acceptance by the Church. Both epistles are known and valued in Rome at a very early date. Hebrews has largely determined the thought, as well as the language, of Clement (A.D. 96) ; and Hermas, a later contemporary of Clement, shows in a number of passages the influence of James. Nevertheless, the Church of Rome declined for more than a couple of centuries to accept either of them as the work of an Apostle. Neither is even mentioned in the *Muratorianum*, which is a list of books accepted (or explicitly rejected) by the Church of Rome at the end of the second century. Eusebius says that the hesitation of Rome in regard to Hebrews lasted down to his own time, A.D. 311 (*H.E.* vi. 20. 3), and James was not admitted to the Roman Canon till about A.D. 350. Again, in regard to both,

Alexandria is the place where we first find evidence of
their acceptance as the writings of Apostles—but here
there is a difference.   The attribution of Hebrews to Paul
was already an ancient tradition in that church in the
time of Clement of Alexandria ; he quotes a theory of
' the blessed Elder ' (presumably Pantaenus, A.D. 180) as
to why Paul omitted to set his name to the epistle.   And
both Clement and Origen wrestle to explain the difference
of style—which was as obvious to the scholarly theologians of Alexandria as to a modern professor—between
this epistle and the rest of the Pauline corpus, in a way
which shows that they were dealing with a work *tradi-
tionally accepted* as Pauline in the Alexandrian Church.
James, on the other hand, is not mentioned by name before
Origen, who, in his Commentary on John (tom. xix. 6)
(after A.D. 232), speaks of it as doubtfully attributed
($\phi\epsilon\rho o\mu\acute{\epsilon}\nu\eta$) to the Apostle ; and it is not clearly *quoted* by
any ecclesiastical writer (save Hermas) until Dionysius
of Alexandria, A.D. 248.[1]

The most noticeable thing, however, about the
attestation of James is the hesitation in regard to it, felt
as late as the fifth century, in the churches of Syria—
where the name of James, brother of the Lord, was held
in special honour, and where Judaistic influences had
been relatively the strongest.   In that part of the world
its first appearance is in the Peshitta, the revised translation of the Syriac made by Rabbula (A.D. 411-435).
It seems to have been accepted by Chrysostom ; but
it is definitely rejected by Theodore of Mopsuestia, A.D.
429, and Theodoret, A.D. 450, both of whom represent the
Syrian tradition.

The slow acceptance into the Canon of a document of

---

[1] There are possible traces of it in 2 Clement, which is also (cf. p. 238 ff.)
an Alexandrian document.

such early date and of such a lofty ethical character would
be easily explained if we could suppose that originally
James, like Hebrews, lacked an opening address giving its
author's name. In that case the first verse of the text as
we have it will have been prefixed in the second century
by some Alexandrian scholar, who, from the internal
evidence afforded by the author's attitude to faith and
works, conjectured that this ancient document was by the
brother of the Lord, whom he knew to have been in the
Apostolic age the leader of those whose thought was at the
furthest remove from that of Paul. The prefixing of the
name of James would revive and extend its circulation ;
and, once attributed to an Apostle, its merits would,
after sufficient lapse of time, secure its admission to the
Canon—especially as the increasingly influential Church
of Aelia-Jerusalem would have warmly championed the
inclusion of a work by their patron saint (p. 42).[1]

Eusebius' attitude to 2 Peter supplies an exact
parallel :

> The tradition received by us is that it is not canonical;
> nevertheless, since it appeared profitable to many, store was set
> by it along with the other Scriptures (*H.E.* iii. 3. 1).

Nevertheless, 2 Peter, in spite of doubts of its genuineness, ultimately got into the New Testament, partly on
its religious and ethical merits, partly, we may surmise,
because it seemed fitting that Peter, as well as Paul and
John, should be represented in the Canon by a plurality
of epistles.

At any rate, however we explain it, it is a fact that,
whereas at the end of the first century both Hebrews and
James were religious classics at Rome, at the end of the
second century no one there even desires to attribute

---

[1] The Liturgy of Jerusalem is attributed to James.

them to an Apostle—and thereby secure for them the admission to the Canon of the New Testament which was at that date a corollary of such attribution. Of this the only explanation I can see is, that the Roman Church originally knew the names of the actual authors, and therefore never thought of ascribing their works to Apostles.

It may be objected that, from the standpoint of theological development, Hebrews and James are at too far a remove from one another to make it likely that they represent the same church at approximately the same date. To this I would reply, that the evidence of Clement and Hermas shows that, wherever they were written, both were found acceptable by some Christians in Rome at an early date. Rome, it must be remembered, differed from other churches in that its membership must from the first have included persons from all parts of the Empire, and presumably, therefore, of a wide range of views.

The Christian community at Rome was not only one of the largest, but also was highly representative of the various currents of thought, tradition, and practice of the whole Christian church. It is not an exaggeration to say that Rome became very early the great laboratory of Christian and ecclesiastical policy, and that it contributed more than any other Church . . . to the defeat of the internal forces which [in the second century] were leading Christianity to a complete disintegration.[1]

There is a link between the two documents. Both Hebrews and James exhibit, though in very different ways, interesting points of contact with the Lukan writings—which there is reason to associate with Rome. Clement of Alexandria tried to account for the Greek style of Hebrews on the hypothesis that it was a trans-

---

[1] G. La Piana, *Harvard Theological Review*, July 1925, p. 203.

lation by Luke of an epistle written by Paul in Hebrew.
No one now holds this view ; but the linguistic affinities
between Hebrews and the Lukan writings are striking.[1]
And though the author of Hebrews had perhaps not read
the Gospel, his obvious reference to Gethsemane (v. 7 f.)
suggests that he knew the story with the addition (including the ' bloody sweat ') found in Luke (xxii. 43 f.) in
the Western and Byzantine texts. In this case I believe
these texts preserve the true reading. But if it be
an interpolation, it only the more evidently reflects a
tradition current at Rome ; for it was known to Justin
Martyr. The contacts between Luke and James are
of another character. ' There is the same fusion of
Wisdom-ideas with the tradition and formation of the
evangelic logia, and the same attitude towards wealth
which has led many writers to ascribe a sort of Ebionistic
sympathy to Luke.' [2]

Matthew, in his attitude towards wealth, shows by
contrast a desire to beat a retreat from a too literal insistence on the commands of the Lord ; he omits the
story of the widow's mite in Mark, he explains the beati-
tude as applicable to ' the poor *in spirit* ', and he omits
(if this stood in his source) the ' Woes ' to the rich and
fortunate, which are so striking a feature in Luke's
version of the Great Sermon.

The verbal reminiscences in James of sayings of
Christ are also on the whole nearer to Luke than to
Matthew. But occasionally they reflect more nearly
the wording of Matthew ; Luke slightly Hellenises his
sources, so it would look as if the author of James had
read Q in the recension known to Luke.

---

[1] Cf. J. Moffatt, *Introduction to the Literature of the New Testament*, 3rd ed.,
p. 435 f.   [2] Cf. Moffatt, *op. cit.* p. 466—where parallels are given.

That the epistle to the Hebrews was addressed to the Church of Rome, or to some section of it, is a view which has of late years won a very general acceptance. Apart from the fact that the epistle first appears in Rome and had made a mark on Roman thought as early as Clement, the allusions to persecution in which many had been made a spectacle of (θεατριζόμενοι) (x. 32 ff.), and to the noble end (ἔκβασιν) of the leaders who had converted them (xiii. 7), may be read naturally as references to the persecution by Nero. So, too, the words ' Those from Italy (οἱ ἀπὸ τῆς Ἰταλίας) salute you ' (Heb. xiii. 24). The translation ' They of Italy ' in A.V. and R.V. is unfortunate ; it suggests a greeting sent by persons living in Italy to some place outside, whereas the Greek favours the converse. It is a greeting sent by Italian Christians living away from their native land at the place of writing ; such a greeting would be most natural in an epistle addressed to Rome.

The place from which the letter was sent we can only guess. The fact that its Christological doctrine bridges the gulf between Ephesians and the Fourth Gospel, combined with the allusion to Timothy's imprisonment (xiii. 23), makes Ephesus the obvious guess. But for our immediate purpose, the actual place of writing is not important. It was addressed to Rome by a person who obviously knew (and was well known by) the Roman Church ; it is, therefore, evidence for the state of things at Rome.

Equally appropriate to the situation at Rome— though the fact is less generally recognised by scholars— is the message of the epistle of James. In Rome—as we should expect and as Clement's letter shows to have been the case—St. Paul's Epistle to the Romans was a church classic. But only the more for that was it liable to misinterpretation. In all ages the Pauline doctrine of Justification by Faith without the works of the Law has been the source, either of intellectual misconception, or of moral antinomianism; and many of the Gnostics were strongly antinomian. In Romans more than in any other of his epistles there are, as the author of 2 Peter puts it,

some things hard to be understood, which the ignorant and unsteadfast wrest, as they do also the other scriptures, unto their own destruction (iii. 16).

One main purpose of James is to protest that mere belief is not enough; right conduct, and that conceived in accord with the ethic of the Sermon on the Mount, is the essential thing (ii. 14-26). Paul would not have denied this; and if the author of the epistle of James had had a deeper insight into Paul's mind, he might have expressed himself differently. But what he is mainly concerned with is, not the inner meaning of Paul, but the misuse by certain persons of texts from Paul to disparage the necessity of good works. Paul cites the *faith* of Abraham; James replies by enumerating his *works*.

The epistle to the Romans was so widely read that a reply to a misunderstanding of this epistle might have been written in any church. But James also cites Rahab the harlot as a case of one who was justified, not by faith, but by works. Why, with all the characters of the Old Testament to choose from, should he select two only— and those Abraham and Rahab? Obviously because these were the two cases most often cited by the persons he would refute. We know why they cited Abraham; Paul had done so—as the outstanding example of justification by faith without works. But why Rahab? It is always in regard to the ethics of sex that anti-

nomians are primarily in revolt; Rahab's profession,
therefore, would specially recommend her to them. But
why, we ask, could they quote her as a person who had
been justified by *faith* ? Doubtless, because her name is
one that occurs in the long roll-call of the heroes of faith
in Hebrews xi.[1] Rahab would not naturally be cited as
a model of faith except in a church where that virtue had
been ascribed to her in a work regarded as a religious
classic. And we know from Clement's epistle that
Hebrews was already such at Rome before A.D. 96;
while, since Hebrews was not yet attributed to Paul, it
could hardly have acquired that position in many other
churches by the date when James was written.

There are two other points in which the language of
James seems specially appropriate if addressed to the
Roman Church.

(*a*) The place where Christians meet for worship is
still called a ' synagogue '; it is so named (three times)
by Hermas, who wrote in Rome a few years later. It
is possible that the use of this word survived in other
parts of the Christian world; but I know of no other
evidence to that effect.

(*b*) Undue deference to the rich, the wearers of ' a
gold ring ', has become a crying abuse (ii. 1-7). The
abuse in question is, unfortunately, one liable to arise in
all times and in all places. But at Rome the gold ring
was an official class distinction; it signified membership
of the Equestrian Order. Archaeological evidence has
accumulated of late—confirming the previously existing
literary evidence—that, towards the end of the first
century A.D., the Church in Rome was gaining, if not
full members, at least ' adherents ', from some of the

---

[1] It is no objection to this view that faith in Hebrews is not used in quite
the same sense as it is by Paul; it is used in yet another sense in James. In
religious controversy, it is commonly words, not their meaning, that matters.

noblest families in Rome, including Flavius Clemens and his wife Domitilla (near relatives of the Emperor), and the Consul Acilius Glabrio. One can imagine the flutter of excitement, in a congregation largely composed of slaves and ex-slaves, when persons of this sort walked into the place of assembly, and the deferential anxiety of those in charge to give them the best seat. It was a situation in which the natural human weakness that inclines the best of us to ' respect of persons ' would be peculiarly difficult to withstand.

The almost Ebionite outlook of the writer is quite compatible with a Roman origin for the epistle. From Philippians it appears that the Judaistic opponents of Paul were extremely active during his imprisonment in Rome;[1] and they were successful in making converts. Paul is large-minded enough to rejoice even in this.

Some indeed preach Christ even of envy and strife ; and some also of good will ; the one do it of love, knowing that I am set for the defence of the gospel ; but the other proclaim Christ of faction, not sincerely, thinking to raise up affliction for me in my bonds. What then ? Only that in every way, whether in pretence or in truth, Christ is proclaimed ; and therein I rejoice, yea, and will rejoice (Phil. i. 15 ff.).

Persecution from without always tends to assuage internal strife. And a persecution like that of Nero must have done much to bring together the warring parties in the Church of Rome. The destruction of Jerusalem also, especially as it was followed by a temporary elimination of the Jerusalem Church, weakened the position of the Judaisers, at any rate outside Palestine. In Rome after the events of A.D. 64, followed

---

[1] It has been suggested that Philippians was not written at Rome, but at Ephesus, during an imprisonment in that city not recorded in the Acts. But even without the evidence of that epistle, it is certain that any church not actually founded by Paul would have included some Judaisers.

by those of A.D. 70, few of the Judaisers would have
declined to throw in their lot with the remnant of the
converts of Paul. During the next hundred years or so
the Church of Rome, like the Church of England to-day,
was notably ' comprehensive '—a state of affairs pro-
ductive of high vitality, but exigent of tact in persons
of position. If, as I believe, the Acts was written in
Rome, it was especially in view of this local situation
that Luke thought it desirable to stress, on the one
hand, the occasions on which Paul went out of his way
to keep some ceremonial injunction of the Mosaic Law,
and, on the other, those on which Peter welcomed
Gentile converts with open arms. At Rome, then, a
marked difference between various parties in regard to
what they deemed to be the essential elements in
Christianity would survive for some generations ; and
the outlook of the author of James is exactly what one
would anticipate in a ' Teacher '—he probably held the
office of διδάσκαλος (iii. 1-2) — whose forbears were
brought up in the Judaistic school of thought.

Assuming, then, that Hebrews and James can be
used as evidence for the early Roman Church, what
light do they throw upon Church Order in this period ?

Hebrews supplies this paragraph :

Obey them that have the rule over you, and submit to them :
for they watch in behalf of your souls, as they that shall give
account, that they may do this with joy, and not with grief :
for this were unprofitable for you (Heb. xiii. 17).

It can hardly be accidental that the only writings
—whether in the New Testament or in the Apostolic
Fathers—which speak of the Christian ministers bluntly
as ' rulers ', are connected with Rome, where the idea of
command was in the very atmosphere. The Pauline
word προΐστασθαι should be translated ' lead ' rather

than ' rule '.   The stronger word ἡγούμενοι occurs three
times in Hebrews (vii. 1 ; xiii. 17 ; xxiv. 1).   It is used
by Clement when exhorting the Corinthians to live up to
the good name they had of old for ' obeying your rulers
and paying due honour to the elders among you ' (iii. 1).
Again, using the compound form προηγούμενοι, he says,
' Let us reverence our rulers ; let us honour our elders '.
And in this form the word is twice used of the church
authorities by Hermas (*Vis*. ii. 2-6 ; iii. 9-7), but is found
nowhere else in the Apostolic Fathers.

In James we find :

Is any among you sick ? let him call for the elders of the
church ; and let them pray over him, anointing him with oil in
the name of the Lord (James v. 14).

It is impossible to build much upon so meagre a
foundation.   At the same time, taken together, these
passages suggest a situation comparable to that implied
in the farewell speech of Paul to the Ephesian elders.
Indeed, supposing, as I believe, the Acts was written
in Rome, it would be quite consonant with the methods
of ancient historians if the phrasing of the speech
attributed to the Apostle were not uninfluenced by
St. Luke's knowledge of the situation at Rome, A.D. 85.
At any rate, both in James and Hebrews ' rulers '
(ἡγούμενοι) and ' elders ' are spoken of in the plural in
a way which, while not actually precluding the existence
of a monarchical bishop, would be unnatural if the
ruling functions were already concentrated in the hands
of a single person.   At the same time both epistles leave
us with the impression that the disciplinary powers and
pastoral responsibility of the presbytery has been consolidated.   In other words, by comparison with the
situation implied in 1 Corinthians or in the *Didache*, the

relative importance of the Pastor, as against the Prophet, has substantially increased.   As we shall see later, Rome at an early date had got its prophets well in hand.

The Epistle of Clement

The historian, before calling documents into evidence, must as far as possible assure himself about their dates. And as the dates of both Clement and Hermas have been disputed, discussion of this question cannot be avoided. All I can do is to try and make this as little tedious as the subject allows.   But a reader confiding enough to accept my results without asking for reasons may skip what follows and start again on p. 213.   For the benefit of such an one, I may say here that I am about to argue that Clement wrote immediately after the terror of Domitian's persecution had been ended by his assassination in A.D. 96 ; and that the first four *Visions* of Hermas were published between this date and the death of Clement—the rest of his book representing visions seen during the next dozen years or so.

Strictly speaking, the so-called First Epistle of Clement is a letter from the Church in Rome to the Church in Corinth, urging the restoration of certain church officers who (in the Roman view) had been wrongfully displaced. The ascription of it to the Clement whose name appears third in the earliest lists of the Bishops of Rome (and who, according to Eusebius,[1] died in the fourth year of Trajan, *i.e.* A.D. 101–102), is already found in a letter (Eus. *H.E.* iv. 23), written to the Roman Church by Dionysius, Bishop of Corinth, *c.* A.D. 170.   Since 1 Clement is written on behalf of the Church of Rome as a whole, the date of writing is more important

---

[1] The duration numbers of Hippolytus, however, favour A.D. 97.

than the name of the person who actually drafted it. Since, however, nothing in the internal evidence provided by the document itself conflicts with the tradition that Clement was that person, it is permissible (and convenient) to speak of it as Clement's, so long as no historical argument is based on his being the actual author. The letter opens with a reference to ' sudden and repeated calamities and disasters ' recently undergone by the Church in Rome. The strength of the language used (early Christians were inured to minor inconveniences)—taken in connection with the fact that later on (lix. 4) prayer is offered for Christians in prison—suggests that the calamities in question were suffered in an outbreak of persecution in Rome which at the time of writing has just ceased.[1]

Now at the end of the year A.D. 96 there was a moment of acute peril for the Church in Rome. Under Trajan the Church in Rome would seem to have been on reasonably good terms with the authorities ; so much so, that Ignatius in his letter to that church is apprehensive that its influence might even extend to procuring a remission of his sentence. But the last years of Domitian were a ' Reign of Terror ' for the Roman aristocracy. The haunting, deadening horror of this still lives for the reader in the grim opening of Tacitus' *Life of Agricola*, written, like 1 Clement, immediately after the assassination of the tyrant allowed Liberty for a moment to draw fresh breath. Seemingly among the victims were persons of high rank who had been attracted

---

[1] Lightfoot makes out a case for interpreting τὸν δηλούμενον (= the aforesaid) in Eusebius (*H.E.* iii. 16) to refer, not to Clement, but to Domitian, in which case Hegesippus stated that the faction in Corinth which called forth Clement's letter was in the reign of Domitian (Lightfoot, *Clement* i. p. 165). If however, as I suspect, Irenaeus (*Adv. Haer.* iii. 1. 3) is following Hegesippus, these words may represent ἐπὶ τούτου τοῦ Κλήμεντος ; and Eusebius may be quoting Hegesippus, not so much as evidence of date, but to show that the letter of the Church of Rome was rightly associated with the name of Clement.

towards Christianity. The most eminent of these was Flavius Clemens, Domitian's first cousin—whose sons he had apparently designated as the successors to the throne. Clemens was put to death early in A.D. 96, and the charge on which he was condemned is stated to have been a religious one ; at the same time his wife Domitilla was sent into exile. There is evidence that the wife at any rate was, or afterwards became, a Christian ; and inscriptions show a Christian cemetery developing during her lifetime on land belonging to her.[1] How many other less important persons connected with the church shared their fate we do not know. But even if the Emperor had decided that it would suffice to make a few conspicuous examples (so that the actual number of martyrs was quite small), the last thing he would do would be to communicate this benevolent resolve to the Church. Whether the actual victims were few or many, the leaders of the Roman Church during the last eight months of his reign would not find it easy to induce a community living in daily expectation of some fresh blow to concentrate its attention on the grievances of some dispossessed clergy at Corinth.

Domitian was assassinated in September A.D. 96. The new government recalled persons whom he had sent into exile, and in many other ways completely and ostentatiously reversed his policy. Among the exiles recalled was Flavia Domitilla, his niece. As the letter of Clement alludes to disasters only in order to explain why the Roman Church had not written before, we may assume that it was written immediately after the cessation of the persecution, that is, in the late autumn of A.D. 96.

[1] Cf. Lightfoot, *Clement* i. p. 33 ff.

THE SHEPHERD OF HERMAS

The Shepherd of Hermas and the Apocalypse of John
are of special interest as being the chief survivals in
literary form of that outburst of prophetism which was
a conspicuous feature in early Christianity — the one
representing Rome, the other Asia. They differ from
all earlier Jewish, and from most Christian, Apocalyptic
writings in that they were published in the author's
own name. But, though both write as prophets, no
contrast could be greater than that between the potter-
ing mediocrity of the timid little Greek and the fiery
brilliance of the impassioned Jew. Hermas is the
'White Rabbit' of the Apostolic Fathers.[1] That is why
we can be certain that he wrote in his own name.
Pseudonymous writers always adopt the style and title
of some great and impressive figure of the past; the
Hermas described in this book is singularly unheroic
—a timid, fussy, kindly, incompetent, middle-aged freed-
man, delightfully naïve, just a little vain of his prophetic
gift, and with a wife and children decidedly out of hand.

Taken in large quantities Hermas is distinctly tedious
—after the first four *Visions*, which are quaintly interesting. Nevertheless there is probably no document which
reflects better the simplicity and genuine piety of the
rank and file of the average church members—largely
recruited as these were from the slave class—in the
sub-apostolic age. That, no doubt, partly explains the
extraordinary popularity that it enjoyed in the first four
centuries, in spite of the frowns of synods and the

---

[1] I quote Lewis Carroll's own description of the ' White Rabbit ' (from an
old magazine, the *Theatre*) : ' Call him " elderly ", " timid ", " feeble ", and
" nervously shilly-shallying ", and you will get *something* of what I meant him
to be. I *think* the White Rabbit should wear spectacles. I am sure his
voice should quaver, his knees quiver, and his whole air suggest a total inability
to say " Bo ! " to a goose.'

strictures of theologians. Hermas is also a landmark, and more than that, a creative departure in the development of the Moral Theology of the Church. He affirms, what the epistle to the Hebrews explicitly denies, the possibility of repentance and forgiveness in the case of grave post-baptismal sin. On that issue the Church of that day was seriously exercised, and remained so for another century and more. That was why so many were ready to attribute plenary inspiration to the revelation of the wider charity given through Hermas.

The place of writing of *The Shepherd* was undoubtedly Rome.[1] Unfortunately in regard to its date we have two quite definite, but quite irreconcilable pieces of evidence. Hermas himself (in a passage quoted p. 210; *Vis.* ii. 4, 3) alludes to a contemporary named Clement whose special business it is to communicate with churches in foreign cities. It is hard to believe that this is other than the Clement associated with the letter from Rome to the Corinthians discussed above. According to Eusebius, this Clement died in the fourth year of Trajan, not later, therefore, than A.D. 101. And this early date is borne out by the internal evidence of *The Shepherd* itself—a book which in every way reflects an extraordinarily primitive state of things. The problem, for example, of distinguishing between false and true prophets is still a live issue in the Church; and the monarchical episcopate does not yet exist at Rome. Indeed no one would ever have doubted that *The Shepherd*, or at any rate its earliest chapters, were written about A.D. 100, but for an explicit statement to the contrary in the fragmentary list of books of the Canon of the New Testament known as the *Mura-*

[1] Hermas has recently been the subject of important studies by American scholars (cf. *Harvard Theological Review*, Ap. 1925, Jan. 1927); the world of scholarship is eagerly awaiting the publication of the recently discovered papyrus of *The Shepherd*, now in the library at Michigan.

torianum. This document affirms that *The Shepherd* was written by Hermas

while his brother Pius, the bishop, was sitting in the chair of the Church of the city of Rome,

and Pius was Bishop of Rome *c.* A.D. 139–154.

It is a mistake to suppose a statement true, merely because it is *not* in Holy Writ! Yet scholars of the sharpest critical acumen have allowed themselves to be terrorised, so to speak, into the acceptance of a date which brings to confusion the history of the Church in Rome, on the evidence of an authority no better than the *Muratorianum.* If we scrutinise other statements characteristic of this document, it is at once clear that few, if any, of them rest on sound tradition. The *Muratorianum* is contemporary evidence as to the views on the Canon of the New Testament held in the Roman Church about A.D. 200—or perhaps a little earlier. For that it is an authority of the first importance. It is a very poor authority on everything else. Its account, for example, of the origin of the Fourth Gospel can only be styled ' a cock and bull story '. This, there is some reason to believe, was derived from the apocryphal *Acts of John* —which is not only a work of pure romance, but one which at that date was not even ancient. Again, the statement that Paul visited Spain may possibly be true ; but as it is known to have occurred in other apocryphal Acts of the same date, the author of the *Muratorianum* probably derived it from these. Lastly, he makes the astonishing affirmation that all the epistles of Paul were written subsequently to the Apocalypse.

Since, however, the work of which the *Muratorianum* is an extract was evidently composed in Rome, it may be urged that its. evidence carries weight when dealing with

The Shepherd—a work originally written in that church.
But in the particular case of Hermas, the author of the
Muratorianum has ' an axe to grind ' ; he wishes to
undercut the position of the Montanists, whose books
he later on expressly condemns.

But *The Shepherd* was written quite lately in our own times
by Hermas, while his brother Pius, the bishop, was sitting in the
chair of the Church of the city of Rome ; and therefore it ought
indeed to be read, but it cannot to the end of time be publicly
read in the Church to the people, either among the Prophets, *who
are complete in number*, or among the Apostles.

The point of this objection is that Hermas was a
prophet ; and the Montanists claimed for contemporary
prophets of their own a plenary inspiration on a level with
that of Scripture. The author of the *Muratorianum* holds
that the Canon of the Old Testament prophets is finally
closed ; [1] and that under the new dispensation plenary
inspiration is confined to Apostles. If he were to admit
a single exception to this rule by including Hermas in the
Canon (as some evidently wished to do), his whole case
against the Montanists would be gone. Origen, who
defends the inspiration of *The Shepherd*, expresses the
belief—doubtless a common one—that its author was
the Hermas saluted by St. Paul (Rom. xvi. 14). To the
opposition, therefore, it is vital to prove that Hermas did
not even belong to the Apostolic age. The name Hermas
was a common one ; no doubt Pope Pius had a brother so
named. How convenient, then, to ascribe to him the
authorship of *The Shepherd* ; for it thus became possible
to waive on one side its claim to authority, as having been
written ' quite lately in our own times '. The phrase ' in
our own times ', occurring in such a context is, of course,
the rhetorical exaggeration of the controversialist. It

---

[1] In some MSS. Hermas seems to have stood among the O.T. prophets.

cannot be pressed, as has been often done, to imply that
the author lived near enough to the time of Pius to be
well informed in the matter.   In any case such language
in early Christian usage allowed considerable elbow-
room.   Irenaeus, for instance, writing about A.D. 185,
says of the Apocalypse, ' It was seen not long ago, but
almost in our own generation, at the end of Domitian's
reign ' (*Adv. Haer.* v. 30. 3 ; Eus. *H.E.* iii. 18).
Domitian died A.D. 96.

Lightfoot thinks the *Muratorianum* is a fragment of an
early work of Hippolytus, A.D. 190.   Harnack—for reasons
which I find not quite convincing—rejects this view,
regarding it as a synodical or episcopal pronouncement
on the Canon.   Even so, since Hippolytus was the leading theologian at Rome at this date, he would be largely
responsible for the content of any such pronouncement.
Lightfoot argues with considerable plausibility that the
list of early popes in the ' Liberian Catalogue ' was taken
from another work of the same doughty controversialist.
It is very remarkable in this list that, while nothing but
the bare names of other early popes are given, to that
of Pius it is added that he was brother of Hermas
who wrote *The Shepherd.*   Hippolytus, then, took a very
special interest in the date of Hermas.   Now Hippolytus
would have heartily despised the *mere* historian, to whom
things like dates are of interest ; he was a man of war, a
malleus haereticorum, and he had a special aversion to the
Montanists.   He takes this opportunity of insisting once
more that Hermas does not belong to the Apostolic age.
Now Hippolytus has given us an account of the proceedings of his rival, Pope Callistus ; anyone who has
read this (I can only call it) ' spicy ' document, will
expect in Hippolytus, when a theological issue is at stake,
not accuracy but vehemence.

The author of the *Muratorianum* was not the only theologian who dreaded allowing too much authority to Hermas. Tertullian (though he had himself at one time accepted *The Shepherd* as inspired prophecy) tells us that more than one synod had rejected it. But synods do not condemn views unless they have sufficient support to be worth condemning. Clearly, the degree of authority to be allowed to *The Shepherd* was a matter of considerable controversy. Especially as many, who did not share the anti-Montanist bias of the *Muratorianum*, would be averse to accepting Hermas as an inspired writer on account of his, for that age lax, teaching as to post-baptismal sin, as well as of a Christological theory which, from the standpoint of later orthodoxy, is deplorable.

Nevertheless Hermas had eminent defenders. Irenaeus and Clement of Alexandria both quote him as ' scripture '. Irenaeus perhaps wrote thus before the attack on him was opened ; and it is just possible that Clement had not yet heard of it. But Origen must have known of it ; he had visited Rome and conferred with Hippolytus. Origen frequently quotes Hermas as an authority, and he lays it down—with the implication that he was aware of a contrary opinion—' in my opinion it is divinely inspired ', and goes on to suggest that it was written by the Hermas mentioned in St. Paul's epistle to the Romans. Origen attributed *The Shepherd* to the apostolic Hermas, because he valued it as inspired; the author of the *Muratorianum* attributes it to the brother of Pius, because he wished to reject that view. Neither statement is that of a dispassionate historical investigator. But there is this to be said in favour of Origen. Of all early Christian writers he was the one most interested in questions of the authenticity of sacred books, and he did approach these questions with the equipment and instincts of a scholar. If he attributed *The Shepherd* to a contemporary of St. Paul it must have been because he knew it had been read and valued in Alexandria for many generations ; and this could not have been the case if it was written by the brother of Pope Pius. On the contrary, his remarks on Hermas read like a definite protest, in defence of a book prized by Alexandrian tradition, against the recent Roman attack on its date and authorship—whether by Hippolytus himself, or by the synod or Pope responsible for the *Muratorianum*. The repute in which *The Shepherd* continued to be held is evidenced by the fact that, of the books which had for a long while hovered on the border line of acceptance into the Canon of the New Testament, *The Shepherd* and the *Didache* alone are thought worthy of mention by Athanasius—who speaks of them much as the XXXIX. Articles speak of the Apocrypha—in the Festal letter (p. 52) which finally settled the list of canonical books.

At any rate, the difficulties involved in accepting the Muratorian date are immense.

(1) Hermas cannot have written while his brother was Pope ; for it is quite clear from his book that he wrote before the monarchical episcopate was established in Rome. He refers to ' the presbyters ', ' the rulers ', ' the bishops '. But these are always mentioned in the plural, and all the references imply in the Church of Rome the same kind of collegiate rule by presbyter-bishops which is evidenced in the epistle of Clement. Yet there can be no reasonable doubt that by the time of Pius, alleged to be the author's own brother, there was at Rome a Bishop in the monarchical sense.

(2) Hermas opens with the words ' The master who reared me sold me to Rome '.[1] This rather looks as if

---

[1] ὁ θρέψας με πέπρακέ εἰς Ῥώμην.

he was a foundling-slave. It was a common practice to expose unwanted babies ; and it was a regular trade to collect and rear such for the slave market. But such a system obviously would rarely, if ever, admit of the foundling knowing the identity of his own parents— much less of a brother, if he had one.

(3) Hermas is commanded in a vision :

Write two booklets, and thou shalt send one to Clement and one to Grapte. So Clement shall send to the foreign cities ; for this is his duty (*Vis.* ii. 4, 3).

If we assume that the Clement named is he who wrote the letter which at once made him famous throughout the whole Church, this would fix Hermas as a contemporary of Clement. Now the early Church took visions seriously, and (unless Hermas was pronounced a false prophet) Clement would as a matter of course obey such an injunction,[1] and would without delay send the book to the principal churches. Here at once is an explanation for the world-wide circulation and universal repute which Hermas certainly enjoyed. It came to the other churches guaranteed as a genuine prophecy by the important Church of Rome. I would add that the early dating of Hermas gives added point to Ignatius' description of Rome as the church which instructed other churches ; for he would then have in mind the fact that, within his own memory, not only the letter of Clement, but also *The Shepherd*, had been officially circulated by the Roman Church.

(4) Irenaeus was certainly in Rome about A.D. 176. If the Muratorian date for Hermas is right, *The Shepherd* had been written within a generation. Yet Irenaeus quotes it with the words, ' Well doth the Scripture say '

---

[1] An example of the serious way in which injunctions in visions were taken is the election of Alexander as Bishop coadjutor of Jerusalem (Eus. *H.E.* vi. 11).

—and Irenaeus is far more sparing in his use of the term 'scripture' than Clement of Alexandria, whom I have already cited as doing the same.[1]

Harnack, followed by many scholars, realising the impossibility of accepting the statement that Hermas wrote while Pius was Pope, tries in effect to 'split the difference' between the earlier and later dates. His suggestion is that Hermas may have been by many years the elder of his brother Pius, and might thus be writing fifteen or twenty years *before* the younger brother became Pope. But the only reason why the author of the *Muratorianum* gives a date at all is to substantiate his contention that Hermas is a recent work written 'in our own times'. If, therefore, *The Shepherd* was written, not (as that writer says) while Pius was Pope, but twenty years or so before, he is making a grave misstatement in a point essential to his argument. It is much simpler to assume that his statement is totally false. Accuracy and veracity were virtues not widely practised in the Ancient World—they would be thought quixotic in dealing with political or theological adversaries. The things said about one another's private life and family antecedents by Demosthenes and Aeschines, the two leading statesmen of an age when Athens still was glorious, go beyond what would now be permissible in two costermongers who had quarrelled over a deal. Even at the present day there are areas of the earth's surface in which language is regarded less as a means of communication than as a weapon, and where politician or trader takes it for granted that

---

[1] There has been an immense amount of discussion as to whether Hermas used the *Didache* or *vice versa*. It would seem practically certain that Hermas used a recension of the *Two Ways*, possibly of the *Didache* as a whole. It is, however, possible that Hermas used a recension of the *Didache* which lacked the 'interpolation' (i³-ii¹) and that the interpolation in the *Didache* was made at a later date by someone who had read Hermas (Mand. ii. 4-6).

the other man is lying, until and unless the contrary is proved.

In politics compromise is often the best solution of a difficulty ; there is less to be said for it in chronology. To accept the Muratorian date for Hermas is to make nonsense of the documentary evidence and, as will appear shortly, of the early history of the Roman Church. Harnack's compromise neither meets the difficulties nor really saves the credit of the *Muratorianum*. Its statement about Hermas not only may, but must be, completely ignored. Pope Pius doubtless had a brother who bore the not at all uncommon name of Hermas ; but it was not he who wrote *The Shepherd*. If so, the attribution to him of *The Shepherd* would be exactly analogous to the procedure of Dionysius of Alexandria in regard to the Apocalypse ; he disliked its millennarianism and therefore attributed it, not to the Apostle John, but to a later personage who bore the same name.

It would seem, however, that only the first four *Visions* were written down, as the Sibyl bade, and circulated in the lifetime of Clement. (1) The word used βιβλαρίδιον, or ' booklet ', implies that the document would not fill a full-size roll (βίβλος) ; *The Shepherd* as a whole is quite half as long again as the Gospel of Matthew, which itself, so far as the information available suggests, would fill a roll of rather above the average length. (2) Considerations of internal evidence show a clearly marked division after the first four *Visions*. (3) The recently discovered Michigan Papyrus would appear never to have contained *Vis*. i.-iv., but to have begun with *Vision* v. There is thus MS. evidence that the latter portion of the work, viz. *Vision* v., the *Mandates* and the *Similitudes*, circulated as a separate volume.[1] And, if so, there is a presumption that the latter portion was originally published as a separate work, and at a different date. (4) The title of the book, *The Shepherd*, is slightly more easy to explain on the hypothesis that the second (and much the longer) part of the book circulated separately. For in this part supernatural communications come to Hermas from an angelic figure called the 'Shepherd'; but he first appears in *Vision* v. 1. There are reasons for supposing that the composition of the latter and longer part of the book was begun after a not inconsiderable interval, and it may have been spread over perhaps another dozen years or so.[2] Nevertheless, it is not safe to quote even the later chapters of Hermas as evidence for a period of later than A.D. 110.

CHURCH ORDER AT ROME

Clement's letter, being addressed to Corinth, is primarily evidence as to the state of things at Corinth ; but he writes throughout as if he took it for granted that the system of Church Order which prevailed—or rather, which he hoped to see restored—at Corinth was not other than that which existed at Rome. Again, there are two passages, which I shall shortly quote, where the authority of the regular ministry is based on its standing in a succession from the Apostles in a way which would be pointless unless such a succession existed in Rome as well as in Corinth. Nevertheless, but for the evidence of Hermas, it would be just possible —though not at all plausible—to maintain that Clement himself, who wrote the letter in the name of the Church

---

[1] Cf. Campbell Bonner in *Harvard Theological Review*, Apr. 1925.
[2] Cf. W. J. Wilson in *Harvard Theological Review*, Jan. 1927.

of Rome, occupied in that church the position of monarchical bishop. But, as has already been pointed out, it
is quite clear from Hermas that the Church of Rome,
clearly in the lifetime of Clement (*i.e. Vis.* i.-iv.), probably till the date of the latest portion of *The Shepherd*,
continued to be governed by a board of persons who are
spoken of alternatively as 'the Elders', or 'the Elders
that preside over the Church' (*Vis.* ii. 4), or as 'the
Rulers', or 'you that are Rulers of the Church and
occupy the chief seats'[1] (*Vis.* iii. 9. 7).

Clement reproaches the Church of Corinth for having
'made sedition against its presbyters' (1 Clem. 47. 6),
some of whom it has dispossessed of office. Several—
though not necessarily all—of the dispossessed presbyters held an office called by the technical name of
ἐπισκοπή or office of bishop.

And our Apostles knew through our Lord Jesus Christ that
there would be strife over the name of the bishop's office. [I
doubt that they knew it was going to last so long!] . . . For
it will be no light sin for us if we depose from the bishop's office
those who have offered the gifts (*i.e.* the Eucharist) unblameably
and holily.[2] Blessed are those presbyters who have gone before
. . . for they have no fear lest anyone should remove them from
their established place (1 Clem. xliv. 4-5).

Again, those who have usurped their place are exhorted to give way, if and when required, to the end that

the flock of Christ be at peace with its *duly appointed*
(καθισταμένων) presbyters (1 Clem. liv. 2).

---

[1] In Hermas the actual word ἐπίσκοπος occurs twice, and on both occasions
in the plural; but it is used in an interpretation of a vision symbolising the
Church Universal, and the context is such as to leave it grammatically an open
question whether in any particular local church one or more persons bore this
name (*Vis.* iii. 5. 1; *Sim.* ix. 27. 2). But Clement's evidence is decisive that
more than one person bore the name at Corinth. They are called "shepherds"
(*Sim.* ix. 31, 5 f.).

[2] Lightfoot, I think by a slip, slightly mistranslates; at any rate, I follow
Harnack in taking τῆς ἐπισκοπῆς with ἀποβάλωμεν rather than with τὰ δῶοα.

But the body of presbyters in its corporate capacity constituted the ruling authority in the Church.

Ye therefore who laid the foundation of the sedition, submit yourselves unto the presbyters and receive chastisement unto repentance (lvii. 1).

' Presbyter ' would seem to be a term connoting not so much office as status. Among those who enjoy the status of presbyter are included a class of episcopoi, and (possibly) also the deacons. At any rate, as in Philippians, bishops and deacons are the names of two kinds of officers. These two offices are spoken of by Clement in a way which excludes the possibility that presbyters is the name of a third and intermediate office.

The Apostles, preaching everywhere in country and town, appointed their first-fruits, when they had proved them by the Spirit, to be bishops and deacons unto them that should believe (xlii. 4).

He goes on to argue that the existence of these two orders in the Church was a fulfilment of Old Testament prophecy—again in a way which excludes there being a third order of presbyters.

It has been written concerning Bishops and Deacons from very ancient times ; for thus saith the Scripture in a certain place, I will appoint their Bishops in righteousness and their Deacons in faith (cf. Isa. lx. 17 in the LXX.).

There is nothing to call forth surprise in this evidence that in Rome and Corinth a system still prevailed not very far removed from that established by Paul. That system prevailed at Philippi for some time longer. It is quite clear from the letter which Polycarp wrote to that church, A.D. 115, sending them copies of the letters of Ignatius, that there was as yet no single Bishop at Philippi. Polycarp himself is mentioned as Bishop of Smyrna, and therefore in writing to Philippi he avoids the word episcopos ; but the persons in authority are addressed collectively as presbyters.

But the new and important thing about the early Roman Church is, not the names or the functions of its officers, but the conception of the nature and source of their authority. Whatever power in the way of personal prestige may have belonged to Clement, there is not a word to hint that he contemplated at Rome or elsewhere any other system than rule by a college of persons alternatively spoken of as episcopoi and presbyters. But, whereas in the *Didache* the episcopoi are represented as *elected* by the local congregation, Clement affirms that they were originally *appointed by Apostles*, who made provision for a regular succession. The principle of Apostolic succession as the basis and rationale of the authority of the ministry is clearly and emphatically laid down—only it appears to be what we should call a collegiate or ' presbyterian ' as opposed to an individual or ' episcopal ' succession.

The Apostles received the Gospel for us from the Lord Jesus Christ ; Jesus Christ was sent forth from God. So then Christ is from God and the Apostles are from Christ . . . They appointed their first-fruits, when they had proved them by the Spirit, to be bishops and deacons, etc. (xlii. 1-4).

The Apostolic commission is still further elaborated a few paragraphs later—though it is important to note that it is qualified by the need for the consent of the whole Church.

For this cause, therefore, having received complete fore-knowledge, they appointed the aforesaid persons, and afterwards they provided a continuance, that if these should fall asleep,

other approved men (δεδοκιμασμένοι ἄνδρες) should succeed to
their ministration. Those, therefore, who were appointed by
them, or afterward by other men of repute (ἐλλόγιμοι ἄνδρες)
with the consent of the whole Church, and have ministered
unblameably to the flock of Christ in lowliness of mind, peacefully
and with all modesty, and for long time have borne a good report
with all—these men we consider are being unjustly thrust out
from their ministration (xliv. 2-3).

I must confess that I am unable to regard as other
than special pleading the arguments of those who
interpret the phrase ἐλλόγιμοι ἄνδρες as implying the
existence at that date of persons qualified to exercise
technically episcopal functions but unattached to any
definite church. They are obviously the same as the
δεδοκιμασμένοι ἄνδρες, i.e. 'approved men' duly ordained
by the Apostles or their successors.

For the people to support irregular, self-appointed
leaders is disobedience to God.

Therefore it is right and proper, brethren, that we should be
obedient unto God, rather than follow those who in arrogance
and unruliness have set themselves up as leaders in abominable
jealousy (xiv. 1).

The necessity of a regular ministry and the authority
due to it is further enforced by two illustrations.

First, the splendid discipline of the Roman Army is
held up as a model for imitation.

Let us mark the soldiers that are enlisted under our rulers,
how exactly, how readily, how submissively, they execute the
orders given them. All are not prefects, nor rulers of thousands,
nor rulers of hundreds, nor rulers of fifties, and so forth ; but each
man in his own rank executeth the orders given by the king and
the governors (xxxvii. 2-3).

Secondly, he appeals to the analogy of the Divine

ordinance in the Old Testament for a worship carried out by an appointed hierarchy.

Now, the offerings and ministrations He commanded to be performed with care, and not to be done rashly or in disorder, but at fixed times and seasons. . . . For unto the High Priest his proper services have been assigned, and to the Priests their proper office is appointed, and upon the Levites their proper ministrations are laid. The layman is bound by the layman's ordinances (xl. 2-5).

He develops this analogy with great elaboration. He can even detect an illuminating parallel between the knowledge possessed by Moses that there would be dissension among the tribes in regard to the Priesthood—brought to an end by the budding of Aaron's rod—and the knowledge which he ascribes to the Apostles that there would be strife ' over the name of the bishop's office '. In a previous lecture (p. 156) I have pointed out how readily the passage last quoted lends itself to a mon-episcopal interpretation of the nature and function of the Christian ministry that goes further than anything which, so far as we can judge, was actually in the mind of Clement when he wrote—and which may have been so interpreted by Ignatius.

Since Clement wrote little more than thirty years after the death of Paul, and at the date of writing was doubtless one of the senior members of the church, his statement that the existing college of presbyters was descended from that of Apostolic times by a method of co-optation by those already in office (subject to the consent of the people) is probably correct—so far as the Churches of Rome and Corinth are concerned. Paul does seem to have appointed colleges of episcopoi and deacons, and to have attached a growing importance to their functions ; and it is also clear from Polycarp's

Epistle to the Philippians, that in the Pauline Church of Philippi the system of two orders only—presbyters and deacons—still survived in A.D. 115. What Clement does is, not to invent facts, but to harden a practice really primitive into the basis of a theory of authority.

But there is one feature in the situation at Rome which must not be overlooked. *At Rome the prophet is definitely subordinated to the regular ministry.* Hermas is admittedly a prophet; yet it is only gradually and tentatively that he is admitted to a seat on the Elders' bench; and he always speaks of the Rulers as if he himself were not reckoned in their number. He has a vision (M. xi.) which embodies in effect a discussion of the problem how the true prophet is to be distinguished from the false—a standing difficulty, we have seen (p. 147 ff.), all over the Christian world at this period. Who is to apply the test he does not say explicitly ; but he doubtless means it to be applied by the persons, said to be ' faithful ', who at the opening of the vision are ' seated on a bench '. These obviously represent the board of Elders who, as in early pictures in the Catacombs, sat facing the assembled church. This conception of the relationship between the regular ministry and persons possessed of spiritual gifts is the more remarkable from the contrast it shows between the state of things at Rome and that implied by the *Didache*. In the church from which the *Didache* issued (p. 150) it is taken for granted that a prophet claims precedence over the episcopoi, and that if a prophet is present he will normally celebrate the Eucharist—the prophet in that case being allowed, or even expected, to extemporise a prayer of thanksgiving in lieu of the fixed liturgical prayer prescribed for the regular minister.

In Clement's letter there are certain hints which suggest that in the disturbance at Corinth the question of the claims of the Prophet as against those of the regular ministry was at least one of the issues. True, Clement nowhere mentions the existence of Prophets. But we must remember that to do so would have placed him in an awkward dilemma. He must either have admitted that they were true Prophets or have denounced them as false. To do the latter would have offended the section at Corinth who were inclined to support them—and Clement's purpose was to reconcile the factions at Corinth. To admit that they were Prophets would be to weaken the case of their opponents, whose cause Clement is supporting. It was thus safer to avoid using the word Prophet. But what Clement says to, or about, the leaders of the party who had dislodged the established ministry, implies that they claimed to be persons of superior spiritual gifts and enlightenment. They are described as persons ' who in arrogance and unruliness have set themselves up as leaders ' (xiv. 1). It is pointed out that, if any individual has any special spiritual gift, humility is only the more incumbent on him.

Let a man be faithful, let him be able to expound a deep saying, let him be wise in discernment of words . . . so much the more ought he to be lowly in mind in proportion as he seemeth to be the greater (xlviii. 5-6).

Again, we are told that regularly-appointed ministers who had served, apparently for many years, without reproach, had been thrust out from their ministration, λειτουργία, and from an office of which a chief function was the offering of the Eucharist (xliv. 3-4). Obviously they must have been thrust out in order to make room for persons deemed by some to have superior qualifications for offering the Eucharist; and in the *Didache* it is clear that a Prophet was, in some churches, regarded as having such. In Clement's letter, then, if we look below the surface, we see Rome already taking a decided stand in the age-long conflict between the Prophet and the Priest.

MON-EPISCOPACY AT ROME

But if at the date when Clement and Hermas were written the government of the Church of Rome was of a type which might not inappropriately be called 'presbyterian', we are compelled to attempt some further investigation of the origin of the monarchical episcopate in that church.

When Hegesippus came to Rome (before A.D. 166), he was able to draw up what he believed to be an authentic list of Bishops of Rome from the beginning until his own time. We must ask, then, is it possible to reconcile the combined evidence of Clement and Hermas, which points to a rule by a college of presbyters, and the monarchical form of government implied in a list of bishops?

Starting with the reflection that at Rome the place where Christians meet for worship is regularly (so three times, in Hermas) called a 'synagogue', the hypothesis presents itself that in Rome the organisation of the primitive Christian community was modelled more nearly than that of some other churches on that of a Jewish Synagogue. The Synagogue was governed by a college of elders, one of whom, styled ἀρχισυνάγωγος, or Ruler of the Synagogue, was in charge of the actual conduct of worship, though in other respects he does not seem to have been superior to his colleagues. The special sanctity attached by Christians to the Eucharist would emphasise the importance of the president in the public worship. If a man of any practical capacity, he might soon become a sort of permanent chairman of the college. But in times of crisis, committee rule works badly—and, for the Roman Church, crisis began under Nero. Indeed, in the capital of the Empire, under the very eye of a central government, the Church could never have been in an easy position. Inevitably, the chairman of the college would insensibly develop into a kind of Managing Director of the Board, especially as the whole tendency of the age was in the direction of autocratic rule. The rapidity of such a development would depend on the strength of character, efficiency, and personal ambition of the presiding presbyters of early times.

Power is most easily achieved by pretending not to want it. At Rome that secret had been divulged to all who had the wit to learn it by Augustus—at home, ever careful to affect the title ' first citizen ', or ' tribune-for-life ', even while consenting to divine honours in the East. It may be that for practical purposes Clement himself held a position of pre-eminence the reality of which was more clearly perceived by outside churches. There is some evidence that at Rome some generations later the ' bishop ' still professed to be nothing more than *primus inter pares* among his colleagues. So at least one would infer from Irenaeus' letter to Victor, protesting against his threatened excommunication of the churches of Asia on the question of the date of Easter (Eus. *H.E.* 5. 24). It looks as if, as late as A.D. 191, the Roman bishops still officially spoke of themselves as ' presbyters '. That Victor's own status, and that of the Bishop of Rome long before his time, was monarchical cannot be doubted ; yet Irenaeus uses the title ' presbyter ' three times (not once, which might be accidental) of Victor's precursors in the Papal chair, and by implication of Victor himself. Irenaeus' aim is to conciliate Victor ; but it would not conciliate a bishop to address him as ' Presbyter ', unless that were, in this particular instance, an official title. The greatest thought of Gregory the Great was the self-chosen style, *Servus servorum Dei* ; but thrust upon him by a provincial bishop, he might have liked it less.

Ignatius, in his letter to the Roman Church, does not mention the bishop ; but that would only prove that there was none if he *did* mention the presbyters and deacons. Actually he salutes the church as a whole, without mentioning any of its officers. Now it is not too much to say of Ignatius that he had episcopacy ' on the brain ' ; to him ' without the Bishop there is not even the name of a Church ' ; he speaks of bishops as established ' throughout the world ' ; and he salutes the Church of Rome as the model of a Christian Church. Such enthusiastic language in him is hard to understand if there was as yet no bishop at Rome. And though he might have misconceived the position of earlier bishops like Clement, Ignatius could hardly have been under a complete delusion as to the state of things in Rome in his own day.

(1) By the time of Ignatius, then, there must certainly have been at Rome some one person who, whatever his powers in regard to the other presbyters of his own church, was at least the head of it in the sense of being its official representative in dealing with external churches—that much I think we must infer to account for the enthusiastic admiration expressed by Ignatius for Rome as a model for other churches. And, that presumption granted, we are entitled to interpret certain infinitesimal pieces of evidence in the light of this presumption,

although apart from it they are not definite enough to carry much weight.

(2) Hermas, or rather the lady who appears to him in a vision, severely blames the rulers of the Church for their divisions.

Now therefore I say unto you that are Rulers of the Church, and that occupy the chief seats . . . Look ye . . . lest these divisions of yours deprive you of your life. How is it that ye wish to instruct the elect of the Lord, while ye yourselves have no instruction ? Instruct one another therefore, and have peace among yourselves (*Vis.* iii. 9. 7-9).

He returns to the subject again later, and makes it clear that the dissensions were due to competition between persons who, though faithful and virtuous, were jealous of one another about first places and a ' certain honour ' (*Sim.* viii. 7. 4). The second reference comes in a prophecy belonging to the later part of Hermas' career, and may be as late as A.D. 110. Thus it is not improbable that ' the honour ' in question, which was the cause of dispute, concerned either the increasing power claimed by, or the next succession to, the Presidency of the Board of Presbyters.

(3) Irenaeus in his letter to Victor, on the ' Quartodeciman ' dispute, reminds him of the policy of ' those Presbyters who governed the Church . . . over which you now preside ', and names them one by one *from Soter back to Xystus*. Ought we to infer from this that names earlier than Xystus in the list of the Roman bishops are names of presbyters who were presiding officers, rather than governors, of the church ? Is it possible that Xystus may have played at Rome a part in the establishment of a definitely monarchical episcopate comparable to that played by John the Elder at Ephesus, and by Ignatius at Antioch ?

This question I proceed to investigate in the light of a brilliant suggestion by G. la Piana.[1] He argues, to my mind convincingly, that this dispute between Rome and the churches of Asia Minor (as to the date of celebrating Easter and of the previous fast) originated from the existence *in Rome* of a group of Christians from Asia who, though permanently resident there, insisted on still observing the Asian custom in this regard. Circumstances at Rome in the second century—when every kind of heresy was competing for recognition, or rather dominance—made the problem of church unity exceptionally acute. Hence the existence of a group of Christians in Rome who insisted on keeping fast and celebrating the greatest of all the festivals at a different time from the rest of the brethren, constituted what might well seem a dangerous anomaly. The visit of Polycarp to Rome, A.D. 155—referred to by Irenaeus in his letter to Victor—was due, probably, to an appeal made to him by the Asian Christians in Rome against an attempt of Anicetus to compel them to conform to the Roman usage. In the result, Anicetus did not feel able to prohibit a practice which so venerable a person as Polycarp affirmed to be Apostolic. He therefore consented to continue a practice which had been that of his predecessors as far back as Xystus : that is to say, while not himself observing or commending the Asian custom, he did not treat it as ground for excommunication, but 'sent the Eucharist to those from the communities (or dioceses, παροικίαι) who observed it' (Iren., *ap.* Eus. *H.E.* v. 24, 14). This 'sending of the Eucharist', la Piana urges, does not mean (as heretofore has been supposed) that the consecrated elements were sent to churches in distant Asia Minor. It is a reference,

---

[1] *Harvard Theological Review*, July 1925, p. 213 ff.

in point of fact the earliest, to a custom, apparently peculiar to Rome, which lasted there till after A.D. 417. A fragment of the Eucharistic Bread consecrated by the Bishop, technically known as the *fermentum*, was sent every Sunday to the celebrating priest in each of the principal churches of Rome, to be by him mixed with the bread which he would himself consecrate. The purpose of this custom is obvious. In a large city like Rome it was impossible for all Christians to attend the Sunday Eucharist of the Bishop; but, in every church to which the *fermentum* was taken, the Eucharist there celebrated could be thought of as being materially, so to speak, as well as spiritually, the Bishop's Eucharist.

If la Piana is right, as I feel sure he is, then, on the evidence of Irenaeus, this practice must have been initiated by Xystus. We may surmise that it was primarily devised to deal with the exceptionally difficult case of those Asian Christians who, though recognised as orthodox, insisted in certain respects on preserving their own usages, but was extended to other churches in the city. Thus, from the time of Xystus to that of Soter, the Asians living in Rome formed a kind of 'Uniat' church in that city.[1] It was this state of things that Victor wished to end when he excommunicated those who declined to conform to the Roman usage—thereby precipitating the open breach with the churches of Asia

---

[1] Irenaeus, it will be noted, omits to mention Eleutherus, the bishop who intervened between Soter and Victor. We may surmise that the trouble which came to a head under Victor began in the time of Eleutherus. There is evidence of an outbreak of Gnosticism about this time which can be definitely connected with Asian Christians in Rome. The Florinus whom Irenaeus reproached for falling into Gnostic error was at Rome in Victor's time; and he was, or had been, a Presbyter who had once been a disciple of Polycarp; while Eusebius (*H.E.* v. 14) mentions a certain Blastus as forming a schism in Rome at this time, and it appears from Pseudo-Tertullian (*Adv. om. haer.* viii.) that he was a Quartodeciman—and therefore presumably belonged to the Asian group. If the Asian group was in danger of becoming a nursery of Gnostics, Victor's action in regard to the Quartodeciman issue was less uncalled for than is usually supposed.

Minor, which called forth notable letters from Irenaeus and Polycrates of Ephesus.

But the practice of sending the *fermentum* is one that carries with it large implications. If it was begun by Xystus, it means that from his time onward participation in the Bishop's Eucharist becomes the essential test of full communion with the Church. Inevitably the Bishop, as the recognised centre and symbol of church union, would become more and more the arbiter of orthodoxy, and thus the supreme fount of authority.

In this connection, consider the following passage from Ignatius :

Shun divisions, as the beginning of evils . . . let no man do aught to things pertaining to the Church apart from the Bishop. Let that be held a valid Eucharist which is under the Bishop or one to whom he shall have committed it. Wheresoever the Bishop shall appear, there let the people be ; even as where Jesus may be, there is the catholic church. It is not lawful, apart from the Bishop, either to baptize or to hold a love-feast (Smyrn. viii. 1 ff.).

I venture to put forward the hypothesis that the policy of Xystus, attested by Irenaeus in regard to Christians from Asia, marks the beginning of a new epoch at Rome as regards insistence on the unique position of the Bishop—and that this is directly due to the influence of Ignatius himself. For if I am correct in the suggestion which I make (p. 276) as to the date of the martyrdom of Ignatius, he will have reached Rome a few months later than the appointment of Xystus (whose tenure is ordinarily dated A.D. 115–125)[1] as ' Bishop ', or, perhaps, President of the presbytery at Rome.

On these assumptions, let us envisage the situation at Rome on the arrival there of Ignatius at the very end

---

[1] Cf. Lightfoot, *Clement*, i. p. 340.

of the year A.D. 115. Ignatius had sent on ahead of him
a letter which would have reached Rome a fortnight or
so before his own arrival. His letter to the Roman
Church is a striking document; it made a profound
impression on the mind of the early Church at large,
becoming, as Lightfoot puts it, ‘in some sense a *vade-
mecum* of martyrs in the subsequent ages’.[1] His name has
found its way—at what date we do not know—into the
list of martyrs daily enumerated in the Canon of the Mass.
At once on his arrival the leaders of the Roman Church
would have waited upon him in prison; there is no
reason to suppose that they would have been allowed
less freedom of personal communication with him than
were the bishops of the churches of the cities in Asia
Minor which he had already passed through on his way
to Rome. Recall the personality of the man, aglow with
religious exaltation as martyrdom drew near; picture its
effect upon minds already deeply moved by his letter—
his lightest word would seem full of consequences tremendous. And of what did he speak? When a man
has an *idée fixe*, we know for certain of what he will
speak whenever the slightest occasion presents itself for
doing so. We may be quite sure that, in every interview
he had with the leading Christians at Rome, he reiterated
with passionate conviction what is the main theme of
all his other letters—the supreme necessity of concen-
trating power in the hands of a single bishop.

Remember also that Ignatius was a prophet—and to
the early Church, once a prophet was accepted as a true
prophet and no impostor, his words came with the
authority of the voice of God. Now supposing Ignatius
discovered, as he doubtless soon would, that, in the
matter of the centralised authority of the Bishop, Rome

---

[1] For evidence, see Lightfoot, *Ignatius*, ii. p. 186 f.

was not quite the model church he had believed ; psychologically it would be almost inevitable that, in this
supreme emotional crisis, the prophetic frenzy would
come upon him, and he would speak ' in the spirit '.
And what would he have said ? He has himself told us
how, only a few weeks earlier, at Philadelphia, under
control of the prophetic spirit,

I cried out, when I was among you ; I spoke with a loud voice,
with God's own voice, ' Give ye heed to the bishop and the
presbytery and deacons ' (Philad. vii. 2).

Ignatius spoke as a prophet, and he spoke to a church
already strongly imbued with the Roman sense of discipline. Is it likely that his exhortations fell upon un-
heeding ears ? And, this message spoken, he was led
out to the Colosseum to die a martyr. That would
have lent his message double power.

He had prayed, he had worked, he had written, he
had fought, to strengthen everywhere the Bishop's power ;
and he had longed for the martyr's palm. But he had
accomplished more, and other, than his heart's desire, if
—on that day when he realised his dream to be ' God's
wheat, ground by the teeth of wild beasts '—the Papacy
was born.

As in the Empire, so in the Church, there was constant
interaction between the capitals of East and West.
Rome sent the legions to Antioch ; in the result, deplored
by patriotic satirists, ' the Orontes drained into the
Tiber '—bringing, amid a wash of Eastern cults, the
Christian Church. From Rome came the Gospel of
Mark ; it came back again from Syria vastly enriched,
and with the Apostolic name of ' Matthew '—and that
enrichment includes the words which give the Keys to
Peter. From Rome came the letter of Clement, bringing

to Antioch the idea of Roman discipline in the ordering
of the Christian Church ; there came back the fervour
of Ignatius which, if I am right, gave Rome a line of
bishops ready later on to make a grander claim upon
those Keys.

On the balance of exchange Rome was not the loser.

VII

ALEXANDRIA AND THE PATRIARCHATES

SYNOPSIS

THE DEARTH OF EVIDENCE

ABOUT A.D. 180 Pantaenus founded the Catechetical School at Alexandria, which was to be the nursery of the creative minds of Greek theology—Clement, Origen, Athanasius, Cyril. But before this date the dearth of evidence for this church is remarkable.

Hence, to assign to Alexandria the 'Epistle of Barnabas' and the 'Second Epistle of Clement' is to fill an important gap in Church history.

Neither Barnabas nor 2 Clement claims to be by the authors with whose names tradition connects them. They are not pseudonymous, but merely anonymous. The author of 2 Clement should therefore be called, not 'Pseudo-Clement', but 'Deutero-Clement'.

THE EPISTLE OF BARNABAS

Three reasons for connecting 'Barnabas' with Alexandria.

The exact date is disputable; but it must be somewhere between the first destruction of Jerusalem (A.D. 70) and the second (A.D. 132).

DEUTERO-CLEMENT

Discussion of the theory of Harnack, that Deutero-Clement emanated from Rome, and that of Lightfoot, that it was written at Corinth. On examination both theories completely break down.

But a strong case can be made out for connecting the document with Alexandria. This summarised under four main heads.

CHURCH ORDER AT ALEXANDRIA

The author of Barnabas would seem to belong to the order of Teachers. After high flights of allegorical exegesis he ends on the simple moral teaching of 'The Two Ways'—another recension of that found in the *Didache*. This emphasis on the primary place of ethics in the Christian life characteristic of the Catholic Church as against the Gnostics.

Harnack's theory that Deutero-Clement held the office of Reader—an office which (at any rate in Syria) ranked next after that of Presbyter and implied the duty of interpreting, as well as of reading, Scripture.

Alternative theory of Dr. Vernon Bartlet that the writer of Deutero-Clement was President of the Board of Presbyters. The case for this theory stated.

The theory would fit in with the evidence that well into the third century the Bishop of Alexandria was elected from among themselves by the twelve Presbyters and consecrated Patriarch by them.

Until Demetrius there was no Bishop in Egypt except the Bishop of Alexandria. Demetrius, and his successor Heraclas, appointed Bishops in other cities. These naturally remained dependent on the Bishop of Alexandria, who thus at one step attained the position of Patriarch.

THE PATRIARCHATES

With the death of the Apostles and the destruction of Jerusalem the Church lost its natural centre—especially as the fact that it was regarded by the State as a more or less illegal association, made impossible the calling of large Synods, much less an Oecumenical Council.

Of necessity, therefore, the decision of most important questions was left in the hands of the churches of the greater capitals—supplemented by conferences of a more or less secret and informal character between representatives of the Great Churches.

This explains the exceptional authority accorded to the Patriarchs of Rome, Antioch, and Alexandria, and the authority in their own provinces of the Metropolitans of smaller capitals like Ephesus or Caesarea.

The position of the Patriarch of Alexandria has a special explanation ; but the position accorded to the Apostolic sees—Rome, Antioch, and (in the second century) Ephesus—goes back to sub-Apostolic times. It is implicit in Clement's letter to the Corinthians, and in the special courtesy shown by Ignatius to the Churches of Rome and Ephesus, and assumed by him to be due to himself as representing the Church of Antioch. Thus, to speak paradoxically, the office of Archbishop would seem more primitive than that of Bishop.

VII

ALEXANDRIA AND THE PATRIARCHATES

THE DEARTH OF EVIDENCE

OF the early history, at any rate in outline, of the Church in Syria, Asia Minor, and Rome, a clear view can be derived from the New Testament and from the writings of those Apostolic Fathers of which we have so far made use. By contrast the early history of the Church of Alexandria is darkness itself. There is a tradition that it was founded by the evangelist Mark; but this first appears, A.D. 311, in Eusebius, with the significant quali-fication, ' it is said that . . .' (*H.E.* ii. 16). The tradi-tion is ignored—rather curiously, as Duchesne has pointed out, if it be authentic—in a discussion of the career of Mark, as given in the New Testament, by Dionysius of Alexandria (*ap.* Eus. *H.E.* vii. 25). And there is no hint of it in the by no means exiguous surviving writings of Clement and Origen, themselves members of this church. In the *Clementine Homilies* Barnabas appears as the founder of the Church in Alexandria. And though this is a work of fiction, and in no sense authentic history, it does afford negative evidence that, *c.* A.D. 220, Syrian tradition did *not* attribute that distinction to Mark.

A letter of Hadrian to the consul Servianus (he was consul A.D. 134), of which the genuineness is disputed, in a satirical allusion to the medley of religions in Egypt, mentions Christianity as one of them.[1] The Gnostic Valentinus, c. A.D. 130, and Carpocrates a little later, started off to teach in Alexandria. The recently discovered *Epistle of the Apostles*[2]—which, if the Coptic text is correct (§ 17), must be dated before A.D. 150—is thought by some scholars to be of Egyptian origin. But we do not reach the firm ground of definite historical evidence until the statement by Clement of Alexandria that Pantaenus founded in Alexandria, apparently about A.D. 180, the Catechetical School, which was destined to be the nursery of so many great philosophical theologians. Immediately thereafter begins the sequence—including Clement, Origen, Athanasius, Cyril—of the creative minds in the history of Greek theology.

During the period of darkness there is reason to think that the Church of Alexandria developed on relatively independent lines. It was characterised by width of outlook, and a more tolerant attitude than other churches towards Greek thought and even Gnostic speculation. We find also that the line between canonical and uncanonical books of Scripture is drawn less rigidly here than elsewhere. Apocryphal Gospels, too, the *Gospel according to the Hebrews*, and a *Gospel according to the Egyptians*—extracts from one of which probably survive in the Oxyrhynchus Logia—are often quoted, not indeed as canonical, but as reputable, authorities.

The writings of Clement of Alexandria, intellectually the most latitudinarian of the Saints, have an added interest if regarded as the bridge over which the thought of Alexandria passed on its way from the too gnosticising liberalism of the second century to the highly cultured

---

[1] See below, p. 254. The text is given in full and the genuineness defended by Lightfoot, *Ignatius*, i. p. 480 f.

[2] Dr. James includes a translation of this in his *Apocryphal New Testament*. He assigns to Egypt the *Preaching of Peter* (frags.). Lightfoot and Harmer (*op. cit.* p. 488 f.) suggest Pantaenus as author of *Ep. Diognetus*, xi.-xii.

orthodoxy of the third. To Clement the instructed
Christian is the only real Gnostic. He is the possessor of
a ' gnosis '—a knowledge, or, perhaps better, wisdom—
which includes, but far transcends, the best which the
divinely given faculty of human reason has heretofore
achieved. He grasps Reality, for he not only securely
' apprehends the First Cause ', but can also clearly define
Good and Evil and comprehend the teaching of the
Lord. He is calm in danger, firm against the lures of
pleasure, frugal and serious, making ' knowledge ' his
chief pursuit. He is a student of music, mathematics,
astronomy, logic, and metaphysics—all of which are
means of elevating the mind from earth to heaven—and,
' studying ever divine things ', he ascends ' to the knowledge of Him who created them '.

But [he goes on] the generality are as frightened of Greek
philosophy as are children of hobgoblins—afraid that it will run
away with them. But if their faith—I could not call it knowledge—is such that it will be upset by specious argument, let it be
upset ; and therefore the more let them confess that they are not
[persons] likely to get hold of (ἔξειν) Truth, for Truth, it is said, is
invincible, falsehood is ever overthrown (cf. *Strom.* vi., ix.-x.
78-81).

The discipline of philosophy was given to the Greeks, as
the law was given to the Jews, as the schoolmaster to
bring them to Christ (*Strom.* i. v. 28).

Just because of the remarkable lack of information
about the early history of such an important church, a
special interest (quite apart from the question of the
Church Order which they imply) attaches to the possibility
of assigning to Alexandria two early documents which so
far have not been discussed, though usually classed under
the general name of 'the Apostolic Fathers'—the Epistle
of Barnabas and the ' Second Epistle ' of Clement to the

Corinthians. Both titles are misleading; but in neither case are they due to the original authors.

(1) Barnabas is a homily sent as a letter. It makes no claim to be the work of the Apostle; the writer's name was doubtless known to its earliest readers, but, like the name of the author of Hebrews, the epistle to Diognetus, and many other ancient writings, it has been forgotten. Or, if his name was actually Barnabas, then he never supposed his readers would confuse him with the Apostle.

(2) The 'second epistle' of Clement is not an epistle at all, but a homily. In the MSS. it follows the genuine (so-called 'first') epistle of Clement of Rome, which we have discussed in previous lectures, and is attributed to the same author. But no scholar now accepts it as the work of this Clement; and the document itself makes no pretence of being by him. I propose, therefore, to speak of him, not as Pseudo-Clement—which might imply that he professed to be Clement—but as Deutero-Clement. The unfortunate student of Church history will then the more easily distinguish him both from Clement of Rome (A.D. 96) and the later Clement of Alexandria (A.D. 200).

I labour the point that we are not here dealing with pseudonymous documents, which are often difficult of interpretation because they purport to be of authorship other than they are. It is important to grasp that we have here authentic documents of which the authorship —and, therefore, also the date and place of writing— *happens* to have been forgotten.

The Epistle of 'Barnabas'

For believing that the epistle of Barnabas was written by an Alexandrian there are three main reasons.

(1) The epistle exhibits in the most extreme form the

application to the interpretation of the Old Testament of
the method of allegory, which in Alexandria had been
developed, more especially by Philo, to a degree of
elaboration unparalleled elsewhere. I give as a specimen
an exegetical effort of which (as appears from the concluding sentence) the author was particularly proud.

Learn therefore, children of love, concerning all things abundantly, that Abraham, who first appointed circumcision, looked
forward in the spirit unto Jesus, when he circumcised, having
received the ordinances of three letters. For the scripture saith :
'And Abraham circumcised of his household eighteen males and
three hundred'. What then was the knowledge given unto him ?
Understand ye that He saith the 'eighteen' first, and then after
an interval, 'three hundred'. In the 'eighteen' I stands for
ten, H for eight [i.e. in the Greek system of notation in which
numerals are represented by letters of the alphabet]. Here thou
hast Jesus (IHΣOΥΣ). And because the cross in the T was to have
grace, He saith also 'three hundred'. So He revealeth Jesus in
the two letters, and in the remaining one the cross. He who
placed within us the innate gift of His covenant knoweth ; no
man hath ever learnt from me a more genuine word ; but I know
that ye are worthy (Barn. ix. 7-9).

(2) The epistle is quoted by Clement of Alexandria
as 'scripture' and is attributed by him to 'the apostle',
or 'the prophet', Barnabas, whom he identifies with the
companion of Paul. Origen also cites it as 'the catholic
epistle of Barnabas'. But elsewhere in the Church it
is practically ignored; and by Eusebius it is not even
reckoned in the list of books 'disputed though they are
well known and approved by many', but definitely among
those classed as 'spurious'.

(3) The two great fourth-century MSS. ℵ B seem to
preserve the text of the New Testament in the form
specifically characteristic of Alexandria.[1] The end of

---

[1] Cf. *The Four Gospels*, p. 54 ff.

B is missing ; but in א Barnabas follows immediately after the Apocalypse. In no other MS. is it associated with the canonical books.

There are therefore solid reasons for connecting the epistle with Alexandria ; and there are none for connecting it with any other church.

About the connection of Barnabas with Alexandria scholars are generally agreed. In regard to its date there is a wide difference of opinions. It contains a reference to the destruction of Jerusalem by Titus, A.D. 70, but does not refer to that under Hadrian, A.D. 132. Within these limits a plausible case can be made out for more than one date ; all depends on which interpretation of certain obscure references a particular critic may prefer. Lightfoot would place the epistle before A.D. 79 ; Gebhardt and Harnack incline to a date about A.D. 120.

DEUTERO-CLEMENT

In Deutero-Clement we have another document of which it is difficult to determine the date, but not, I hold, the place of origin. Lightfoot would put it between A.D. 120–140; Gebhardt and Harnack, A.D. 130–160.

The Alexandrian origin of Deutero-Clement has not been recognised by the great editors. Lightfoot assigns it to Corinth, Harnack to Rome. The view that it originated in Alexandria occurred to me spontaneously some years ago ; it was not till after the actual delivery of these lectures that I made the discovery—which fortified my confidence in the correctness of my view— that it had been previously propounded by Dr. Vernon Bartlet.[1]

Lightfoot completely succeeds in demolishing Har-

[1] In *Zeitschrift f. N.T. Wissenschaft,* vol. vii. 123 ff.

nack's case ; but, no less completely, he fails to establish his own. The case for Rome was attractive only in conjunction with Harnack's conjecture that Deutero-Clement is really the letter of Pope Soter mentioned by Eusebius (*H.E.* iv. 23. 9), which seems to have been read in public worship, as well as that of the real Clement, in the Church of Corinth. Obviously this conjecture rests entirely on the assumption that Deutero-Clement is a *letter*—an assumption which was possible, and even natural, so long as the last chapters were missing. It collapsed when in 1875 for the first time a complete text, containing the missing end, was made known, derived from the same unique MS. that includes the one surviving copy of the *Didache*. It then became certain that Deutero-Clement is not a letter at all, but a sermon. In support of the theory of Roman origin it was also urged that the conception of the Church, and of the pre-existent Christ as spirit, in Deutero-Clement has some points of contact with Hermas. These points on examination are seen to amount to very little. But even if dependence on Hermas were certain, it would constitute no evidence for a Roman origin of Deutero-Clement. Hermas, we know, was (as commanded in the vision, p. 210) circulated among the churches of the Empire *in the lifetime of its author* ; in the second century it was widely regarded as ' scripture ', and in Alexandria its prestige was greater, and lasted far longer, than in Rome (p. 208 f.). Dependence on Hermas, if such can be proved, is really quite as strong an argument for Alexandria as for Rome.

For a Corinthian origin Lightfoot adduces two arguments. The first of these is best given in his own words :

The allusion to the athletic games, and presumably to the Isthmian festival, is couched in language which is quite natural if addressed to Corinthians, but not so if spoken elsewhere.　When the preacher refers to the crowds that ' land ' to take part in the games without any mention of the port, we are naturally led to suppose that the homily was delivered in the neighbourhood of the place where these combatants landed.[1]

But are the games referred to those held on the isthmus of Corinth ?　This inference—and therefore its corollary that the audience addressed must have lived hard by—is in no way justified by the evidence which Lightfoot adduces.　This evidence stands or falls by the correctness of the word ' land ' as a translation of the verb καταπλεῖν ; and Lightfoot, by a curious slip of memory, renders this by ' land ' in his general discussion, but by ' resort to ' in his translation of the text :

> So then, my brethren, let us contend, knowing that the contest is nigh at hand, and that, while many *resort to* the corruptible contests, yet not all are crowned, but only they that have toiled hard and contended bravely.　Let us then contend that we all may be crowned.　Wherefore let us run in the straight course, the incorruptible contest.　And let us *resort to* it in throngs and contend, that we may also be crowned (2 Clem. vii. 1-2).

I have quoted the passage from Lightfoot's own translation in order to call attention to the fact that he twice translates the Greek καταπλεῖν by the English words (which I have italicised) ' resort to '.　That this translation is not an accident appears from his note on the word, at its first occurrence, where he supports this rendering by a passage of Plutarch.　Yet, having done this, unaccountably, and without alleging any reason, he adds, ' But καταπλεῖν can hardly be so explained here '.[2] Then, on the very same page, he himself proceeds to explain the word thus on its second occurrence in the passage quoted above—translating it, in his note, ' go

[1] *Clement*, ii. 197 f.　　　[2] *Clement*, ii. 223-4.

there '. ' Let us not only take part in this race, but let us *go there* ' (the italics are mine) ' in great numbers '.

If the verb καταπλεῖν occurs twice in the same context, and on the second occurrence clearly means ' to go there ', we cannot in the first occurrence press its literal meaning ' to land '. But on this possibility rests the whole case for supposing the games mentioned to be the Isthmian.

But if the passage quoted above be approached without any *a priori* preconception, it reads quite naturally if Deutero-Clement is merely after the manner of preachers echoing the well-known words of St. Paul :

Know ye not that they which run in a race run all, but one receiveth the prize ? Even so run that ye may attain. And every man that striveth in the games is temperate in all things. Now they do it to receive a corruptible crown ; but we an incorruptible (1 Cor. ix. 24-26).

St. Paul's first epistle to the Corinthians is quoted by Clement of Rome, by Ignatius, by Polycarp, and by Hermas, more clearly and more frequently than any other of the Apostle's writings. At a very early date it had become a classic read everywhere throughout the whole Church. Moreover, in Greek life the games were as prominent a feature as is football in English or American life, and metaphors drawn from them are a regular feature in ancient literature. The notion, then, that this passage of Deutero-Clement would be in any degree more appropriate to a Corinthian than it would be to any other audience is quite unfounded.

Lightfoot's only other argument for a Corinthian origin of Deutero-Clement is the hypothesis that its attribution to Clement would be most easily explained if it had been copied without a title into some early MS.

R

immediately after the genuine epistle of Clement, so that the two writings were, by subsequent scribes, taken to be by the same author. But why, we ask, is this more likely to have happened at Corinth than anywhere else ? On the contrary, if it had happened at Corinth and at an early date, the evidence for the two letters *circulating together as Clement's* ought to be much earlier and stronger than is actually the case. Eusebius, for example, though he knows of the existence of a second epistle reputed to be by Clement, is quite clear that only the first is authentic. Evidently, at the time he wrote, MSS. of the genuine letter did *not* as a rule contain the second epistle.

Deutero-Clement first appears under Clement's name towards the end of the fourth century, in the *Apostolic Constitutions*, which undoubtedly originated in Syria. The author of this work, which purports to be instructions from the Twelve Apostles to the bishops of the churches, transmitted through their disciple *par excellence* Clement of Rome, includes *two* epistles of Clement (as well as the *Apostolic Constitutions*, itself considered as a work of Clement) in his list of canonical books of the New Testament. The next witness to Deutero-Clement—one who gives, in Lightfoot's phrase, ' the earliest reference to its contents '—is a work (± A.D. 400) (falsely ascribed to Justin) which Harnack and Lightfoot agree in supposing ' to have emanated from the Syro-Antiochene Church '.[1] But it is not till the fifth or sixth century that the two works are generally spoken of together and accepted as Clement's. And so late as the ninth century a learned writer like Photius of Constantinople pronounces the second spurious. From these facts the natural inferences are :

---

[1] Lightfoot, *Clement*, ii. p. 200.

(1) The attribution of the writing to Clement is *not* an early one.

(2) It was first made in Syria. In Syria, as we have already seen (p. 154 f.), they had a passion for foisting works on to Clement. At Corinth they would probably have known better. The church where the homily was written would be the last, not the first, to make mistakes about its authorship ; just as Rome, to which the epistle to the Hebrews was originally written, was the last church to accept it as by Paul.

Thus I venture to affirm there is simply no case at all for assigning Deutero-Clement either to Corinth or to Rome. But quite a strong one can be made out for Alexandria.

(1) Deutero-Clement evidently used at least one written Gospel ; for he introduces a saying of Christ by the words, 'For the Lord saith in the Gospel'. He gives three sayings of Christ which are not to be found in our Gospels. He also quotes several sayings of Christ which in substance occur in the canonical Gospels, but nearly always in a form strikingly different. Clearly, then, he uses some authority for the sayings of Christ other than the canonical Gospels. It is possible that all his quotations come from this source ; or, if he does use any of our Gospels, he treats them and his apocryphal Gospel as on the same level. Of the three uncanonical sayings given by Deutero-Clement, one (in a slightly different form) is quoted by Clement of Alexandria as coming from the *Gospel according to the Egyptians*. This, or the *Gospel according to the Hebrews*, is probably the source of the other untraced quotations given in Deutero-Clement. Both these Gospels are treated with respect as sub-canonical authorities by the Alexandrian

Fathers. They must, then, have been documents of some antiquity. The very name of the first suggests it was of Egyptian origin ; and there is no evidence that it was ever read, much less quoted on a level with the other Gospels, outside Egypt.

(2) Deutero-Clement develops a curious doctrine of the pre-existent *ecclesia* incarnate in Christ—related to Christ, as female to male—by means of a mystical interpretation of Gen. i. 27. Lightfoot compares it with that of Paul in Eph. i. 3 ; and goes on to say :

> The language of our preacher stands midway in point of development, and perhaps also about midway in point of chronology, between this teaching of St. Paul and the doctrine of the Valentinians, who believed in an eternal aeon ' Ecclesia ', thus carrying the Platonism of our Pseudo-Clement a step in advance.[1]

Quite so, and what conclusion follows ? Valentinus was born in Egypt, and was educated in Alexandria. He taught there *before* he went to Rome ; and he reached Rome sometime in the episcopate of Hyginus, who died A.D. 140. If Valentinus, as Harnack and Lightfoot agree in thinking, represents a *later* development of a doctrine regarded as orthodox in the church to which Deutero-Clement was addressed, the natural inference is that this was the church in which Valentinus started to develop his views. We have thus another reason for supposing that Deutero-Clement wrote in Alexandria.

(3) Hilgenfeld in his edition argued, on the ground of certain points of contact in thought and style, that Deutero-Clement was an early work of Clement of Alexandria, attributed by a curious error to the Roman writer of the same name. His view has met with so little acceptance that it is not necessary to discuss it.

---

[1] *Clement*, ii. p. 243.

I would, however, point out that the coincidences of thought or style which struck Hilgenfeld—given that any of them be accepted as sufficiently striking to establish a connection between the two writers—would be completely explained on the view that Clement of Alexandria had read, and been influenced by, a homily which by his time had become a kind of religious classic in Alexandria.

(4) Since Barnabas is generally admitted to be Alexandrian, the existence of a number of resemblances between this epistle and Deutero-Clement cannot but add something to the case for connecting him with the same church.

(a) Both these writings show an exaggerated sense of the breach between the religion of the Old Testament and the New. Barnabas, for instance, holds not only that the Law of Moses was superseded, except in an allegorical sense—which is the view of the author of Hebrews—but that it had never been meant to be taken literally. He draws the sharpest contrast between Jews and Christians :

Now let us see whether this people or the first people hath the inheritance, and whether the covenant had reference to us or to them (Barn. 13).

In a like spirit Deutero-Clement interprets the words of Isaiah liv. 1, which form, as it were, the ' text ' for his sermon,

the children of the desolate are more than of her that hath the husband,

as meaning

our people [*i.e.* Christians] seemed desolate and forsaken of God, whereas now, having believed, we have become more than those [*i.e.* the Jews] who *seemed* to have God (2 Clem. ii. 3).

In another passage (i. 6) he speaks as if he himself, and the whole of the church he addresses, had been converted from idolatry.

(*b*) Barnabas and Deutero-Clement agree in a high incarnationist doctrine of the person of Christ :

The Lord endured to suffer for our souls, though he was Lord of the whole world, unto whom God said from the foundation of the world, ' let us make man after our own image and likeness ' (Barn. 5).

So Deutero-Clement opens with a passionate protest against any ' low Christology ' :

Brethren, we ought so to think of Jesus Christ as of God, as of the Judge of quick and dead. And we ought not to think mean things of our salvation : for when we think mean things of Him we expect also to receive mean things.

This makes it the more remarkable that neither of them employs the term Logos. Possibly in the city of Philo the gulf from abstract to concrete implied in the phrase ' the Word was made flesh ' was more visible than elsewhere. Or, possibly the use made of the Logos in Egyptian theosophic speculations, like those that survive in the *Poimandres* of Hermes Trismegistos, made it somewhat suspect. More probably it had never occurred to anyone to connect together the Logos of Hellenistic philosophy and the conception of the pre-existent Christ. Once the equation was made, it seems so natural that we wonder how anyone of that age could have overlooked it. But most epoch-making discoveries seem obvious, once they have been made.

It is one more striking piece of evidence for my thesis of the independent development of the Great Churches, to find documents, whose incarnationist doctrine is practically identical with that of the Fourth

Gospel, just stopping short of the word Logos which later theology made fundamental. Incidentally, I would remark, this complete ignoring of the Fourth Gospel, combined with a free use of the *Gospel according to the Egyptians*, are marks of an early date—before A.D. 140 at the latest. It cannot be explained by attributing to Deutero-Clement semi-Gnostic tendencies ; for the Gnostics favoured the Fourth Gospel. In the dogmatic controversies of the later Church, Antioch is always inclined to emphasise the more literal, the more Hebraic, the more 'adoptionist' of two possible interpretations ; Alexandria champions the more allegorical, Platonic, incarnationist. If we contrast the *Didache* and the Gospel of Matthew, on the one hand, with Barnabas and Deutero-Clement on the other, we trace the difference between these two great churches—as we should expect—back to the sub-Apostolic period.

(c) Three minor points of contact between Barnabas and Deutero-Clement may be noted. Both use the allegorical method of interpreting the Old Testament in an advanced form ; both are familiar with the *Two Ways* ;[1] both quote our Lord's saying, 'I came not to call the righteous, but sinners, to repentance'—a coincidence the more interesting in view of the doubt whether either of them used the canonical Gospels. If these stood alone, nothing could be inferred from them ; but they are congruent with other evidence that both documents came from the same church—the Church of Alexandria.

Church Order at Alexandria

The evidence in regard to Church Order to be derived from Barnabas and Deutero-Clement is extremely scanty ;

---

[1] Deutero-Clement is not here dependent on Barnabas, for he quotes a phrase from the *Two Ways* which occurs in the *Didache* but not in Barnabas.

but it makes up for this by being of an unusual character.
In the documents discussed in earlier lectures there has
been frequent allusion to the office of Teacher. It is
therefore of very great interest to note that Barnabas
twice alludes to himself in a way which makes it evident
that he held this office.[1]

The document is in form a letter. It opens with
the conventional phrase of greeting ($\chi a\acute{\iota}\rho\epsilon\tau\epsilon$); and the
expression, 'I was eager to *send* you a trifle', implies
absence from those to whom the message is given. It
was perhaps written by a revered Teacher of the
Church of Alexandria to the church in one of the small
towns in Egypt, which he had recently visited, in order
to provide them with some record of the essential
features in his teaching. If, then, we wish to use
Barnabas as evidence for the kind of thing a Teacher did,
we must read it not so much as a single sermon but
rather as a summary statement of what the author
conceived to be the various heads of his special message
—including his choicest (and most original) efforts in
the way of allegorising the Old Testament. It is,
perhaps, lest he should seem only to care for the more
'high-brow' members of the church, that he concludes
(chs. xviii.-xxi.) with 'another gnosis and teaching'—
the simple old-fashioned moral instruction of the *Two
Ways*.

At any rate his selection for the final, and therefore
the most important, element in his message, not of his
own daring and original flights of exegesis—though he
was very proud of these—but of the simple traditional
exhortation to righteousness of life, is significant. It was
just this exaltation of sound conduct over intellectual
brilliance which differentiated the Catholic Church from

---

[1] $\dot{\epsilon}\gamma\grave{\omega}$ $\delta\grave{\epsilon}$ $o\dot{\upsilon}\chi$ $\dot{\omega}s$ $\delta\iota\delta\acute{a}\sigma\kappa a\lambda os$ $\dot{a}\lambda\lambda'$ $\dot{\omega}s$ $\epsilon\hat{\iota}s$ $\dot{\epsilon}\xi$ $\dot{\upsilon}\mu\hat{\omega}\nu$ (i. 8); cf. (iv. 9).

the Gnostic sectaries. It is the conduct of daily life, love of the brethren and the homely virtues, that Barnabas, like the writers of the New Testament, puts first. That was the strength of the 'great' Church ; even to Ignatius, preoccupied as he is with questions of ecclesiastical discipline and theological orthodoxy, the main count against the heretics is moral :

They have no care for love, none for the widow, none for the orphan, none for the afflicted, none for the prisoner, none for the hungry and thirsty (Smyrn. vi. 2).

Harnack has made the interesting suggestion that the author of Deutero-Clement belonged to a class of church officers which so far we have not heard of : he was a *Reader*.[1] In the standardised Church Order of the fourth century the Reader, or Lector, is one of the ' Minor Orders ', along with officers like doorkeeper and exorcist. But at an earlier period, in Syria at any rate, and possibly in other churches,[2] the Reader was, it would seem, an important officer, who in certain respects ranked next after the Presbyters. The work known as *The Apostolic Church Ordinances*[3] embodies older sources

---

[1] *Sources of the Apostolic Canons*, E.T. (Black, 1895.)

[2] Harnack's discussion too rashly assumes that in these matters what is evidence for one church is presumptive evidence for all, and that 2 Clement is evidence for Rome.

[3] *Die apostolische Kirchenordnung*, so called by its editor, J. W. Bickell. But in the MS. it is called *The Constitutions of Clement and Ecclesiastical Canons of the Holy Apostles*. The full text in Greek—which includes the *Two Ways*—is given by Harnack in his edition of the *Didache* (*Die Lehre der zwölf Apostel*, Leipzig, 1884), p. 225 ff. The regulations on church offices are given in English in the above-mentioned work by Harnack, *Sources of the Apostolic Canons*, which contains his extremely important discussion of the ' Origin of the Readership '. Harnack thinks the *Apostolic Church Ordinances* to be of Egyptian origin; but the regulation, that a small church wanting a bishop shall apply to the neighbouring churches ' where any of them is a settled one ', does not seem to suit Egypt, where the Bishop of Alexandria appointed all local bishops. On this ground, Prof. C. H. Turner maintains (in an unpublished lecture) that, like the *Apostolic Constitutions* and (probably) the *Didascalia*, it represents Syria.

containing a number of regulations in regard to the appointment and function of church officials. These regulations Harnack regards as earlier than the year A.D. 200. Here, after the sections dealing with the Bishop and the Presbyters, and immediately before that dealing with the Deacons, occurs this regulation :

For Reader, one should be appointed, after he has been carefully proved ; no babbler, nor drunkard, nor jester ; of good morals, submissive, of benevolent intentions, first in the assembly at the meetings on the Lord's day, of a plain utterance, and capable of clearly expounding, mindful that he assumes the position of an Evangelist; for whoever fills the ear of the ignorant will be accounted as having his name written with God.

From this it is clear that in some churches in early times the status of Reader was a relatively high one ; and that his office entailed, not merely the reading of the Scripture (for which a good voice would suffice), but the exposition of what he read ; for his work is compared to that of an Evangelist, and he gains honour in the sight of God if he guides the ignorant aright.

In Syria—where, to judge from the *Didache*, prophets were numerous till a later date than elsewhere—the office of Reader was of a quasi-prophetic character. An ancient prayer, to be used at the admission of a Reader, is preserved in the *Apostolic Constitutions* (viii. 22) and includes the words :

Look upon him now being admitted to read thy Holy Scriptures to thy people, and give him a holy spirit, a prophetic spirit ; thou who didst make wise thy servant Esdras to read thy laws to thy people, now also in answer to our prayers make wise thy servant. . . .

Wisdom, it is obvious, is a prime requisite, not for reading the Scripture aloud, but for expounding it.

In the (earlier) *Didascalia* (ii. 20) occurs the sentence :

And if there is a Reader, let him too receive (an allowance) like the Presbyters, as ranking with the prophets.

In light of these three quotations Harnack interprets the following remark of Deutero-Clement :

Therefore, brothers and sisters, after the God of Truth hath been heard [*i.e.* after the lesson from Scripture] I read to you an exhortation to the end that ye may give heed to the things which are written [*i.e.* the Scripture], so that ye may save both yourselves and him that readeth in the midst of you[1] (2 Clem. xix. 1).

He concludes that Deutero-Clement was a Reader ; and that the document we have is his exposition of a portion of Scripture, written out beforehand and read to the congregation at the conclusion of the Scripture lesson.

I have summarised the main points in Harnack's theory, because, whether or no we accept his view of Deutero-Clement, the evidence as to the existence and nature of the office of Reader is of considerable interest to the student of early Church Order. When I first wrote this chapter I was disposed to accept the suggestion that the author of Deutero-Clement held the office of Reader ; but Dr. J. Vernon Bartlet has since communicated to me an alternative theory which he has recently developed, and has kindly given me permission to make use of it. I gladly avail myself of this—adding that he is not to be held responsible in detail for the way in which I have here worked it out.

It would appear from Justin Martyr that at Rome the Sunday service began with reading from the Gospels and the Old Testament. The procedure is thus described :

[1] Cf. Rev. i. 3 : 'Blessed is he that readeth, and they that hear the words of this prophecy and keep the things which are written therein'. Harnack thinks this implies the existence of a special Reader.

The memoirs of the Apostles or the writings of the Prophets are read as long as we have time. Then, when the Reader has finished, the President speaks, admonishing, and exhorting us to the imitation of these excellent things. After that we rise all together and offer prayer. And when the prayer has ended, bread and wine and water are presented. . . . (Justin, *Apol.* i. 76).

From this it would appear that the preacher and the reader were *not* as a rule the same person. The preacher was normally the Bishop, but he would take his text from the Scripture-lesson which had just been read. We cannot, of course, be certain that the practice of Alexandria was identical with that of Rome. But the assumption that it was so in this particular respect, provides an illuminating explanation of the passage quoted above from Deutero-Clement. A portion of Scripture has been read—and is followed by a homily, exhorting the congregation to ' give heed to the things ' they have just heard read. There is nothing here to suggest that the person who had read from the Scriptures was the same as he who reads the homily still preserved to us in Deutero-Clement. On the contrary, on the analogy of the practice of the synagogue, what we should expect of a reader is that (if and when he did more than read the bare text) he would, at most, venture on a kind of paraphrase or running commentary— related to the lection much as the Targum to the Hebrew text. What Deutero-Clement does is to select from a lection taken from Isaiah—presumably one of considerable length—certain verses (especially Isa. liv. 1), which he treats much in the way that a modern preacher does the text of his sermon. He speaks, too, with authority; he takes upon himself to censure and to warn. Now a Bishop may do this ; but hardly (we should suppose) a mere Reader.

We ask, then, was the author of Deutero-Clement a Bishop ?   To answer that question we must consider the two allusions which he makes to the Presbyters.

And let us not think to give heed and believe now only while we are admonished by the Presbyters.   But likewise when we have departed home let us remember the commandments of the Lord and not suffer ourselves to be dragged off the other way by our worldly affections (xvii. 3).

Admirable advice, and not yet out of date !   Again, a few sentences later, the obdurate are represented as destined to say at the Last Judgment :

Woe unto us, for Thou wast and we knew it not, and believed not ;   and we obeyed not the Presbyters when they told us of our salvation (xvii. 5).

The allusions to the Presbyters are susceptible of alternative explanations.   Either the writer is *not* himself a Presbyter (but a Reader, or other such officer), or he is a Presbyter entitled to speak as representing that body—just as the Vicar of a modern church where there are several curates might ask the congregation to pay attention to ' the Clergy '.   In view of the tone of authority assumed by the writer, and also of the fact that both the passages quoted imply that preaching and admonishing belong specially to the office of Presbyter, the more probable alternative is, that the writer is the President of the body of presbyters.

We infer, then, that at Alexandria at this date there was a President of the board of presbyters ;   but that he was still called by the title Presbyter, and was not yet, or not yet quite, in the position of a monarchical bishop.

This hypothesis would explain why, when mon-episcopacy did arise in Alexandria, it retained, at least until some date in the third century, a notable feature. The Bishop was elected by the twelve presbyters of the

city churches, and was by them consecrated to his office.
When the see was vacant, we are told, the twelve
presbyters chose one of themselves, and the remaining
eleven laying their hands on his head, blessed him, and
created him patriarch. Evidence for this practice is
given in detail in the well-known ' Dissertation on the
Christian Ministry ' appended to Lightfoot's *Philippians*
(p. 230 ff.) ; it has been slightly increased by fresh discoveries since he wrote.[1]

Lightfoot calls into evidence the letter of Hadrian to
Servianus, mentioned above, to prove that already by
A.D. 134 the offices of Bishop and Presbyter were clearly
distinguished in Egypt. Hadrian, enlarging on the
fickleness and instability of the Egyptians, says :

> There, worshippers of Serapis are Christians, and those who
> say they are *bishops* of Christ are devotees of Serapis. There is
> no Ruler of a Jewish Synagogue, no Samaritan, no *presbyter* of
> the Christians, who is not an astrologer, a soothsayer, a quack.

Hadrian, it should be noted, speaks of ' bishops ' in
the plural ; but, as we shall see later, a hundred years
after his time there was still only one bishop in Egypt.
Lightfoot thinks Hadrian may have used the plural
through misapprehension—taking it for granted, from his
knowledge of Christianity elsewhere, that there would be
bishops in Egypt outside Alexandria. But in view of the
evidence afforded by Deutero-Clement—which Lightfoot,
of course, did not regard as Alexandrian—it is far more
likely that Hadrian was *not* mistaken on this point. His
letter is evidence that in Alexandria—as in the usage of
the New Testament, Clement of Rome, and Hermas—the
same persons could be called alternatively Bishops or
Presbyters.

It cannot, however, have been many years after

[1] *J.T.S.* ii. p. 612 ff.

Hadrian wrote before there was a monarchical bishop in Alexandria. True, the first bishop of this church about whom we have any very definite information is Demetrius, who was appointed about A.D. 190. But it is clear that the office to which he was appointed was one of old standing and of universally recognised authority; and from the moment of his election he was able to exercise very autocratic powers. His own position was so secure that he could afford to make fresh departures outside Alexandria, of a kind which imply that mon-episcopacy was already an old-established institution. Until Demetrius, we are told, the Bishop of Alexandria was the only bishop in Egypt. Demetrius initiated an entirely new policy, and appointed bishops in other cities of Egypt. His successor, Heraclas (A.D. 233), continued this policy, and largely increased their number.

Incidentally, though not perhaps accidentally, this policy reacted on the position of the Bishop of Alexandria itself. The newly founded sees naturally remained subject to his supreme authority. Thus the Bishop of Alexandria attained at one step to the position of a Patriarch.

The Patriarchates

After the death of Peter, Paul, and James, and the destruction of Jerusalem, the Church's natural centre, the theoretical ideal of a Church one and indivisible became a thing extremely difficult to realise in actual practice. The centrifugal tendencies inherent in that diversity of local usage and outlook, which was the inevitable result of the spontaneous and almost haphazard character of the earliest mission, had no longer an effective counterpoise. The position was made more difficult by the political situation. *Divide et impera* was the

maxim of Roman rule. The Government was tradition-
ally and on principle jealous of anything that savoured
of combination and co-operation, even when the objects
of such combination were regarded as of the most highly
respectable character ; [1] and the persecution of Nero
established a precedent, after which Christianity was,
in the eye of the law, a *religio illicita*. This made conference on disputed questions impracticable on any large
scale. The law in its full rigour was rarely enforced
against Christians, and persecution of a serious character
appears to have been intermittent and sporadic. But
in the first two centuries, to hold anything like a provincial synod, much less an Oecumenical Council like
those of later Church history, would have been quite
impossible. The Church was a secret society suspect by
the police. In order to survive, it had to adapt itself
to this difficult environment.

One result of this necessity of avoiding public attention would be that important questions would often have
to be decided by the churches of the great provincial
capitals, without formal consultation either with one
another or with the smaller local churches. Again, local
churches would be compelled to depend for support and
guidance less on one another than on the church of the
provincial capital; for it was easy for delegates of a small
church to find a pretext for visiting the capital without
attracting notice. Thus on large points of policy the
affairs of the church local would in practice be decided
by the churches of the provincial capitals; while questions
affecting the Church universal could only be settled by
occasional conference, necessarily of a more or less secret
and informal character, between representatives of the
Great Churches.

[1] Cf. Trajan's letter to Pliny, x. 97.

By the third century we find the Patriarchs of the churches of the greater capitals, Rome, Antioch, Alexandria, and the Metropolitans of provincial capitals like Ephesus or Caesarea, exercising a large authority over the smaller churches in their province. Historians have often commented on the obscurity of the origin of this Patriarchate and Metropolitan jurisdiction. How and by what stages did the bishops of the Great Churches acquire their predominant position in regard to the lesser churches of a province ? The answer to this question is that the primacy of the metropolitan churches was not a thing that had to be acquired ; in its essential features it was, in effect, primitive. The case of Jerusalem was exceptional (p. 43). Again, in Egypt at definite dates, and by definite acts, the bishoprics of the smaller churches were constituted in accordance with a clearly determined policy by bishops of Alexandria ; and naturally their appointees continued to be regarded as their subordinate officers. But elsewhere this patriarchal and metropolitan authority grew insensibly and inevitably out of the circumstances of the sub-Apostolic age—only in the earliest period the authority would seem to have resided rather in the metropolitan church as such than in the person of its bishop.

This is exactly as we should expect. Anyone who has any knowledge of the way in which successful ' movements '—whether religious, political, or otherwise—are ' run ' at the present day, is aware that it is precisely in the early stages that local branches depend most upon ' headquarters '. Whenever a crisis or a difficulty occurs in a struggling branch, advice is sought at the national headquarters or at a provincial head office. On all points, whether in regard to organisation or to ' platform ', a deputy from the central office is listened to with a respect

s

which is almost pathetic. It is at a later stage, when a local branch feels that it is firmly rooted, that it is apt to ' take the bit between its teeth ' and to cause head-quarters much trouble. In new movements the primitive stage is that in which dependence of local branches on the great centres is at its maximum. And if this is so in the democratic England or America of the twentieth century, how much more would it hold good in the patriarchally minded semi-oriental civilisation of the bureaucratically governed Roman Empire.

It is not, of course, suggested that the pre-eminence of the Great Churches was of the nature of a rigidly defined legal jurisdiction—all the evidence points the other way. For the first hundred years or so all church organisation must have been more or less informal, and a matter of moral prestige rather than of legal right. Still less is it to be supposed that the smaller churches of the whole of the Roman Empire were neatly parcelled out among certain Great Churches definitely labelled ' metro-politan '. The churches of all important cities would enjoy a certain pre-eminence in their own neighbour-hood. But the fight with Gnosticism led to a growing stress on the tradition of churches founded by Apostles. Hence arose a widespread feeling that both a special pre-eminence and a special responsibility belonged to the churches in the three capitals which could also claim to be ' Apostolic Sees '—Antioch, Ephesus, and Rome.

Tertullian speaks of those ' Apostolic Churches which are the wombs and origin of the faith '.[1] Irenaeus regards them with similar respect. Neither Irenaeus (of Lyons) nor his younger contemporary, Tertullian (of Carthage), was himself a member of one of the great Apostolic Churches ; and both of them were prepared

---

[1] *Matricibus et originalibus fidei* (*De Praescr. Haer.* 21).

on occasion to denounce in strong language high-handed action by a Roman bishop. Hence their testimony to the influence of the Apostolic Sees upon the Church at large is by that much the more impressive.

The question whether the position occupied by a man like Clement of Rome in relation to his presbyters was comparable to that of a bishop to his clergy, or of a dean to his canons, is one which has been much disputed. It is not disputable that the position taken up by Clement, writing in the name of the Roman Church to the Church at Corinth, implies a sense in the larger church both of responsibility and of moral authority, in which lie the germs of the legal authority claimed by later Popes. It is not less significant that Ignatius of Antioch speaks more than once as if conscious of a similar responsibility for the Church throughout Syria ; and that the Bishop of Ephesus, as will shortly appear, seems to occupy a similar position in Asia.

Martyrdom was not a rare thing in the early Church. Why, then, did deputations, including in every case the bishop, come, often from a considerable distance, to wait upon Ignatius ? Why does he feel it incumbent on him to write letters of good advice to churches in Asia which he had never seen or only once passed through ? The alternations of mood between extreme self-esteem and exaggerated profession of humility which occur in almost every letter, I have explained (p. 168 ff.) as partly neurotic. But a neurotic, except his case is very serious, is more likely to exaggerate something which actually exists than to imagine the non-existent. Why, then, in writing to the Roman Church does Ignatius feel it necessary to say, ' I do not command you as though I were Peter and Paul. They were Apostles, I am a convict ; they were free, but I am a slave, to this very hour ' ?

Martyrdom in the early Church conferred upon a man a claim to exaggerated respect. But that alone would not put Ignatius in a position in which a disclaimer of equality with Peter and Paul could seem an expression of humility. Ignatius, as we have seen, grossly ' overdoes it ' ; but there would be reason, or at least excuse, for his protestations, if he knew that his post as president of the Church of Antioch was generally recognised as one of a quasi-Apostolic character. In that case it might seem a tactful courtesy to disclaim the intention of speaking to the Church of Rome in that capacity ; while his own position would be one for the responsibilities of which it would behove the holder to remind himself— though not quite so often other people—of his personal unworthiness.

That the See of Ephesus enjoyed a certain distinction in Asia I have inferred from the Pastoral Epistles and the minor epistles of John. It should be noted also that Ephesus heads the list of the Seven Churches of Asia in the Apocalypse. We are not, then, surprised at the marked difference in the tone in which Ignatius writes to the smaller churches, and that he adopts in his letter to Ephesus. The special compliments which he pays to this church are significant. He obviously regards the Apostolic Church of Ephesus, as well as that of Rome, as being of a dignity comparable to that of his own Church of Antioch.

Thus already in the time of Ignatius there are at least three churches enjoying a pre-eminence in which is implied more than the beginnings of the later provincial system. This pre-eminence was evidently no new thing. In fact—to put it paradoxically—the office of Archbishop would seem more primitive than that of Bishop.

EPILOGUE

OUR survey of the evidence is ended. Much of it is unambiguous ; much admits of more than one interpretation. Of necessity, there will be a corresponding variation in the degree of certainty which attaches to the several conclusions reached. Of these, some are as firmly established as anything can be that rests on ancient testimony, others are no more than, in Huxley's phrase, ' scientific guesses '. But whatever else is disputable, there is, I submit, one result from which there is no escape. In the Primitive Church there was no single system of Church Order laid down by the Apostles. During the first hundred years of Christianity, the Church was an organism alive and growing—changing its organisation to meet changing needs. Clearly in Asia, Syria, and Rome during that century the system of government varied from church to church, and in the same church at different times. Uniformity was a later development ; and for those times it was, perhaps, a necessary development.

In a book which aims at being a contribution to historical research, a discussion of issues which are a matter of controversy in the Church of to-day would be out of place. It would, however, be futile to pretend that the historical conclusions here reached are without relevance to practical questions keenly debated at the present time. All over the world—more especially in India, China, and Africa—disunion among Christians is recognised as a force of weakness amid surrounding paganism. The obstacles to be overcome are many; and they are real. No one who has given serious study to the question will condemn out of hand those who are apprehensive lest ill-considered attempts at premature reunion may hinder rather than advance the cause. But perhaps the greatest obstacle is the belief—entertained more or less explicitly by most bodies of Christians —that there is some one form of Church Order which alone is primitive, and which, therefore, alone possesses the sanction of Apostolic precedent. Our review of the historical evidence has shown this belief to be an illusion. In the Primitive Church no one system of Church Order prevailed. Everywhere there was readiness to experiment, and, where circumstances seemed to demand it, to change.

To offer any suggestions in regard to the practical problems and current controversies of the present day would be to go outside the province of strictly historical investigation proper to this book. Yet it is permissible to hint that the first Christians achieved what they did, because the spirit with which they were inspired was one favourable to experiment. In this—and, perhaps, in some other respects—it may be that the line of advance for the Church of to-day is not to imitate the forms, but to recapture the spirit, of the Primitive Church.

APPENDICES

263

APPENDIX A

THE importance of this document has been strangely overlooked. For if any historical value whatever be allowed to it, the case for the residence of the Apostle John in Asia can no longer be sustained. Lightfoot allows it none.

Unhappily it has no points of contact with authentic tradition. If it contains any grains of truth, we have no means of sifting them from the huge heap of falsehood.[1]

Similarly the Bollandist, Fr. H. Delehaye, dismisses the Pionian *Life* as a fourth-century fiction in the conventional hagiological manner.[2]

To me any such estimate of its historical value appears to be gravely in error. No doubt the author revels in stories of miracle; and he is obviously inclined to rewrite and embellish his original sources for purposes of edification. Biographers of saints all do this—and so, though in a slightly different way, do most biographers of sinners. St. Bonaventura did in *The Life of St. Francis*, which became the official ' legend ' of the Franciscan Order. A tendency to ' idealise ' creates no presumption at all against the probability that, like Bonaventura, the author of *The Life of Polycarp* had access to early and valuable sources.

Of the miracles, the great majority occur lumped together in one section of *The Life* (§ 25-32). This looks as if they came from a different source from the rest of the story; and the author virtually says so, § 27 (p. 271). Probably they represent a collection of stories told by guides to pilgrims to the martyr's tomb. Apart from the author's taste for miracles, the ground on which Lightfoot rules him absolutely out of court is his complete ignorance

---

[1] Lightfoot, *Ignatius and Polycarp*, i. p. 435 f. In vol. iii. of the same work will be found the text in full and a translation.

[2] *Les Passions des Martyrs et les genres littéraires.* (Bruxelles, Office of the Bollandists, 1921.)

of the residence of the Apostle John in Asia, and of the appointment of Polycarp as Bishop of Smyrna by that Apostle ; and the
fact that he gives an account of the life and career of Polycarp
quite incompatible with Polycarp's having had any connection
whatever with the Apostle.[1]

Lightfoot accepts unreservedly all that Irenaeus says about
Polycarp's relations with the Apostle John ; and also those of
Tertullian, whose statements he regards as those of an independent witness, and not as a mere rhetorical amplification of
what he read in Irenaeus. Lightfoot, therefore, can take no
other view than he does of the historical value of *The Life of
Polycarp*. Supposing, however, we have, on other grounds,
begun to suspect that the tradition of the Apostle's residence in
Asia may have arisen out of a confusion between him and the
Elder John, then the mere fact that the author of *The Life* never
mentions the Apostle John in Asia, and seems never to have
heard of any connection between him and Polycarp, compels to
a patient hearing of the case in favour of its historicity.   The
belief that John the Apostle lived in Ephesus soon became universal.   The *Acts of John*, which presuppose it, had a great vogue.
The works of Irenaeus, who makes the connection of Polycarp
with St. John one of the corner-stones of his argument against the
Gnostics, had a wide circulation and repute.   And his statements
about St. John in Asia, along with those of Polycrates and others,
were republished by Eusebius, A.D. 311, and thus gained still
wider currency.

Now the author of *The Life of Polycarp* wished above all things
to glorify his hero.   He had read Irenaeus,[2] who asserts :

Polycarp was not only instructed by Apostles and lived in
familiar intercourse with many that had seen Christ, but was also,
by Apostles in Asia, appointed bishop of the Church in Smyrna; whom
I also saw in my early youth.

How, then, can we possibly account for the fact that he totally
ignores Polycarp's connection with any of the Apostles, and represents him instead as the *protégé* and pupil of an insignificant
and wholly unknown bishop, Bucolus ?   Only, I suggest, on the
hypothesis that this maligned writer was doing what he tells us

[1] Lightfoot, *op. cit.* iii. p. 430 f.
[2] Lightfoot, *op. cit.* p. 428.

he is doing, *i.e.* drawing his facts from an ancient document based on authentic Smyrnaean tradition.

That the author made use of *some* older documents we know. *The Life*, as we have it, is incomplete. Lightfoot shows that the Letter of the Smyrnaeans, commonly known as *The Martyrdom* of Polycarp, was originally included in *The Life*; and it follows it immediately in the sole surviving MS. of *The Life*. (The other MSS. of *The Martyrdom* are all derived, not from the Letter in its *original* form—most of which is also reproduced by Eusebius (*H.E.* iv. 15)—but from the version of it reproduced in *The Life*.) Lightfoot also shows that the miraculous incident of the dove—which does not appear in Eusebius' version—is an embellishment of the original letter made by the author of *The Life*. Another ancient document originally contained in *The Life* was the genuine letter of Polycarp to the Philippians (§ 12). It certainly included a list of early Bishops of Smyrna (§ iii.), an account of Polycarp's scriptural expositions (§ xx.), a dream, in which Polycarp appeared to the author, ' as I will declare in the sequel ' (*Martyrdom*, xxii. 4). I shall argue later that in addition it contained a notice of Polycarp's visit to Rome. Some of this lost material may have stood in the lacuna between §§ 28 and 29 ; but most of it probably occurred, either between the end of the part of *The Life* which survives and *The Martyrdom*, or after *The Martyrdom*.

The author makes the definite assertion that the earlier part of *The Life* was based on an ancient source or sources. He begins his work :

Tracing my steps farther back and beginning with the visit of the blessed Paul to Smyrna, as I have found it in ancient copies, I will give the narration in order, thus coming down to the history of the blessed Polycarp.

There follows a paragraph in which a visit of St. Paul to one Strataeas, who had heard him in Pamphylia, is described. In this the Apostle lays down the true doctrine in regard to the Quartodeciman controversy. The details of the Apostle's discourse are of course purely apocryphal and reflect—as one would expect in a document written for edification—the views on the subject regarded as orthodox, and *therefore Apostolic*, by the author of *The Life*.

Lightfoot says of the author :

He does not scruple to appeal to documents, where these documents have no existence.

The only ground for this condemnation is that he asserts of Polycarp :

He wrote many treatises and sermons and letters, but in the persecution . . . certain lawless heathen carried them off. Their character, however, is evident from those still extant, among which the Epistle to the Philippians was the most adequate (*ἱκανωτάτη*). This we will include in its proper place (§ 12).

Lightfoot argues that it is highly improbable that there were in existence any other letters than that to the Philippians which still survives. But in fairness to our author it should be observed that, though he asserts that other letters were extant, he only professes to have access to this one.[1]

But there is an independent reason for thinking that his account of the interview between St. Paul and Strataeas is a rewriting of an older source. One of the great moments in the career of Polycarp was the visit to Rome in the time of Anicetus (A.D. 155), in which he stoutly upheld the tradition of the churches of Asia on the Quartodeciman issue, as being primitive and Apostolic, against the tradition of Rome. The firm stand made by Polycarp for the customs of Asia, and Anicetus' friendly 'agreement to differ' on the matter, form one of the main precedents in the 'case for Asia' in the letter of Irenaeus cited above (p. 222), when the churches of Asia were excommunicated by Victor of Rome (A.D. 190) (Eus. *H.E.* v. 24, 14 ff.). Some notice of this incident *must* have occurred in a portion of *The Life* that has been lost. But if Polycarp was to be represented as appealing, when at Rome, to the tradition of Smyrna as truly preserving the Apostolic teaching on the Quartodeciman question, it would be natural, if not actually necessary, to prepare the way

---

[1] The statement that Polycarp wrote several letters to neighbouring churches occurs in Irenaeus' letter to Florinus ; and the adjective *ἱκανωτάτη* is applied by Irenaeus (*Haer.* iii. 3, 4) to Polycarp's extant letter. Since both passages are quoted by Eusebius (*H.E.* v. 20 and iv. 14), it has been suggested that the author of *The Life* only knew Irenaeus from Eusebius, and therefore wrote in the fourth century. But the colophon attached to the best (the Moscow) MS. of *The Martyrdom* (originally part of *The Life*) says, ' This account Gaius copied from the papers of Irenaeus. The same lived with Irenaeus.'

for this by setting down early in *The Life* a version of the teaching as originally given by an Apostle.

That the author regards this as the point of the incident, appears from the opening words of the next section (§ 3). ' But after the departure of the Apostle, Strataeas *succeeded to his teaching.*' He means to indicate, no doubt, that Strataeas became Bishop ; but the emphasis is not on his office as such, but on his being a link in the tradition between Paul and Polycarp of Smyrna as to the true doctrine on the Quartodeciman issue. Of course, if St. Paul ever did meet Strataeas (which is not unlikely), he would have found something better to talk about than the Quartodeciman controversy. St. Paul was interested in saving souls, not in the exact date of the termination of the Lenten fast. And no doubt Lightfoot is right in supposing that the actual views attributed to the Apostle are related to the particular stage this controversy had assumed at the time of the author. I am not arguing that the views expressed go back to Polycarp, much less to Paul ; I do urge that the ancient source used by the author of the existing *Life*—if it was a document written in Asia within a year or two of Polycarp's death— *must* have contained something to justify Polycarp's claim to represent Apostolic tradition in regard to this particular question. And that something—partly rewritten—may well be the story with which the Pionian *Life* begins.

Two other considerations suggest the dependence of the Strataeas incident on an early source.

(1) Paul is not stated to have been the founder of the Church in Smyrna. He is represented as visiting it after it was founded. This fits in with the tradition preserved in the *Apostolic Constitutions* which makes Strataeas first Bishop of Smyrna, but does *not* say he was ordained by Paul.

(2) The Apostolic tradition in regard to the Quartodeciman controversy is traced back, not to John—nor even to John and Paul together—but to Paul alone. That is to say, the appeal to Apostolic tradition on a question vital to the independence of the churches of Asia against Rome is made to depend, not on the joint authority of John and Paul, who together might fairly balance the Roman appeal to Peter and Paul, but solely on that of Paul.

We are now entitled to give their due weight to other little bits of evidence. The facts are mentioned by Lightfoot, though he is obliged to minimise their significance.

(1) The author shows a good deal of local knowledge of Smyrna and the neighbourhood. I need not reproduce the details, which are fairly summarised by Lightfoot (*op. cit.* iii. p. 430).

(2) A miracle story (in which figures a certain Camerius) opens with these words:

> Now among others, whom Polycarp appointed Deacons, was one named Camerius, who also became Bishop, the third in succession from him, and next after Papirius (§ 27).

Of Papirius nothing more is said. The allusion to him is a mere parenthesis; but the name is mentioned in the letter of Polycrates of Ephesus to Victor of Rome (Eus. *H.E.* v. 24) as a prominent upholder of Asiatic custom in regard to Easter at this date.

(3) Our author tells how the body of Bucolus was taken

> to Smyrna, to the cemetery in front of the Ephesian Royal gate, and placed where in our day a myrtle tree sprang up after the burial of the body of Thraseas the martyr (§ 20).

Lightfoot (*op. cit.* i. p. 510) dates the martyrdom of Thraseas within the years A.D. 155–164. And in his note on the passage quoted above, he remarks: ' There would seem therefore to be an anachronism in the νῦν, " in our day " '. If the passage, as Lightfoot holds, was originally penned in the fourth century, there would certainly be an anachronism; a more natural view is that we have here preserved the actual wording of a second-century source.

The question whether *The Life* was written by the Pionius who was martyred A.D. 250 in the Decian persecution and who is known to have had a special veneration for the memory of Polycarp, has been hotly debated since Lightfoot wrote. Corssen and others have maintained that the martyr was the author. Delehaye argues for a date *c.* A.D. 400. Personally I incline to think that the attribution to Pionius, though not provable, is at least probable. I find it hard to believe that, after the publication of Eusebius' *History*, a *Life of Polycarp* written in the spirit of enthusiastic hero-worship could have absolutely ignored the unique distinction there claimed for him as a personal disciple of St. John, consecrated Bishop by Apostolic hands. All, however, that I am here concerned to show is that, whoever wrote *The Life*, and however freely he may have dealt with his materials, he was working upon old and valuable sources, or rather that one of his sources was such.

The author definitely states that he had access to an ancient document. And that such a document once existed we might, on independent grounds, have surmised, though I believe the fact has not heretofore been noticed. At the close of the *Martyrdom of Polycarp* there is a sentence which suggests that the letter of the Church of Smyrna, which we call the *Martyrdom*, was merely intended as an instalment :

Ye indeed required that the things which happened should be shown unto you at greater length : but we *for the present* (κατὰ τὸ παρόν) have certified you as it were in a summary (ὡς ἐν κεφαλαίῳ) by the hand of our brother Marcianus (§ 20).

This looks as if, at the time of writing, the authorities of the Church of Smyrna contemplated something like a *Life of Polycarp*. If they carried out that intention, there is not the slightest reason why Pionius, who was a prominent member of the Church of Smyrna and whose devotion to Polycarp was of the nature of a ' cult ', should not have got possession of a copy.

Be this as it may, the first part of *The Life* purports to be based on an ancient document. It is, therefore, the more important to note that, in introducing the collection of miracle stories about the saint, the author speaks as if he was here dependent on a *different* source—apparently oral tradition. ' I will now record such of the miracles wrought by his hands as *have been handed down* to us ' (§ 25). In mediaeval times—the most famous examples are St. Francis and St. Thomas of Canterbury—we have instances of collections of miracles being made at a slightly later date, as supplements to an original biographical sketch. I suggest that in this, and in some other respects, the Pionian *Life of Polycarp* started a fashion.

The question, however, whether or not *The Life* is actually the work of the Pionius who was martyred in A.D. 250, does not affect my main argument. Nevertheless it has some historical interest. For, if *The Life* be dated before A.D. 250, it becomes early evidence for the prevalence in Asia of the custom that, for the consecration of a bishop, bishops should be summoned from neighbouring churches. The Council of Nicaea, A.D. 325, made it a matter of canonical rule that at least three bishops should take part in the consecration. Such a rule implies a widespread previous custom. The practice is implied in the document miscalled *The Egyptian Church Order*, which is really a recension of *The Apostolic Tradition* of Hippolytus of Rome (*c.* A.D. 220).[1] If it can be carried back to the ancient source used in *The Life of Polycarp*, the hypothesis suggests itself that it was a practice that originated in Asia. In Asia, earlier than elsewhere among the Gentile churches, mon-episcopacy had been established ; and in Asia the close propinquity of a number of churches dating from the Apostolic age (cf. ' The seven churches of Asia ') made it both natural and easy for bishops from neighbouring churches to assemble for such a purpose.

[1] *Texts and Studies*, viii. 4 (Camb. Univ. Press). In the Verona MS., the best witness for the text in its oldest form—here supported by the Sahidic—the Canon reads as follows : Episcopus ordinetur electus ab omni populo ; quique cum nominatus fuerit et placuerit omnibus, conueniet populum una cum praesbyterio et his qui praesentes fuerint episcopi die dominica . . . unus de praesentibus episcopis ab omnibus rogatus inponens manum ei qui ordinatur episcopus, orat ita dicens, etc. (Similarly the Sahidic, G. Horner's edition, p. 306).

APPENDIX B

THE LETTERS OF IGNATIUS AND POLYCARP

THE genuineness of the seven short letters written by Ignatius, Bishop of Antioch, on his road to martyrdom in the Colosseum at Rome, was finally established by the monumental work of Lightfoot. Otto Pfleiderer, quite the ablest of the later Tübingen School, was converted by Lightfoot from a complete rejection, to an enthusiastic advocacy, of their authenticity. But while accepting their genuineness, he wished to bring down their date to about A.D. 130—on the ground that the Gnostic views combated in the Epistles resembled those of Basilides and Saturninus, who flourished in the reign of Hadrian.

Lightfoot had already shown the fully developed views of these two leaders to be precisely *not* the kind of Gnosticism implied by the strictures of Ignatius. And as a result of more recent research it is now recognised that Gnosticism represents essentially a pre-Christian tendency; so that we must push back to an earlier date the beginning of the infiltration into Christianity of Gnostic views.

The evidence for the view that Ignatius perished under Trajan, who died in the latter part of the year A.D. 117, though it comes a long way short of being conclusive, is adequate, in default of evidence to the contrary.

(1) Origen in his *Homilies on Luke* (ch. 6), written about A.D. 231, speaks of

Ignatius, who was second Bishop of Antioch after the blessed Peter, and during the persecution fought with wild beasts in Rome.

Evidently Origen regarded Ignatius as belonging to the sub-Apostolic period; while the phrase ' the persecution ' is appropriate to Trajan's reign, under whom Symeon, Bishop of Jerusalem, was martyred, besides a number of Christians in Bithynia when Pliny was governor. Trajan, on the whole, discouraged persecution ; but Hadrian, the next Emperor, went a stage further than Trajan in this direction.

(2) In Fotheringham's edition of Jerome's version of the *Chronicon* of Eusebius the martyrdoms of Symeon of Jerusalem, Ignatius, and the Bithynian Christians are mentioned one after the other continuously in the space opposite the numbers X and XI (but, perhaps by accident, IX is omitted), which perhaps means that they are assigned vaguely to the ninth, tenth, and eleventh years of Trajan (*i.e.* A.D. 107–8). C. H. Turner (*Studies in Early Church History*, p. 137) argues that the ninth year is the date intended in the Armenian version of the *Chronicon*, Lightfoot having misunderstood the method of arrangement adopted by the scribe in the case of specially long entries. And Lightfoot himself shows that the concurrence of the ' Roman ' and of Antiochene Acts, and also of the *Chronicon Paschale*, which all agree in assigning his death to the ninth year of Trajan, is to be explained by their dependence on the *Chronicon* of Eusebius. But there is no reason for supposing that the date assigned by Eusebius is more than an approximation. Indeed, in the *Ecclesiastical History* he treats of Ignatius *after* his account of the persecution carried out by Pliny—thus reversing the order in which these events are given in the *Chronicon*. (The date of Pliny's persecution can be fixed as A.D. 112.) At any rate the words ' in their time ' (*H.E.* iii. 36) show that Eusebius was not professing knowledge of the exact year. The earliest of the various legendary accounts of Ignatius' martyrdom—the ' Antiochene Acts ', which Lightfoot dates *c.* A.D. 440—confronts Ignatius with the Emperor Trajan in Antioch, and makes the Emperor himself pronounce sentence upon him. Lightfoot has shown that these Acts have the most shadowy claim to be treated as historical evidence. To the arguments he adduces I would add the consideration that, if sentence had been passed by the Emperor in person, there would have been no possible ground for the apprehensions expressed in Ignatius' letter to the Romans that members of that church might be successful in procuring a reprieve. Moreover, Trajan, when in Antioch, would have been much too busy organising his projected campaign in Mesopotamia to concern himself with trying unimportant criminals—and as such he would certainly regard Ignatius. Nevertheless, it is just possible that

in synchronising the condemnation of Ignatius with the Emperor's visit to Antioch, these Acts preserve an authentic tradition.

(3) While Trajan was in Antioch there occurred a prodigious earthquake, which caused enormous havoc in the city. Now, whenever in the early centuries some great natural catastrophe occurred, the populace at once leapt to the conclusion that it was an expression of the anger of the gods for permitting the ' atheist ' Christians to exist.

> If the Tiber rises as high as the city walls, if the Nile does not send its waters over the fields, if the heavens give no rain, if there is an earthquake, if there is famine or pestilence—straightway the cry is, ' The Christians to the lion.' And what a mouthful ! (*Tantos ad unum ?*) (Tertullian, *Apol.* 40 ; cf. *Ad Nationes*, 9.)

It may be taken for granted that an earthquake of exceptionally devastating character would stir the mob of Antioch to seek out the persons who had earned for the city the vengeance of heaven. Ignatius, as his letters show, was one of those fiery spirits whose existence in any community cannot be hidden ; and if, as is probable, he was wont to denounce the gods of the heathen as violently as he does heretics and Jews, he would be marked out clearly as a victim. On this view, no difficulty is presented by Ignatius' belief that Christians in Rome might, if they tried, procure a reprieve. In A.D. 112 Trajan had written to Pliny saying that Christians were not to be sought out for punishment, nor arrested on anonymous information ; and that, even if publicly accused, they were to be given an opportunity to recant and thereby obtain pardon. It would be known by those in authority that the Emperor's policy was, so far as possible, to turn a blind eye towards Christians ; and at Rome there would be no mob demanding expiation for the crime of having brought down the anger of the gods upon the community.

This hypothesis fits in sufficiently well with the evidence as to the time of year. The earthquake took place during winter ; probably in January, possibly in December, A.D. 115.[1] The day of the month, though unfortunately not the year, is given by Ignatius himself in his letter to the Romans. This was written from Smyrna on August 24, and we know that he had been

---

[1] A late sixth century chronographer, Malalas, gives the exact date as Dec. 13, A.D. 115. Dion merely says ' in winter ' ; and Lightfoot argues for a date early in A.D. 115 (*Ignatius*, ii. p. 413 ff. and p. 436 ff.).

brought to Smyrna from Antioch by road, a journey which would take some little time. Lightfoot thinks that the soldiers in charge of him were commissioned to pick up criminals condemned to the amphitheatre at various places on the route travelled—for a single prisoner a guard of ten seems unnecessarily large. This would probably mean delays at various stages. Allowing, therefore, time for periods of imprisonment before and after the trial, the six months' interval required could easily be filled.

Trajan died A.D. 117, and there is not the slightest ground for rejecting the tradition that the martyrdom of Ignatius took place in his reign. If, however, the *Didache*, as I have argued, originated in the Church of Antioch, it would allow more ample time for a development from the situation implied in that document to that implied in the letters of Ignatius, if we assume that his death took place towards the end of that Emperor's reign. Apart, therefore, from the conjectural datum afforded by the earthquake, the date A.D. 115 is one that reasonably satisfies the available evidence. It is, however, worth while to add that, should evidence turn up which established a date some ten years later, no position taken up in this book would require to be surrendered, and some would be the more easy to defend.

The date of the Ignatian Epistles cannot be considered altogether apart from that of the epistle of Polycarp to the Philippians. On this point an interesting suggestion has been communicated to me by Dr. P. N. Harrison. I have urged him to publish this, presenting the evidence in detail ; in the meantime, he permits me to state it in outline.

He asks whether what has come down to us as the epistle of Polycarp to the Philippians is not really *two* letters—a short letter, comprising ch. xiii. and xiv., written at the time of the death of Ignatius, and a longer letter (ch. i.-xii.) written ten years or more later ? The shorter letter (ch. xiii. and xiv.) is a covering letter, obviously authentic, sent to the Philippians, along with copies of such of the letters of Ignatius as Polycarp had been able to procure—probably the collection which has descended to us :

The letters of Ignatius which were sent to us by him, and others as many as we had by us, we send unto you, according as ye gave charge ; the which are subjoined to this letter.

Polycarp wrote this *before* he had received definite news that the martyrdom of Ignatius had actually taken place :

Moreover concerning Ignatius himself and those that were with him, if ye have any sure tidings, certify us.

The main reason for referring ch. i.-xii. to a later date is the contents of ch. vii. This seems to be directed against Marcion, whose views we know were regarded by Polycarp with special aversion :

For everyone who shall not confess that Jesus Christ is come in the flesh, is antichrist ; and whosoever shall not confess the witness of the Cross, is of the Devil ; and whosoever shall pervert the truths of the Lord to his own lusts, and say there is neither resurrection nor judgment, that man is the first-born of Satan.

First, notes Dr. Harrison, comes a quotation from 1 John, originally no doubt directed against the Docetists of ±A.D. 90. Polycarp is evidently applying this to someone in his own day who failed to acknowledge that Jesus Christ came ' in the flesh '. Now Marcion taught that ' clothed in a visionary body in the likeness of a man of thirty years old, the Son made His appearance, etc.' (This and subsequent summaries of Marcion's views are quoted from Harnack.) Further, somebody or other is now failing to confess ' the witness of the Cross '. Marcion, again, saw in the Crucifixion an act of the Demiurge—a ' crime ' for which He was forced to make amends. Marcion's view of the Old Testament would make it impossible for him to appreciate the early Christian interpretation of a witness of the prophets in general, and of Isaiah liii. in particular, to a conception of the Cross which makes it in a real sense an act of the good God. Further, this preacher of devil's doctrine is taking liberties with the oracles ($\lambda \acute{o} \gamma \iota a$) of the Lord to suit his own perverse inclination, which looks like a reference to Marcion's mutilation of the Gospel of Luke. He says there is ' no resurrection ' : Marcion taught that ' only the spirit of man is saved by the good God ; the body, because material, perishes '. He teaches that there is ' no judgment ' ; here again, ' according to Marcion, the good God never judges, but everywhere manifests his goodness. . . . Men who do not believe the Gospel, the good God does not judge, but merely removes from his presence '. Finally, Polycarp says that the teacher of these doctrines is ' Satan's first-born ' ; and we know from Irenaeus (*Haer*. iii. 3, 4) that Polycarp, when he met Marcion in the Baths, addressed him in these very words.[1]

Dr. Harrison also points out that the reference to ' the blessed Ignatius ', along with Paul and the rest of the Apostles (ch. ix.), reads more naturally if it was written sometime after the martyr-dom of Ignatius. One does not include in a list of the glorious dead the name of a man as to whose fate one *in the same letter* asks for information, and who, for all one knows, may be still alive.

Some further considerations in favour of the hypothesis that ch. i.-xii. are a letter written at a later date have occurred to me.

(1) Irenaeus tells us (cf. p. 268, *n*.) that Polycarp was in the habit of writing letters to neighbouring churches ; there is, there-fore, nothing surprising in his having written a second letter to the Philippians.

(2) The letter was written *in reply to a request* from the Church of Philippi for Polycarp's advice (ch. iii. 1). His com-ments on the case of the erring presbyter Valens and his wife (ch. xi.) look as if the advice was asked for at least partly in regard to this affair. Such a request by a distant church could only have been made to a man of great and established repu-tation. And the whole tone of the letter, with its fatherly exhortations to purity in doctrine and conduct, is far more appropriate in a letter sent by Polycarp in his venerable old age, when he had become a quasi-apostolic figure, than in one written at the time of the death of Ignatius (when he was approximately forty-five years of age)—more especially as he was writing to a church other than his own.

(3) There is some reason to suspect that another letter addressed to the Philippians (that of the Apostle Paul) is made up of two letters written on different occasions pieced together so as to read like one—Phil. iii. 2–iv. 1 being from a different letter.

(4) The benediction, ' Now may God the Father, etc.', and the call for prayer—ending with the words ' that ye may be perfect in Him '—with which the first part concludes, read as if they were intended as a kind of peroration (to a letter which is all but a sermon), and therefore originally stood at the end.

---

[1] Lightfoot—arguing against the view that the *whole* letter was directed against Marcion, and *therefore spurious*—asks, ' If Marcion was the object of attack, why is his dualism spared ? ' The objection proves too much ; the early Docetae were also dualists.

APPENDIX C

ORIGIN AND DATE OF THE 'DIDACHE'

THE *Didache* circulated mainly, if not exclusively, in Syria and Egypt. But as the place of origin Egypt is ruled out. The Eucharistic prayer (§ 9) speaks of the corn of which the bread is made as having been 'scattered upon the mountains'. This would be unnatural in Egypt; it would be appropriate in many districts of Syria, including its capital Antioch, which is close to a range of mountains. The undeveloped Christology, resembling that of the early chapters of Acts, suits Syria far better than Alexandria. Barnabas, the earliest document we have from Alexandria, already shows, we have seen (p. 246), that tendency towards a high Christology which in later times was characteristic of Alexandrian as contrasted with Antiochene theology. The fact that the moral teaching given in the opening chapters of the *Didache* is practically identical with that of the latter chapters of Barnabas, only emphasises the more the contrast between their doctrinal outlook. The ethics of the *Two Ways* Barnabas accepts; but the theology implied in the rest of the *Didache* he has left far behind.

There are seeming echoes of the *Didache* in Ignatius.[1] This does not prove that the *Didache* was written in Antioch, but it suggests that it was valued in Antioch before the time of Ignatius.

It is even possible that Ignatius directly refers to it. In the collocation of 'the Gospel', 'the Apostles', and 'the Prophets' (Philad. v. 1-2), the Prophets are clearly those of the Old Testament, and the Gospel, which is 'as it were the flesh of Christ', must be a book (doubtless our Matthew) which makes His humanity real.[2] In what sense, then, can he urge that one takes

---

[1] Cf. Magn. v. 1; other phrases which suggest that Ignatius was familiar with the *Didache* are pointed out by Prof. C. H. Turner, *Studies in Early Church History*, p. 8.

[2] Both Lightfoot and Harnack miss the point, believing (on purely *a priori*

279

refuge in the Apostles 'as in the presbytery of the Church', unless they also were available in written form? The epistles of Paul go far to give this exhortation meaning; but Ignatius uses the plural 'Apostles', and elsewhere he speaks of 'the ordinances (διατάγματα) of the Apostles' (Trall. vii. 1). May not the *Didache*, regarded as being what it claims to be, viz. teaching given by the Twelve, have been at Antioch on the way to inclusion in the New Testament Canon alongside the epistles of Paul?

The *Didache*, as I have shown elsewhere,[1] quotes from (and tells its readers to refer to) the Gospel of Matthew—and (if *Did.* i. 3–ii. 1, which appears to conflate Matthew, Luke, and Hermas, be regarded as an interpolation) apparently no other. It must, therefore, have been produced in an area where Matthew was the Gospel officially recognised. If we could accept the tradition that the Gospel of Matthew was written in Palestine, we might assign the *Didache* to the same province. But this so-called 'tradition' is merely a repetition by later writers of the statement (which I quote, p. 187) made for the first time by Irenaeus, A.D. 185. And this we have seen (p. 19) is merely an *inference* drawn from the famous, but highly enigmatic, statement of Papias, 'Matthew wrote τὰ λόγια in the Hebrew tongue'. The inference that a book written in Hebrew was written in Palestine is natural; but, as it is quite certain that our Gospel of Matthew is not a translation from Hebrew (being dependent on the Greek Gospel of Mark), the deduction is fallacious. Yet on this deduction depends the whole case for the Palestinian

---

grounds) that εὐαγγέλιον could not yet have been the name of a book. The use at such an early date of the word 'Gospel' as the title of a book (cf. also *Did.* xv. 3 f.) need excite no surprise. I have suggested (*The Four Gospels*, p. 507) that it originated soon after the publication of Mark, from the (Jewish) practice of using a striking word in the first sentence as the title of a book or a section of it. εὐαγγέλιον is the striking word in Mark i. 1. At any rate a Hebrew punning transliteration of the Greek word εὐαγγέλιον is so used in a story about the wife of Rabbi Eleazer, A.D. 100, in which a Christian judge quotes a saying very like Matt. v. 17 from a book called *The Gospel*. Cf. the essay by G. F. Moore in *Essays in Modern Theology and Related Subjects* (Papers in honour of C. A. Briggs), p. 101 ff. (Scribner, 1911). The story is also given and discussed by R. T. Herford in *Christianity in Talmud and Midrash*, p. 146 ff. (Williams & Norgate, 1903). In a conversation with Prof. G. F. Moore I raised the question whether the reference to the 'evangelion' belonged to the original story; he gave reasons for believing it to be original.

[1] *The Four Gospels*, p. 507.

origin of the Gospel. Against such an origin there is, to my mind, one fatal objection, *i.e.* the character of the *narrative* additions which this Gospel makes to the story as told by Mark. If Matthew was really written in Palestine, we should expect it to exhibit additions to the narrative material derived from Mark, both considerable in extent and palpably authentic—whereas in fact the precise contrary holds good. In the matter of the *teaching* of Christ, the additions made to Mark by Matthew are of the utmost value ; and that is explained by his use of *written* documents like Q. But the *narrative* additions are not of a character that suggests that they are derived from authentic local tradition ; most, if not all, of them are of the nature of ' Haggada '—*i.e.* imaginative homiletic expansion—on the text of Mark, whose narrative they presuppose.

But though the Gospel of Matthew can hardly have been written in Palestine, it is undoubtedly used by Ignatius, Bishop of Antioch. To him, moreover, Matthew is evidently *the* Gospel. For this and other reasons I myself incline to the view that it was compiled in Antioch. At any rate, the *Didache* and the Gospel of Matthew both emanate from the part of the world covered by the wide term Syria ; and the circulation and prestige which both enjoyed are not easily explained unless the general position which they represent was one which about the year A.D. 90 was congenial to important churches in an area in which far the most important church was Antioch.[1]

The historian is liable to draw false conclusions as to the date of an ancient document unless he first asks the question how exactly the text in front of him represents what the original author wrote. The *Didache* survives in a single manuscript dated by the scribe who wrote it in the year A.D. 1056. Now if we take any one average MS. of the Gospels of that date, we find a number of complete sentences and a very large number of individual words which editors like Westcott and Hort or Tischendorf (who base their text on the oldest MSS.) will not allow us to regard as authentic. For example, every Greek MS. but one of the Gospels later than the year A.D. 1000, so far as I recollect, gives Mark xvi. 9-20 as part of the authentic text of that Gospel. It is obvious

---

[1] To the view that the *Didache* emanated from Caesarea the main objection is the absence of points of contact with the strains of Gospel tradition preserved in Luke which we have some reason (p. 57) to connect with Caesarea.

to any critic that the author of those twelve verses made use of the Gospel of Luke and the Acts—from which fact it would, if the passage were authentic, be a necessary inference that the date of Mark is later than that of Luke and Acts. Only because those verses do not occur in the oldest MSS. are we free to accept without qualms the convincing evidence afforded by the rest of the Gospel that Mark was not only earlier than, but actually used by, Luke.

The text of the *Didache* presents an exact analogy. Near the beginning there is a passage (i. 5) which appears to contain a quotation from Hermas. But of the *Two Ways*, the first six chapters of the *Didache*, we have an old Latin version ; and the *Two Ways* also appears in Greek as the conclusion of Barnabas ; and both these authorities omit a considerable section (i. 3–ii. 1) in the middle of which the quotation from Hermas occurs. True, most scholars believe that the *Two Ways* (ch. i.-vi.) was an earlier document incorporated independently by the authors of Barnabas and of the *Didache*. And it is possible that the Latin version may be derived directly from this earlier document and not from the *Didache* itself; though it is more likely that it represents a truncated version of the *Didache*, made after the Church Order and other directions in ch. vii.-xvi. had become obsolete. But even if that be so, we have evidence that in the third century there existed texts of the *Didache* itself which lacked the ' interpolation ' ; for precisely that same section is omitted by the author of *The Apostolic Church Ordinances*, and he read the *Two Ways* as an integral part of the *Didache* itself (p. 285). Admittedly the ' interpolation ' is an early one ; it is found in texts of the *Didache* both in Egypt and Syria before the end of the fourth century. Curiously enough a papyrus fragment of that date (cf. *Oxyrhynchus Papyri*, vol. xv. p. 14) which contains only a few lines of the *Didache* happens to include one sentence of the ' interpolation ' ; it was also in the copy used about the same date by the author of the *Apostolic Constitutions*. In this matter, therefore, the text of our surviving MS. can be carried back to the fourth century. But this does not prove the reading authentic ; texts of St. Mark's Gospel containing the last twelve verses can be shown to have existed as far back as the *second* century, for Irenaeus, A.D. 185, used such a text. The analogy of the text of the

Gospels would lead us to expect that this is by no means the only place where the text of our one MS. of the *Didache* is not to be regarded as infallible. The tiny papyrus fragment I have mentioned has several minor variants ; so also, it would appear, had the MS. used by the author of the *Apostolic Constitutions*.

There is also evidence that the *Didache* circulated in more than one recension. Thus a couple of phrases are found, both in the *Apostolic Church Ordinances* and in the version of the *Two Ways* at the end of Barnabas, which are absent from our text of the *Didache* ; and, as already mentioned, both these omit *Did.* i. 3–ii. 1, ' the interpolation '. The old Latin version, how-ever, while agreeing with Barnabas and the *Apostolic Church Ordinances* in omitting the ' interpolation ', does *not* have the two short inserted phrases. Again, the striking phrase ' dead gods ' (*Did.* vi. 3), which does *not* appear in the parallel in Barnabas, is found also in the document I have styled Deutero-Clement (iii. 1), where it is presumably an echo of a MS. of the *Didache* slightly different from that used by Barnabas.

It has been necessary to discuss the state of the text, and in particular the ' interpolation ', at some length, because the main argument advanced by scholars so distinguished as Prof. von Harnack and Dr. Armitage Robinson for assigning to the *Didache* a relatively late date is the fact that it quotes Hermas. But apart from this section (which on textual grounds we conclude not to have been penned by the original author) the case for such quotation is too flimsy to bear any serious weight.

Dr. Robinson's theory that the *Didache* represents a fancy picture by some antiquarian romancer of later date, who was endeavouring to depict what he (falsely) conceived to be the state of things existent in the Primitive Church, is one that I cannot bring myself to take seriously.[1] There survive several attempts in the third and fourth centuries to depict what their authors conceived as the discipline and order of the Apostolic Age. But then, even more than now, the customs of the Primitive Church were regarded as an authoritative guide for present-day practice. What these writers are concerned to do is to project back into the Apostolic Age, either the conditions which existed at their own time, or else conditions which seemed to them a slightly

---

[1] The theory is discussed in detail in the admirable little edition by A. S. Maclean, *The Doctrine of the Twelve Apostles* (S.P.C.K., 1922).

improved variety of contemporary usage. That a later writer, of Montanist proclivities, should have admired, and desired to depict as primitive, the state of things reflected in the *Didache*, is possible—there are no limits to the idiosyncrasy of individuals in any age. What is incredible is that, had he done so, his work —running so absolutely counter as it does to the ideals and tendencies of the time—should at once have secured such wide influence and prestige.

A second theory, that the *Didache* represents a state of things which actually existed at an early date, but only in some out-of-the-way church, is less intrinsically absurd. Nevertheless it goes shipwreck on the fact, for which I shall shortly adduce evidence, that the influence of this little book on the later literature dealing with Church Order has been perhaps greater than that of any other work outside the New Testament. Wherever, and by whomsoever, it was composed, it must have been accepted as authoritative, and that almost at once by the most important churches of Syria and Egypt. But this could not have happened unless the situation which it implies was one that actually existed in these churches, so that the advice given in the document supplied something of which they felt an actual need.

I proceed to recall certain facts which attest the exceptional prestige which once attached to this ancient writing.

(1) It hovered on the verge of acceptance into the Canon until the fourth century.

Athanasius, in the notable 39th Festal Letter (A.D. 367), which practically settled the Canon of the New Testament, classes the *Didache* and *The Shepherd* along with certain books of the O.T., *i.e.* Wisdom, Ecclesiasticus, Esther, Judith, and Tobit, which he pronounces extra-canonical. All these he characterises as

books not admitted into the Canon, but appointed by the fathers to be read to those who are just coming to us and desire to be instructed in the doctrine of godliness.[1]

This special mention of the *Didache* and Hermas is the more significant because of the omission of all mention of books like

[1] Rufinus, writing in Italy about the same time, gives practically the same list, if, as is probable, the work *Duae Viae sive Judicium Petri*, of which he speaks, is a recension of the *Didache*, or at least of the *Two Ways*. Athanasius' 39th Festal Letter and the list of Rufinus are conveniently printed in Westcott's *Canon of the New Testament*, p. 554 ff. and p. 569 f. (Macmillan, 1889).

1 Clement, Barnabas, and the Apocalypse of Peter, which at one time were also serious candidates for admission to the Canon.

(2) The *Didache* must have been regarded as an ancient classic by the author of the, probably Syrian (p. 249, *n.*), manual on Church Order of the third century called by its editor, J. W. Bickell, the *Apostolic Church Ordinances*. Both open with the *Two Ways*. But in the *Didache* this introductory section is explicitly affirmed to be a manual of instruction for candidates for Baptism ; and is then followed by directions about the ritual of Baptism, about Prayer, the Eucharist, and the Ministry. This arrangement is natural and intelligible. The *Apostolic Church Ordinances*, however, begins with a series of extracts from the *Two Ways*, and then goes on to elaborate at great length a new Church Order, quite unlike that of the *Didache*, but conformed to the views of a later period.[1] No one *starting fresh* to set out a Church Order would have prefaced it with the *Two Ways*, still less with a mutilated version of it. Such a proceeding, however, is quite explicable in an author who wished to capture for his own ideas on Church Order the ' good-will ' of a primitive document, which claimed to be the work of the Apostles and was commonly regarded as the classical treatise on the subject.[2]

(3) A similar effort to bring the Church Order of the *Didache* ' up to date ' is found in the seventh book of the *Apostolic Constitutions*. This author incorporates the text of the *Didache* practically whole. But he gains his object by tendencious additions. But why trouble to do this, unless the *Didache* was regarded as an ancient standard authority for the practice of the Apostolic Age ?

(4) To a somewhat less extent the *Didache* has been made use of in an earlier Syrian Church Order known as the *Didascalia* ; also in a treatise by Athanasius, *Syntagma Doctrinae*, and in other less important works, such as the Pseudo-Athanasian *De Virginitate*.

The evidence summarised above proves that both in Syria and Egypt the *Didache* was a document which enjoyed immense

---

[1] A single sentence, however, in this latter portion betrays its author's knowledge of the latter part of the *Didache*.

[2] The Greek text of the *Apostolic Church Ordinances* and that of the relevant portions of the *Apostolic Constitutions* are printed in Harnack's *Lehre der Zwölfe Apostel*, Leipsig, 1884, passages derived from the *Didache* being in different type.

prestige. Just for that reason, it was a *cause of considerable embarrassment* to the authorities on account of the striking contrast between the type of Church Order which in the third and fourth centuries they wished to believe Apostolic and that which the *Didache* implies. Hence the various attempts to get rid of the difficulty by producing up-to-date versions of it. The *Didache* purports to represent the teaching of the Twelve Apostles in this matter ; it must, therefore, have been *accepted as Apostolic*—in character if not in actual authorship—in Syria and Egypt *before* the Church Order it implies had become obsolete in those countries. And this was certainly obsolete by A.D. 130. We must go further and say that the *Didache* must have reached these churches at a time when its teaching was actually in *advance* of the needs of the actual situation. The main object of the second half of the *Didache* is to give advice to communities which are in difficulties owing to the lack of an established ministry and to help them in that direction. Now there are always people in this world ready to give unnecessary advice—but there are few who accept it with enthusiasm. And the *Didache* would never have attained such widespread popularity unless, at the time when it reached these churches, the advice it gave was felt to be really needed. But the stage when churches like Antioch and Alexandria keenly felt the need of the precise advice which the *Didache* gives can hardly have lasted much later than A.D. 110. Beginning about A.D. 130, there was a spate of literature, mostly Gnostic in origin, purporting to represent the teaching of one or more of the Apostles. But by A.D. 250 all of this which the Great Churches were not ready to accept as consonant with Apostolic teaching was officially discredited. The *Didache* remained respectable, in spite of reflecting a type of Church organisation which at that date these churches would have vehemently declined to consider Apostolic. This is difficult to explain unless the work in question was known to be of immemorial antiquity, was believed by some to be actually Apostolic, and had reached these churches at much about the same time as some of the books of the New Testament itself.

External evidence, then, is against a date much later than A.D. 100. On the other hand, the reference by the *Didache* to the Gospel of Matthew as a standard authority (xv. 3, 4) makes it impossible to date it much earlier than A.D. 90.

To the historian it has long been something of a puzzle to account for the way in which already in the second century the Gentile churches looked back on the work of the Twelve Apostles, as if to them, quite as much as to Paul, was due the mission to the Gentiles—in spite of the clear evidence of the New Testament to the contrary. No doubt a number of different causes contributed to this result. But to those which have been suggested by previous writers, I would add another—the great repute and the wide circulation of the Message of the Twelve to the Gentiles which we name the *Didache*.

APPENDIX D

IRENAEUS AND THE EARLY POPES

In Lightfoot's classical discussion of ' The Early Roman Succession ' occurs this sentence :

Whether Irenaeus directly copied the Catalogue (of Roman bishops) of Hegesippus, or whether he instituted independent inquiries, we cannot say (*Clement*, i. p. 205).

I hope to find the answer to the question which Lightfoot here leaves open—by showing that Irenaeus derived from Hegesippus, not only his Catalogue of Bishops, but also a good deal more. Lightfoot's brilliant identification of the Catalogue of Bishops in the *Panarion* of Epiphanius (xxvii. 6) with that compiled by Hegesippus has been further consolidated, and defended from objections raised by Harnack and others, in Dr. Lawlor's *Eusebiana*. I do not propose, except incidentally, to re-state here a case so adequately presented elsewhere. Nevertheless, while my main object is to answer the question posed above, the considerations I advance do, if they hold good at all, materially strengthen Lightfoot's argument.

My starting-point is the statement of Eusebius (*H.E.* iv. 22) as to the identity of Hegesippus, supported as it is by a quotation from his work.

Now Hegesippus, in the five *Note Books* which have come down to us, has left behind a very complete record of his personal views. And in his *Note Books* he tells us that on a journey as far as Rome he associated with very many bishops, and that he had received the same teaching from all. In fact, we may listen to what he says, when, after remarks on the epistle of Clement to the Corinthians, he adds as follows :

'And the Church of the Corinthians continued in the true doctrine until Primus was bishop of Corinth. . . . With them I associated on my voyage to Rome, and I abode with the Corinthians many days ; during which we were refreshed together in the true doctrine. But when I came to Rome, I made for myself a succession-list as far as Anicetus; whose deacon was Eleutherus. And from Anicetus Soter received the succession; after whom came Eleutherus. And in every succession and in every city, that prevails which the Law and the Prophets and the Lord proclaim.'

There are here two points—of which, to the best of my knowledge, the full significance has heretofore escaped the notice of scholars—that call for comment. First, in the original work of Hegesippus the paragraph quoted by Eusebius stood 'after some remarks on the epistle of Clement to the Corinthians'. Secondly, the sound doctrine with which Hegesippus was mainly concerned was the affirmation that the God who created the world and revealed Himself in the Law and in the Prophets was *also* the God and Father of Jesus Christ, and not (as the Gnostics maintained) a Demiurge, *i.e.* a secondary, and ethically inferior, creator. Now in the middle of his Catalogue of the Bishops of Rome, Irenaeus has a long paragraph giving an account of the contents of the epistle of Clement to the Corinthians, elaborating its teaching in regard to this very point. (*Adv. Haer.* iii. 3.) The digression occurs at the mention of the name of Clement, the third bishop after the Apostles, in whose time

the Church in Rome wrote a most effective letter to the Corinthians, urging them to be at peace together, and renewing their faith and setting forth the tradition which it had recently received from the apostles: which tradition proclaims One God Omnipotent, Maker of heaven and earth, the Creator of man, who brought on the Deluge, and called Abraham, who led the people from the land of Egypt, spake with Moses, ordained the law, and sent the prophets. . . . Those who will, may learn from this very writing that He, the Father of our Lord Jesus Christ, is (the God) preached by the churches, and may understand the apostolical tradition of the Church; since the epistle is more ancient than those who now utter false teachings and fabricate another God, above the Artificer and Creator of all things that exist.

The occurrence of this digression is notable in two ways. First, it is a clumsy interruption in the list of Roman bishops. Secondly, as a matter of fact, Clement's letter betrays not the slightest interest in, or knowledge of, the controversy about the God of the Old Testament. His epistle is remarkable for the large number, and the great length, of its quotations from the

U

Old Testament ; and he takes it for granted that this is Holy Scripture—indeed the only Scripture, since he writes before the books of the New Testament had attained canonical authority. But the point of Clement's quotations from the Old Testament is the duty of peace and good-will and similar practical problems, not their bearing on the unity of God—a doctrine which in his day had been called in question by few (if any) who claimed to be Christians, and was not the matter in dispute at Corinth.

Both facts are explicable on the hypothesis that this account of Clement's letter occurred in the middle of the Catalogue of Hegesippus, and reproduces substantially the ' remarks on the epistle of Clement to the Corinthians ' mentioned in the excerpt quoted above by Eusebius. The testimony to the faith given in a letter of the Church of Rome to the Corinthians written in the time of Clement would be highly appropriate in a context dealing with the purity of the Apostolic doctrine preserved at Corinth till the time of Primus.

I suggest, therefore, that Irenaeus had never himself come across Clement's letter. But he was interested to find, on the authority of Hegesippus, that such strong and definite anti-Gnostic teaching occurred in the work of a person so near the age of the Apostles. Hence he thought it worth while to summarise it, even though it here formed a cumbrous digression in his Catalogue. Clement's letter, though highly prized in the East, was hardly read in the West. In the passages quoted in the editions of Lightfoot, and of Gebhardt and Harnack, as evidence for use of the epistle by later writers, the only clear quotation by a Western writer is this very passage of Irenaeus which we are now discussing ; and nowhere else does Irenaeus himself display any knowledge of the epistle.

We next note that Epiphanius, too—in the same place in his Catalogue of the Roman Bishops—has a long digression about Clement. (This is mainly concerned with reconciling the occurrence of the name Clement as third from the Apostles in the Catalogue with the alternative tradition, derived from the Clementine Romance, that Clement was appointed bishop by Peter.) And Epiphanius, also, in the course of *his* digression, quotes from Clement's letter. But the sentence he quotes (' I depart, I go away, only that the people of God be in good case ') was derived,

he expressly states, not direct from the original, but 'from one
of Clement's letters in certain Note Books (ὑπομνηματισμοῖς)'.
And ὑπομνήματα is the title given by Eusebius as that of the
work of Hegesippus. Again, Lightfoot and Harnack agree in
affirming that Epiphanius, though he quotes certain spurious
letters of Clement, seems *not* to have read the genuine letter.
If, then, Epiphanius derived his Catalogue of Bishops from Hegesippus, the natural inference is that he found this quotation
from Clement's letter in Hegesippus, in the exact context (in the
Catalogue) in which he quotes it.

Thus two persons, who elsewhere show no knowledge of
Clement's letter, quote it at the mention of the name Clement in
a digression in the middle of a Catalogue of Bishops of Rome.
The presumption that both derived the list from the same source
and that this source quoted from Clement's letter is very high.
The words quoted by Epiphanius from Clement are in the
original an exhortation to any individual who is a focus of dissension to sacrifice himself for the sake of the peace of the church ;
Irenaeus also, though his summary of Clement is mainly concerned
with its doctrinal content, speaks of the letter as ' urging them
to be at peace together '.

Hegesippus, then, said rather more about the purpose of the
epistle being to urge peace than is preserved by either Irenaeus
or Epiphanius. That is only natural. No one who was making
at first hand a summary of the epistle could fail to stress this
point, seeing that it was really the sole purpose for which it was
written. But in Irenaeus this aspect of the epistle is barely
mentioned, and if we knew nothing of it but what he tells us, we
should suppose that its main purpose was to oppose the doctrinal
teaching of certain Gnostics. This, however, is readily explicable
if he only knew Clement at second hand, and was excerpting from
Hegesippus the part of his summary of the epistle which was most
germane to the subject of his own book.

Epiphanius, after naming Clement, adds, ' whom Paul men-
tions in the epistle to the Romans '. This is an error ; it is in
Philippians that mention is made of a person of the name Clement.
Either Epiphanius or his source Hegesippus has made a slip.
Irenaeus omits Paul's reference to Clement, but substitutes a
similar remark about Linus, ' of this Linus Paul makes mention

in the epistles to Timothy '. As these epistles purport to have
been written *from Rome*, this is to the point. There is little
force in saying that a Clement, named as the third Bishop of
Rome, is mentioned by Paul as living *in Philippi*. It looks as if
the slip goes back to Hegesippus ; Irenaeus detected it, but it
suggested to him the substitution of a statement about Linus
which is both correct and to the point.

The Catalogue of Bishops occurs in the third book of Irenaeus'
Against Heresies ; in a totally different context (bk. i. 25) he has
an account of the observances of the Carpocratians, and of a
certain Marcellina, who spread their doctrine in Rome under Pope
Anicetus. In Epiphanius an identical account of Marcellina and
the Carpocratians occurs, but curiously mixed up with the
Catalogue of Bishops. There is an almost word-for-word agreement between Irenaeus and Epiphanius in what they jointly say
about Marcellina and the Carpocratians ; but it is clear that
Epiphanius is *not deriving his information from Irenaeus*, but
from a source which *also* contained the Catalogue of Bishops. A
brief résumé of Epiphanius will make this clear.[1] He begins :

Now there came upon us (ἦλθεν δὲ εἰς ἡμᾶς) some time ago a
certain Marcellina who had been led into error by them [the Carpo-
cratians].   She was the ruin of a great number of persons in the time
of Anicetus, bishop of Rome, who succeeded Pius and his predecessors.   [Irenaeus has the above sentence in all but identical terms,
save that he writes ' to Rome ' instead of ' upon us '.]   For in Rome
there were first Peter and Paul, both Apostles and Bishops, then
Linus, then Cletus, then Clement, a contemporary of Peter and Paul,
of whom Paul makes mention in his epistle to the Romans (*Pan.*
27. 6. 1 f.).

Then comes the long digression already discussed—explain-
ing why it was that, since Clement was a contemporary of the
Apostles, they did not make him the first bishop, instead of the
third—in the course of which occurs the quotation from Clement's
letter derived, not from the letter itself but from ' certain *Note
Books* ' (*i.e.* from Hegesippus).

After the digression Epiphanius starts off again on the
Catalogue :

---

[1] The student who has access to Dr. Lawlor's *Eusebiana* will find there the
passages of Irenaeus and Epiphanius to be discussed printed conveniently in
parallel columns.

But however this may be, this is the succession of Roman bishops. Peter and Paul, Linus and Cletus, Clement, Evaristus, Alexander, Xystus, Telesphorus, Hyginus, Pius, Anicetus, *whom shortly before I have named in the Catalogue.* And let no one be surprised that I have gone so minutely into these details ; for always by means of these is the truth established. In the time, then, as I have said, of Anicetus the above-mentioned Marcellina coming to Rome, and vomiting out the poison of Carpocratian doctrine, corrupted and drove to their destruction many in that place. . . . [Here follows a section giving certain details about the Carpocratians which occurs almost word for word in Irenaeus (i. 25, 6) immediately after *his* mention of Marcellina.]

Three points require notice :

(*a*) The words, ' whom shortly before I have named in the Catalogue ', can only be a quotation carelessly copied unaltered from his source by Epiphanius ; for in his own work the Catalogue of Bishops occurs, not before, but *after* this reference to it.

(*b*) The Marcellina incident is twice alluded to—the first time in words found also in Irenaeus (and therefore derived from the common source), the second time in Epiphanius' own vituperative paraphrase. Evidently in the source (*i.e.* in Hegesippus) the Marcellina incident stood in the second of these two contexts— the one where Epiphanius has reproduced it in paraphrase. The words identifying Anicetus as the bishop, ' whom shortly before I have named in the Catalogue ', must have originally followed the mention of his name (in the former of the paragraphs quoted above) as the Pope in whose time Marcellina came to Rome. The words which *there* follow the mention of his name (which do not occur in Irenaeus), 'Bishop of Rome, who succeeded Pius and his predecessors ', are an addition by Epiphanius, who had just read the Catalogue, which in his source stood a few sentences earlier.

(*c*) The words ἦλθεν δὲ εἰς ἡμᾶς are translated by Lightfoot, ' paid us a visit ' ; and he interprets the presence of the first person plural in the text of Epiphanius as a survival of the actual language of Hegesippus carelessly reproduced by Epiphanius. K. Holl, in the edition of the *Panarion* in the Berlin Corpus, argues that the words, in the usage of Epiphanius, should be translated ' There has come to our knowledge how Marcellina . . . ' ; and he concludes that Lightfoot's whole theory that Epiphanius is here using Hegesippus therewith falls to the ground. Personally I prefer to translate the words 'came upon us', *i.e.* 'effected an entrance into our society'—in which case Lightfoot is right in supposing that we have here preserved the actual language of Hegesippus. I note that there is other evidence here of careless copying of an earlier source. The final letter of $\mathring{\eta}\lambda\theta\epsilon\nu$ is only in place if followed by $\epsilon\mathring{\iota}\varsigma$; the $\delta\acute{\epsilon}$ has been added to make a connection with the previous sentence by some one (whether Epiphanius himself or his secretary) who forgot to cut out the superfluous consonant. But even if Holl is right in the matter of translation, the dependence of Epiphanius upon Hegesippus, both for the incident of Marcellina and for the Catalogue of Bishops (which, as we have already seen, must have stood in the *same* source), is an hypothesis still needed to account for the following facts :

(i.) Unless the whole argument of this Appendix has been nonsense, Irenaeus and Epiphanius each used a source which contained an identical account of Marcellina and the Carpocratians, and also a Catalogue of Bishops substantially identical,[1] and in each case broken by a digression in which 1 Clement was quoted.

(ii.) Hegesippus says that while in Rome, $\delta\iota\alpha\delta o\chi\grave{\eta}\nu\ \mathring{\epsilon}\pi o\iota\eta\sigma\acute{\alpha}\mu\eta\nu$ $\mu\acute{\epsilon}\chi\rho\iota\varsigma$ $\mathring{A}\nu\iota\kappa\acute{\eta}\tau o\upsilon$, which is naturally to be translated, 'I drew up a succession-list of bishops as far as Anicetus'. This implies in some degree individual research; the idea that such a succession-list had an apologetic value was evidently his own. Irenaeus visited Rome ten or twelve years after Hegesippus, so that the probability that he would have known his work is extremely high.

(iii.) The confluence of four independent streams of information at the name of Anicetus must be explained. Under Anicetus

---

[1] The only difference between the Catalogue of Irenaeus and that in Epiphanius is that, while Epiphanius gives the name of the second bishop as Cletus, Irenaeus gives it as Anencletus. The name occurs in the shorter form in the Canon of the Mass. Liturgiologists believe that the first three names of Roman Bishops in the Canon represent the remnant of what was originally an enumeration of all the bishops down to a certain (unknown) date. In such a list a shorter would naturally be preferred to a longer name ; it is even possible that the shortening came about in the rapid utterance of a recital constantly repeated. Eastern Christians often went to Rome—Epiphanius himself was there in A.D. 382 ; but that was after he wrote the *Panarion*—and it is quite likely that the form Cletus is due to a correction by Epiphanius of the original list of Hegesippus to make it conform to the list of names as there recited in the Canon.

Marcellina comes to Rome ; in the time of Anicetus Hegesippus visits Rome ; he made a Catalogue of Bishops ending with Anicetus ; with Anicetus ends the Epiphanian Catalogue of Bishops.

Hegesippus saw apologetic value against Gnostics in a Catalogue of Bishops ; moreover, his journey from Palestine to Rome to visit the Apostolic churches was inspired by the idea that any doctrine in which they all agreed must be Apostolic. In the light of these facts let us consider the comment of Epiphanius in the passage last quoted in the Catalogue of Bishops, ' Let no one be surprised that I have gone so minutely into these details ; for always by means of these is the truth established '. In the context in Epiphanius' own work there is nothing to show how or why this kind of detail has any bearing at all on religious truth. But all is clear if we suppose that Epiphanius is here summarising an argument of Hegesippus that the succession of bishops is, against the Gnostics, the great guarantee of the apostolicity, and therefore the truth, of the orthodox faith. Now this is the precise point made by Irenaeus (iii. 3, §§ 1-2) in the paragraphs with which he introduces his Catalogue of Bishops. I suggest, therefore, that Irenaeus derived the substance of these introductory paragraphs, as well as the Catalogue itself, from Hegesippus. If so, Hegesippus, though not ' the father of Church History ', *is* the real father of the argument from tradition, guaranteed by the succession of bishops in the great Churches, which is the subject of this famous opening of the third book of Irenaeus.

The question how much more of the lost work of Hegesippus is preserved in other parts of Irenaeus' treatise is one which I commend to the investigation of scholars.

APPENDIX E

A GNOSTIC HYMN

(*The Acts of John*, §§ 94-95)

JESUS gathered all of us together and said : Before I am delivered up unto them let us sing an hymn to the Father, and so go forth to that which lieth before us.   He bade us therefore make as it were a ring, holding one another's hands, and Himself standing in the midst He said : Answer Amen unto Me.   He began, then, to sing an hymn and to say :

> Glory be to thee, Father.
> And we, going about in a ring, answered Him : Amen.[1]

THE HYMN OF JESUS

Glory to Thee, Father !	Amen.
Glory to Thee, Word !	Amen.
Glory to Thee, O Grace !	Amen.
Glory to Thee, Holy Spirit !	Amen.

> Glory to Thy Glory !
> We praise Thee, O Father ;
> We give thanks to Thee, O shadowless light !   Amen.

Fain would I be saved :	And fain would I save.
Fain would I be released :	And fain would I release.
Fain would I be pierced :	And fain would I pierce.
Fain would I be borne :	Fain would I bear.
Fain would I eat :	Fain would I be eaten.
Fain would I hearken :	Fain would I be heard.

---

[1] The introductory paragraph I have taken from Dr. James.   The Hymn itself I have given in the free but fine version prepared by Mr. Gustav Holst for his musical setting, with his kind permission and that of the publishers, Messrs. Stainer & Bell.

Fain would I be cleansed :   Fain would I cleanse.
I am Mind of All !   Fain would I be known.
Divine grace is dancing :   Fain would I pipe for you.
Dance ye all !   Amen.

Fain would I lament :   Mourn ye all !   Amen.
The Heav'nly Spheres make music for us ;
The Holy Twelve dance with us ;
All things join in the dance !
Ye who dance not, know not what we are knowing.
Fain would I flee :   And fain would I remain.
Fain would I be ordered :   And fain would I set in order.
Fain would I be infolded :   Fain would I infold.
I have no home.   In all I am dwelling.
I have no resting place :   I have the earth.
I have no temple :   And I have Heav'n.

To you who gaze, a lamp am I :
To you that know, a mirror.
To you who knock, a door am I :
To you who fare, the way.   Amen.

Give ye heed unto my dancing :
In me who speak, behold yourselves ;
And beholding what I do,
Keep silence on my mysteries.
Divine ye in dancing what I shall do ;
For yours is the passion of man that I go to endure.
Ah ! Ye could not know at all what thing ye endure,
Had not the Father sent me to you as a Word.
Beholding what I suffer, ye know me as the Sufferer.
And when ye had beheld it, ye were not unmoved ;
But rather were ye whirled along.

Ye were kindled to be wise.
Had ye known how to suffer, ye would know how to suffer no more.
Learn how to suffer, and ye shall overcome.
Behold in me a couch : Rest on me !   Amen.

When I am gone ye shall know who I am ;
For I am in no wise that which now I seem ;
When ye are come to me, then shall ye know ;

What ye know not, will I myself teach you.
Fain would I move to the music of holy souls !

Know in me the word of wisdom !
And with me cry again :—

        Glory to Thee, Father !   Amen.
        Glory to Thee, Word !   Amen.
        Glory to Thee, Holy Spirit ! Amen.

INDEX OF NAMES

INDEX OF SUBJECTS

THE END

Printed in Great Britain by R. & R. CLARK, LIMITED, *Edinburgh.*

BY CANON STREETER

Third Impression. 8vo. **21s.** *net.*

THE FOUR GOSPELS
A STUDY OF ORIGINS

TREATING OF

THE MANUSCRIPT TRADITION,

SOURCES, AUTHORSHIP, AND DATES

The late Bishop RYLE wrote to the publishers: "I regard it as the most important, substantial, and constructive addition to the study of New Testament criticism that we have had in England since the appearance of Hort's Introduction."

Prof. F. C. BURKITT, in *The Journal of Theological Studies:* "It is impossible to begin to write about this work called 'The Four Gospels' without praise, praise for the justice of its proportions, for the sanity of its conclusions, for the learning it shows on every page, and the ingenuity and persuasiveness of its argumentation. I venture to think 'The Four Gospels' the most important book that has been written upon its august subject for half a generation."

The BISHOP OF GLOUCESTER, in *The Church Quarterly Review:* "The most important contribution which has been made to the criticism of the Gospels for many years, criticism both textual and structural. . . . Will certainly enhance Canon Streeter's reputation for originality and acuteness, and also, may we add, for great sobriety of view."

Prof. JAMES MOFFATT, in *The Hibbert Journal:* "Dr. Streeter has given us a volume of real importance upon the origins of the Gospels. There is no book in English where the results of criticism are so conveniently arranged; he has surveyed the broad field of research, and disentangled the salient issues with skill. The reader who will bring patience to this book will receive a clearly cut impression of the modern position reached by investigators into the four Gospels. . . . No more stimulating and fascinating study of the problem has been given us, in English or indeed in any language, since Wellhausen wrote his five small books."

LONDON : MACMILLAN AND CO., LTD.

BY CANON STREETER

REALITY : A New Correlation of Science and Religion. *9th Impression.* 8vo. 8s. 6d. net.

Times Literary Supplement.—" A brilliant survey of the field of thought as it appears to-day ; more than that, it is a brilliant strategic occupation of it in the interests of a spiritual philosophy."

The Times.—" No sketch of the main argument can take in the many brilliant observations and fresh lines of thought that branch off from the central stem."

Nature.—" In classing this volume with apologetic literature in general, we should not be acting fairly to Canon Streeter. It is a work of a very different type ; one which all earnest students of the natural sciences would do well to read."

Saturday Review.—" The outstanding merit of Dr. Streeter's book is to have shown the right method *at work*, and to have marked out the path for 'any future' approach to Reality. . . . He has demonstrated to younger students the right way to tackle the problem, and his own answer to it leaves us satisfied."

STUART HODGSON in *Daily News.*—" As for the little essay on Immortality, it is in its kind one of the most touching and beautiful things that has been written in our times."

ADVENTURE : The Faith of Science and the Science of Faith. By B. H. STREETER, C. M. CHILCOTT, J. MACMURRAY, and ALEX. S. RUSSELL. *3rd Impression.* 8vo. 7s. 6d. net.

The Times.—" The intense actuality of life makes itself felt through all that Canon Streeter writes, and here his colleagues in this latest book are at one with him. . . . It is an appeal that recalls the great ages of theology."

The Guardian.—" A really important symposium. Mr. Macmurray is brilliant in discussing the nature of divine personality."

The Expository Times.—" Very emphatically we would state, underline, and insist that it is a book to get. . . . A better gift-book for a minister we cannot conceive. . . . For the lay reader . . . the book may be very cordially recommended likewise."

The Spectator.—" The ethics of sex have seldom been more boldly or more wisely handled."

LONDON : MACMILLAN AND CO., LTD.

BY CANON STREETER

THE SPIRIT : God and His Relation to Man considered from the Standpoint of Philosophy, Psychology and Art. By A. SETH PRINGLE-PATTISON, LILY DOUGALL, J. ARTHUR HADFIELD, C. A. ANDERSON SCOTT, CYRIL W. EMMET, A. CLUTTON-BROCK, and B. H. STREETER. *5th Impression*. 8vo. 1os. 6d. net.

Canon A. W. ROBINSON in *The Guardian*.—" On no matter is there more need and more desire for light than this . . . and many will turn to these pages in the hope that they may be found to furnish some helpful direction, or at least some useful suggestions. I can say at once that the hope will not be disappointed. I do not know of any book that gathers up more effectively, both for the student and the general reader, what ha been said and written from the side of mental and moral science in regard to spiritua experiences during the course of recent years."

IMMORTALITY : An Essay in Discovery ; co-ordinating Scientific, Psychical and Biblical Research. By B. H. STREETER, A. CLUTTON-BROCK, C. W. EMMET, J. A. HADFIELD and the author of *Pro Christo et Ecclesia*. *4th Impression*. 8vo. 1os. 6d. net.

Canon BARNES, now Bishop of Birmingham, in *The Challenge*.—" I feel it to be of great importance. . . . Its writers are able, thoughtful, and wide in sympathy and understanding."

Dean INGE in *The Guardian*.—" The volume is important, interesting, and stimulating. . . . There is much for which we may cordially thank Canon Streeter and his colleagues."

CONCERNING PRAYER : Its Nature, its Difficulties, and its Value. By the author of *Pro Christo et Ecclesia*, HAROLD ANSON, EDWYN BEVAN, R. G. COLLINGWOOD, LEONARD HODGSON, RUFUS M. JONES, W. F. LOFTHOUSE, C. H. S. MATTHEWS, N. MICKLEM, A. C. TURNER, and B. H. STREETER. *5th Impression*. 8vo. 1os. 6d. net.

Dr. TEMPLE, now Archbishop of York, in *The Challenge*.—" Of supreme value and importance."

The Church Quarterly Review.—" A book to be thankful for. . . . We have here the work of minds which are penetrated with the Christian faith, and find in the religious life their deepest interest, and yet are at the same time keenly alive to the intellectual movements of the day."

LONDON : MACMILLAN AND CO., LTD.

3

BY CANON STREETER

FOUNDATIONS : A Statement of Christian Belief in Terms of Modern Thought. By Seven Oxford Men : B. H. STREETER, R. BROOK, W. H. MOBERLY, R. G. PARSONS, A. E. J. RAWLINSON, N. S. TALBOT, W. TEMPLE. 10th Impression. 8vo. 10s. 6d. net.

The Times.—"It is the endeavour to put into fairly popular language the . . . position of the young men who seem to claim that they can speak on behalf of their generation. They have gone further than their Victorian predecessors. They believe that they have gone deeper down to the 'Foundations.' It is an unmixed gain that we should have their statements presented to us in a form so free from the jargon of party and from the distressing discord of controversy."

The Hibbert Journal.—"A book which deserves to be treated very seriously. The ability of the individual writers is of a high order, but the importance of the work as a whole is much greater than that of any individual essay in it. . . . It may be that this book will constitute a turning-point in the history, not of a party, but of the Church of England and of the Church in England."

RESTATEMENT AND REUNION : A Study in First Principles. 2nd Impression. Crown 8vo. 2s. 6d. net.

The Church Quarterly Review.—"This is an admirable book—admirable alike in its sincerity, its faith, and its all-embracing charity. We may doubt whether Mr. Streeter's position is tenable in the Church of England, but even those of us who most disagree with him will wish that it might be so. . . . Of Mr. Streeter's second and third chapters it is difficult to speak with too much praise. We hardly know whether more to admire the wisdom and truth of what he says, or the sympathy and understanding with which he speaks of those with whom he disagrees."

THE SADHU : A Study in Mysticism and Practical Religion. By B. H. STREETER and A. J. APPASAMY. 9th Impression. Crown 8vo. 5s. net.

(This book has been translated into six different European languages.)

Dean INGE in *The Evening Standard.*—"One of the most fascinating books that I have read for a long time. . . . I urge my readers to read *The Sadhu.*"

Miss EVELYN UNDERHILL in *The Westminster Gazette.*—"Canon Streeter and Mr. Appasamy have put all students of religious experience under a debt of gratitude by producing this excellent and sympathetic study."

LONDON : MACMILLAN AND CO., LTD.